W9-AXF-596

STEEL DRIVIN' MAN

STEEL DRIVIN' MAN

JOHN HENRY, THE UNTOLD STORY OF AN AMERICAN LEGEND

SCOTT REYNOLDS NELSON

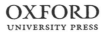

OXFORD
UNIVERSITY PRESS
2006

OXFORD

UNIVERSITY PRESS

Oxford University Press, Inc., publishes works that
further Oxford University's objective of excellence
in research, scholarship, and education.

Oxford New York
Auckland Cape Town Dar es Salaam Hong Kong Karachi
Kuala Lumpur Madrid Melbourne Mexico City Nairobi
New Delhi Shanghai Taipei Toronto

With offices in
Argentina Austria Brazil Chile Czech Republic France Greece
Guatemala Hungary Italy Japan Poland Portugal Singapore
South Korea Switzerland Thailand Turkey Ukraine Vietnam

Copyright © 2006 by Scott Reynolds Nelson

Published by Oxford University Press, Inc.
198 Madison Avenue, New York, NY 10016
www.oup.com

Oxford is a registered trademark of Oxford University Press

Library of Congress Cataloging-in-Publication Data
Nelson, Scott Reynolds
Steel drivin' man : John Henry, the untold story of an American legend
/ Scott Reynolds Nelson.
p. cm
ISBN-13: 978-0-19-530010-9
ISBN-10: 0-19-530010-6
1. Henry, John William, 1847?–ca. 1875.
2. African Americans—Biography.
3. Railroad construction workers—United States—Biography.
4. John Henry (Legendary character).
5. African Americans—Music.
6. African American art.
7. Henry, John William, 1847?–ca. 1875—Homes and haunts.
8. Nelson, Scott Reynolds—Travel—Southern States.
9. Southern States—History, Local.
10. Chesapeake and Ohio Railway Company—History.
I. Title
E185.97.H455N45 2006
973'.04960730092—dc22 [B] 2006045346

1 3 5 7 9 8 6 4 2
Printed in the United States of America
on acid-free paper

To my grandfather, David George Brown.
A big man who died too young.

CONTENTS

STEEL DRIVIN' MAN

1

THE SEARCH FOR JOHN HENRY

THE STORY GREW among black day laborers, men who laid track, drilled steel, and drove mules for the railroads in the days before gasoline. John Henry, they said, was the strongest man there was. And from his first days on the line he knew that his hammer would kill him.

As a young man, John Henry drove steel on the tunnels of the Chesapeake & Ohio Railroad, striking a hand drill all day with his nine-pound hammer. John Henry sang while he hammered, his partner swapping out chisels as they dulled from the blows.

> Ain't no hammer
> Ain't no hammer
> In these mountains
> In these mountains
> Rings like mine

One day, as the work progressed, an engineer brought a steam-powered drill out to the site. The workmen at the tunnel resented it immediately, but John Henry boasted that no man or machine could beat him at his task.

> Before I let that steam drill beat me down
> I'll die with this hammer in my hand
> I'll die with this hammer in my hand

Thus began their contest, man and machine, side by side, in a race to the bottom. John Henry took the right-hand side, with the steam drill on the left.

By sundown John Henry had drilled fourteen feet; the steam drill had only made nine. Then, just as John Henry finished his work, he collapsed.

> John Henry, O John Henry,
> Blood am runnin' red!
> Falls right down with his hammah to th' groun',
> Says, "I've beat him to th' bottom but I'm dead, -
> Lawd, - Lawd, -
> I've beat him to th' bottom but I'm dead."

He knew the end was coming, and, like Samson, he asked for a cool drink of water before he died. According to legend, "they took John Henry to the white house and buried him in the sand," and forever after steam engines paid their respects as they passed.

> Every locomotive comes roarin' by
> says yonder lies a steel-drivin' man.

There are almost two hundred recorded versions of the ballad of John Henry. It was among the first of the songs that came to be called "the blues" and was one of the first recorded "country" songs. Folklorists at the Library of Congress call it the most researched folk song in the United States, and perhaps the world.[1]

Particularly among African American men and women, John Henry is an icon. In Philadelphia, men ask one another, "How's your hammer hangin'?" Cardiologists have coined the term "John Henry syndrome" to describe black men's propensity for hypertension and heart attack. In the schoolrooms of working-class Cleveland and rural West Virginia, teachers recite his exploits to inspire black boys and girls to think about their own history. For more than a century, most historians and folklorists have assumed that John Henry was just a legend, a story designed to inspire pride, an invention. When I began my research, I too started out looking for a legend, but in the end I found a real man. I discovered how John Henry came to be a steel-driver on the C&O, how he lived, and where he was buried. But how he died remained a mystery, and I set out to uncover the truth behind one of America's most powerful legends.

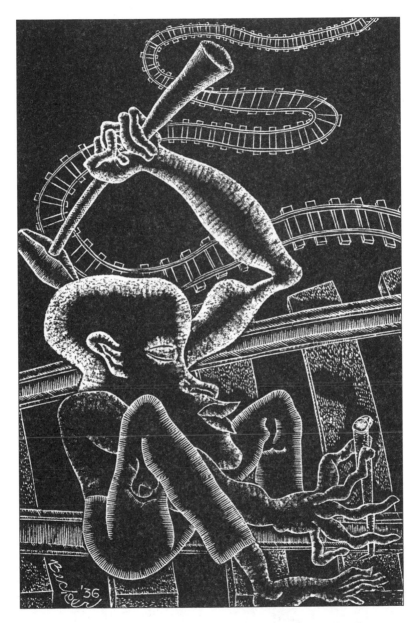

John Henry Building a Railroad, drawn by Fred Becker for the Federal Art Project of the Works Progress Administration. (Author's collection)

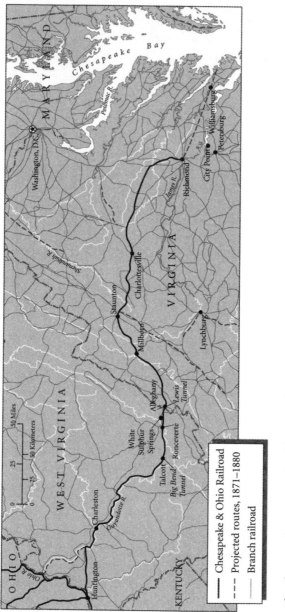

After the tunnels were completed in 1873, the C&O stretched west from Richmond to the Ohio River. Adapted from 1873 map.

I knew that John Henry's fate was tied to the rise of Southern railroads in the years just after the Civil War. Virginia and West Virginia, sundered by war but hoping for a miracle, had turned over all their stock and right-of-way to railway baron Collis Potter Huntington, provided that freight trains could run from the eastern Tidewater to the Ohio River by the summer of 1872. Huntington, the tall and barrel-chested Republican who created the C&O, had agents in Prussia selling ten million dollars in mortgage bonds, all beginning to pay off creditors in 1872. Huntington was accustomed to buying legislators, inspectors, even U.S. congressmen to get what he wanted. Only Virginia's western mountains stood in the way.[2]

Huntington knew what he was doing. He had already done something like it on the West Coast. The "Big Four," himself included, had amassed one of the largest fortunes in the world when their Central Pacific Railroad put a tunnel through the Sierra Nevada Mountains during the Civil War. Huntington had two instruments that he thought would guarantee him success in Virginia. Nitroglycerin, brewed up on the site, would blast massive holes into the mountains. Steam drills would make enough pilot holes to allow the nitroglycerin blasts to follow one another in rapid succession. Theoretically, steam drills and nitroglycerin together could bore through these mountains. Of course, in those days no one had successfully used steam drills in the South, particularly on the tough slates and shales at the foot of the Appalachian Mountains. Here was ancient mantle, hundreds of miles deep, which had been driven up millennia ago by tectonic shifts. Whatever made it through those mountains must have been a marvel.[3]

There are many mountain tunnels in the South, and many Southern states have made claims on John Henry. There are roadside historical markers in north Alabama, Arkansas, and even Texas that mark the spot where John Henry is supposed to have fought the steam drill and died. But the musical clues always seemed to lead to the Big Bend (or Great Bend) Tunnel along the C&O line near Talcott, West Virginia.

> When John Henry was a little boy,
> He was sitting on his mama's knee;
> Says, "The Big Bend Tunnel on the C and O road
> Is going to be the death of me, Lord, Lord,
> Is going to be the death of me."

Scholars in the 1920s found many West Virginians who knew the ballad of John Henry, as well as some evidence of hard drilling at the tunnel

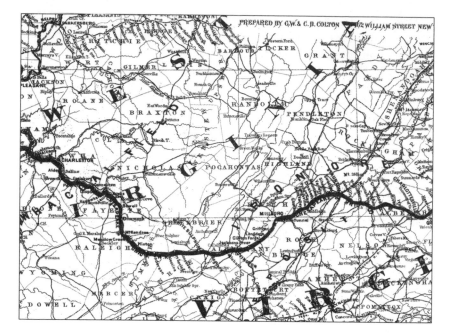

Three long tunnels were built near the Virginia–West Virginia border. The Lewis and Allegheny tunnels, each under a mile, lie just east of White Sulphur Springs on the Virginia–West Virginia border. The Big Bend Tunnel, more than a mile long, is in Talcott, approximately twenty-nine miles west of the border. Detail from 1873 map. (Library of Congress)

at Big Bend. Musicians as different as Leadbelly and Johnny Cash told their listeners that John Henry had died there, and the Jim Beam distillery donated thousands of dollars in the early 1970s to erect a statue of John Henry in Talcott. Colson Whitehead's humorous 2001 novel, *John Henry Days*, imagined an overhyped press tour at the annual John Henry festival in nearby Summers County to commemorate the minting of a John Henry postage stamp. The weight of both history and contemporary legend, it seemed, argued for John Henry's death at Big Bend.

One hundred and thirty years after John Henry fought his contest against a steam drill, I sought to retrace the route of the C&O Railroad as it shot west from Virginia's Tidewater into the West Virginia mountains. I set out for Big Bend in my wife's red Ford Escort station wagon. The eighty-eight-horsepower engine could hardly compete with the two hundred horses behind the steam drills used on the C&O. A "mighty man" could have beaten my engine in the morning and then gone home to lunch.

But my engine persevered. It was a hot midsummer morning; my wife and son had gone to Florida, so I brought my eight-year-old chocolate Labrador, Riley, along in search of John Henry. Windows rolled up, air conditioner wheezing, we put the sun at our backs and headed west. The landscape slowly passed by the windows as I ruminated about the world that John Henry knew, and the steam and steel that replaced him, seemingly in a single day. Every generation imagines that it lives in a time of rapid technological change, but in the late 1870s, within a decade, coal was replacing wood in steam engines, steel had gone from a precious metal to an everyday commodity, steam engines were replacing water races for power, and nitroglycerin was being used instead of gunpowder in blasting. In short, mechanical power came unmoored from its source. Power no longer meant horses, a waterfall, or human muscle. It was suddenly portable, cheap, and efficient.[4]

From Williamsburg, Virginia, our route to the railroad tunnels of West Virginia took us over Interstate 64 along a path that had been marked by the wooden crossties and steel rails of the Chesapeake & Ohio Railroad. The railroad stood a few dozen feet on our left most of the way, disappearing occasionally behind hills but usually meeting us again in the deeper gorges and hollows of central Virginia. When railroad builders employed by the Commonwealth of Virginia made their trail toward the western mountains in the 1840s, they followed the stone markings etched in the 1740s by George Washington, surveyor. Below them: Indian trails, deer paths, and roads cut by ancient river bottoms.[5]

Tall pines shaded the journey out of Williamsburg, where I teach American history to students smarter than me at the College of William and Mary. My job as a history professor is to get students to recognize that the past is not dead but surrounds them.

Many things that don't seem historical are infected with the history of dead people. Take the pine trees, for example. For millions of years oaks and hickories had grown along our path to the mountains, but in the seventeenth and eighteenth centuries tobacco farmers saw those hardwoods as stubborn obstacles. Planters girdled and burned them, planting tobacco and Indian corn in the shadow of the stumps. The redbrick suburbs we drove through had been tobacco fields and scrub in the years when George Washington had traveled through here. When richer, blacker land opened

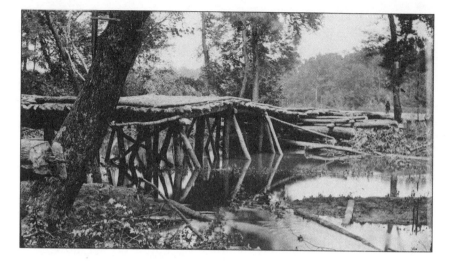

Bridge over the Chickahominy Swamp built by the Fifteenth New York Volunteers, June 1862. (Library of Congress)

up in the Deep South in the nineteenth century, thousands of slave-owning planters took their slaves out of eastern Virginia and let the land turn wild again. These loblolly pines grew in the scrub in the old tobacco fields, filling up and closing off the landscape by the 1850s. A decade later, this newly hatched wilderness of dense, young pines had become an obstacle slowing George McClellan's Union army as it sought to occupy the Virginia peninsula in 1862. That army had tried to build pine bridges across the swamps and failed, only to be nearly destroyed by the Confederate army. Planters had inadvertently left fabulous natural defenses in eastern Virginia. And they were still here. In the 1870s, workmen extended the C&O Railroad through these swamps, replacing the haphazard pine bridges with substantial trestles and steel rails.

With my foot on the accelerator, I outpaced Union armies and wood-fired locomotives as we sped along. Humming old folk tunes to pass the time, I approached Richmond and the West.

> The Captain said to John Henry
> "Gonna bring that steam drill 'round
> Gonna bring that steam drill out on the job

Gonna whop that steel on down, Lord, Lord!
Whop that steel on down."

The Union army took Williamsburg in 1862, but it took them three years to get the remaining fifty miles into the Confederate capital. By tailgating I arrived in Richmond in less than an hour.

Between the 1600s and about 1867, towns like Richmond owed their existence to waterfalls. In the capital city the James River drops a hundred feet at what used to be called the Falls of the James. The falls stopped riverboats from passing farther west, forcing travelers to change from boats to horses; the pause allowed inns, ordinaries, stables, and grogshops to proliferate, catering to travelers going in either direction. The falls also turned waterwheels that transferred power to long, inch-wide leather straps that stretched hundreds of feet. The straps could be strung together with elaborate pulleys, linked throughout a water-age "factory" that could drive

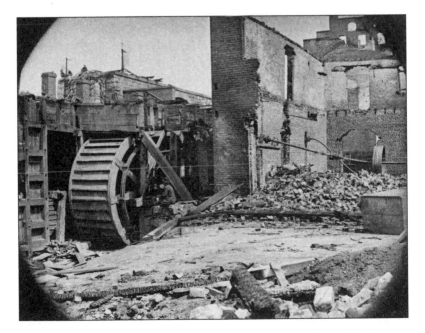

Ruins of a paper mill destroyed in the burning of Richmond, 1865. The James River turned the waterwheel on the left, which provided all of the mill's power. (Library of Congress)

lathes, drills, tobacco presses, and gristmills. A natural source of power, a break in the water like this made cities possible, from Boston to Trenton, Richmond to Raleigh.

When the C&O took control of Virginia's railroads to the western mountains, Richmond was still a world of water and wood. Wood-fired locomotives came into the city from all directions, on iron-tracked railroads. But most traffic still came in by canal, on wide, flat-bottomed wooden bateaux. Wood, stone, and brick construction limited the height of buildings to four or five stories. Factories stood along the James, using the brown, sludgy water for transportation, power, and (unfortunately) drinking.

I saw Richmond differently than the way John Henry would have seen it. The concrete bridges of I-64 carried us high over the swamps east of the city, now populated by golf courses and cemeteries. Steel girders reinforced buildings that climbed two dozen stories. Factories now went anywhere on the power grid. Where I-64 briefly crosses I-95, a quick glance to the left reveals the Powhite Parkway, named after the Powhatan Indians displaced when white settlers established the city of Richmond. The Powhite crosses over the former grounds of the Virginia Penitentiary. Only a photograph can evoke it now, since the Ethyl Corporation replaced it in the 1980s with glass-lined buildings and manicured lawns.

Half an hour west of Richmond, the Blue Ridge mountain range appears. From this distance, in the summer, a dozen shades of green tarnish the hills. Closer to Charlottesville, and on the edge of the passes into the Blue Ridge, the trees proliferate madly. It is tempting to attribute their presence to the hand of Thomas Jefferson, a collector of odd native species. Besides the oaks and hickories that had once covered eastern Virgina, there are maples, dark evergreens, and tropical-looking ten-foot weeds along the highway. Just past Charlottesville lies the town of Crozet, named after the mad French engineer who promised the Virginia legislature in the 1830s that he could pierce the Blue Ridge Mountains with a railroad tunnel. Dreaming of a direct link to the Ohio River, the legislature pledged more and more to support the tunnel's construction. From the 1830s to the 1850s, contractors employed by the Commonwealth of Virginia pushed forward with slaves, Irishmen, and gunpowder. It took dozens of years of hammering and hundreds of barrels of gunpowder before Crozet's men broke through.

That little Blue Ridge Tunnel was an economy-busting project, costing nearly five million dollars. An Irish laborer then made less than a dollar a day; a "prime" slave owned by the C&O's predecessor, the Virginia Central, cost about five hundred dollars. In today's dollars, the project approaches half a billion, and the Blue Ridge Tunnel burdened Virginia with an enormous debt just before the Civil War. Rails were laid through the tunnel in 1858, in time to allow western Virginia militiamen to stream into Richmond if they were needed. Henry A. Wise was the commonwealth's slender and high-strung governor in the years leading up to war. Obsessed by the project, he was ecstatic when he heard that the workmen on both sides of the tunnel had met at the center. He presided at the completion, declaring that Crozet had truly "acupunctured" the mountain and finally tied the capital to the Shenandoah Valley in the west.[6]

Still, there was a higher range of mountains in Virginia to be crossed if Virginia were to be tied to its western border, and Wise well knew it. Past the Blue Ridge, that Shenandoah Valley stretched for about a hundred miles, and beyond it stood the impenetrable Appalachian mountain chain called the Alleghenies. The people who lived in those steep mountain passes were Virginians, but they were foreigners to the plantation owners who controlled Virginia's Assembly in Richmond. Lowland planters called their western neighbors "mountaineers" and laughed at men who would make chairs out of twigs and at women who smoked pipes. Mountaineers, for their part, were generally suspicious of plantation slavery and wanted little to do with men who wore riding gloves, embroidered waistcoats, and socks. Most mountaineers had their roots up North, being granddaughters and grandsons of Scots-Irish servants who had drifted down from Pennsylvania after the Revolution.

Where planters saw the mountains as obstacles to commerce, poorer whites saw opportunities for settlement. They came to the mountains because land was cheap, almost free. Some farm plots, though, were practically vertical. Lowlanders joked that spring planting in the mountains required a shotgun that you filled with seed and fired into the canyons. A few prosperous slave-owning planters lived in the western Virginia mountains, most on the banks of rivers, but the rest of Virginia's mountaineers farmed on small plots with the labor of half-grown children and shavetail mules.[7]

When the Civil War began, the mountaineers of northwestern Virginia kept their distance from the planters and refused to accept Virginia's secession in 1861. Instead, they seceded themselves, from Virginia, creating a new state, later named West Virginia. An efficient route from the Shenandoah Valley through the Allegheny Mountains would have to wait for a generation, for John Henry and the steam drill to arrive.

For more than an hour I drove through the Shenandoah Valley, Crozet's tunnel at my back and the steeper Alleghenies in front of me. In the late nineteenth and early twentieth centuries, this hundred-mile valley was known for horses, apples, and neat farms nestled among gently rolling hills. The farmhouses are still there, looking down grassy hills punctuated by outcroppings of stubborn crystalline rock. But these days the horses and apple trees are mostly gone, the fields dotted with large aluminum Quonset huts filled with genetically engineered chickens and turkeys. Chopped into bite-sized pieces, these animals and their offal will become morsels for Eastern gourmets. Riley perked up at the drifting scents of manure, but we could not stop for lunch. Like the C&O, we were bound for West Virginia: The Shenandoah held no allure for us.

By midafternoon we came under the brow of the Allegheny Mountains, near the border with West Virginia. Cultural difference still marks Virginia's mountains, though the difference is no longer about tobacco pipes or socks. Confederate bumper stickers were slowly being overtaken by those that read UNION YES. Late-model Chevies with throaty V-8 engines came here to die, but not before tearing their hearts out sputtering black smoke as they wheezed up hills with 10 percent grades. I checked my position between mountain ranges and rail lines using photocopies of old railroad maps.

While speeding across a bridge, I noticed—too late—a state trooper parked on the other side. When he walked over to my window I quickly blurted out, "I'm glad you stopped. I thought I was in Millboro, but I can't find it from the signs." He looked puzzled. "Millboro is just an old town with three or four families. Why would you want to go there, sir?" I told him that I was a historian following the construction of the Chesapeake & Ohio Railroad and that convicts owned by the railroad had escaped from there in 1870. "Let me see your map," he said, pointing to the photocopy on the dashboard. When I confessed that my map was drawn in 1872, he smirked and shook his head. Then, with a warning to take it easy on the gas pedal, he gave me directions.

Leaving the trooper behind, I approached the mountains at last. Roadside cuts in the mountainside showed a hundred or more layers of sediment. About four hundred million years ago, shortly after the birth of continents, the East Coast had smashed against the coast of West Africa, and the collision pushed up mountains here in Alleghany County to Himalayan heights of more than four miles. Countless millennia of rain and river had worn three miles off the top of these mountains. By world standards the Alleghenies were small, but impossibly old, dark, and imposing. As we cruised through the narrow valleys, it seemed that the sun rose and fell in the time it took Riley and me to eat the peanut-butter crackers I had packed for lunch.

> The rock was so tall and John Henry so small
> That he laid down his hammah and he cried
> He laid down his hammah and he cried

My first stop in West Virginia was Ronceverte, a prewar lumber town pitched perilously along the Greenbrier River. Ronceverte was about a dozen miles east of Big Bend Tunnel, but it had been one of the biggest towns nearby. Mountaineers would have come here for their salt, seeds, and saddles. The falls would have powered gristmills for corn and a foundry for nails. Doctors' and dentists' offices, shops, groceries, taverns, and stables would have peppered the main street. All of this made Ronceverte a town, but hardwoods had made Ronceverte a little city. The trees were felled upriver and dropped into the Greenbrier, where gravity pulled them down to the Ronceverte falls for milling. After the best trees disappeared by the 1880s, the town became a summer resort. Now it was quiet, with a welfare office occupying the shell of an old grocery store, and junk shops across the street. I would have passed through after taking a few pictures, but from the car I spotted a cherry fiddle in one of the shop windows.

Historians read, and when we look up at the world around us we see dead people. If you think about it, of course, nearly every town and street name refers to dead people, and we're obliged to remember them. But while chasing down the dead is my chosen profession, deeper down, I am a scavenger. I check Dumpsters every semester when the students leave college. I follow abandoned trails and even harvest lumber from collapsed buildings. Bricks, four-by-four crossbeams, and old computers fill my garage. My tendency to worry over artifacts, to reconstruct their histories, was what sent me after John Henry in the first place. Now I was pulled, quite against my will, toward the junk shops of Ronceverte. Riley knew all about these expeditions, and she waited patiently at the door, glad to be out of the car.

After taking a few pictures I wandered in and out of the shops, compulsively turning over coffeepots, colanders, and chain saws. Men in their sixties held court on the front stoop of the junk shop. They talked to the dog and welcomed me to town. I knew that Ronceverte went from river town to boom town in 1872, after the railroad made it possible to load hardwoods onto flatcars. The cheap objects in the junk shop showed me that Ronceverte's palmier days were long gone. I learned from the gentlemen there that the fortunes of Ronceverte had revived a bit when a high-tech lumber mill moved in across the river. Just as in 1872, hardwood along the river had lured investors. Computer controlled and mostly automatic, the lumber factory sliced up oak flooring, along with a little hickory, for customers in the East. No one really needs hardwood for floorboards anymore, as there are cheaper materials, easier to care for, that can line your floor, but hardwood evokes the past, making a new house look solid and seasoned. Now, with rising demand, the remote hardwoods of the Allegheny Mountains seemed less impossible to harvest than even ten years ago. Nearly two hundred people worked at the mill in double shifts, and they sold every stick of flooring they made. But while sliced lumber rode the rails out of Ronceverte, people did not. Amtrak stopped running there in the 1960s. Now the passenger cars stopped at the Greenbrier Hotel farther east, and Alderson Prison farther west.

The chorus of men at the junk shop showed me the drift of the river, the curves and twists of the railroad, and helped me locate the side road from Talcott (pronounced "Toll-cut") leading to the Big Bend Tunnel. "It's supposed to be closed, but you can walk right in," they assured me. I parked near the mountain and walked.

As I approached, the tunnel looked as unimpressive as a pockmark. The Big Bend Mountain had stood for millennia, forcing the Greenbrier River to make a wide loop around it. I saw a long train entering the modern tunnel, built in 1930, and recognized the Big Bend Tunnel just to the right of it. I waited for the train to pass, and then, tying Riley in the shade of an oak, I walked the rest of the way to the Big Bend Tunnel, where some say John Henry died.

Huge stones had blocked the entrance, but they had been pulled away, probably by a truck and tackle, and I scrambled over the soda cans and condom wrappers left by modern explorers. The tunnel is nearly twenty

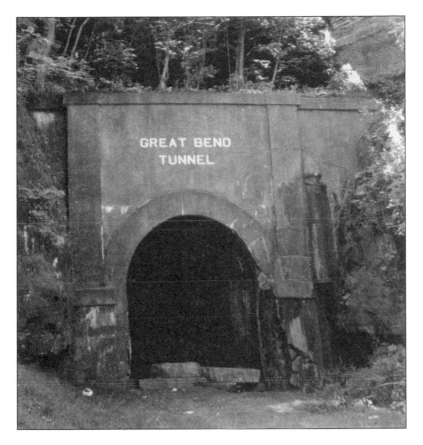

Big Bend (or Great Bend) Tunnel. (Author's collection)

feet high, the height of a double-tall railway car, but is narrower than a road. There would be no passing on the wrong side of the road in the Big Bend Tunnel: Two SUVs wouldn't fit side by side.

I had forgotten a flashlight and so used the flash of my camera to guide me the half mile into the center of the tunnel. The Big Bend Mountain had crumbly rock, "hard red shale crumbling on exposure" according to the tunnel engineers. In 1873, after a cave-in had killed a train crew, the C&O had lined it with six million bricks. The brick made the tunnel feel substantial, and the impression of being covered by a mountain was surprisingly pleasant. I felt comforted, surrounded by thousands of tons of stone.[8]

As I walked back through the tunnel, spying old railway ties and bits of chipped rock, I couldn't resist the urge to grab a fragment that John Henry might have chipped at, though I knew that the tunnel had been cleared and widened in the 1930s. Other historians have been compelled to keep some souvenir from their explorations, though few will admit it, but I do not need that object to be authentic, just a memento. I remembered that Petrarch, when he was exploring a different mountain in 1337, remarked that there were enough pieces of the true cross for sale on the streets of Europe to fill a forest. But history can be summoned up by relics, whether real or man-made, and I still like physical links to the past, a thing that could have been there, even if it wasn't.

> White man says, - "That man's a mighty man,
> But he'll weaken when th' hardes' rock is foun'
> he'll weaken when th' hardes' rock is foun'."

The Big Bend Tunnel was not, in fact, particularly hard rock. Other tunnels like the Lewis Tunnel had cost upwards of $6.50 a cubic yard to excavate. The Big Bend cost only $3.75. I needed to know one more thing about how the tunnel was built, and to do that I needed to do a little trespassing.

When I emerged from the tunnel into daylight again, I began to climb around the side of the mountain. I ran into a few No Trespassing signs. I remembered Woody Guthrie's line from the song "This Land Is Your Land": If you look on the other side of a No Trespassing sign, it doesn't say nothin'. I checked the back of the sign, and he was right. Clearing brush with my feet, I found the faint outline of what I had hoped for: a junk road.

My father had taught me about junk roads when I was ten years old and we lived in Sanford, Florida. Junk roads, Dad said, were the single-lane dirt roads that drifted almost imperceptibly off state highways. This, he said, was where people dumped their stuff. And not just anybody. People with lots of stuff. People too cheap to visit the county dump. Here, Dad said, were the treasures of old civilizations, left behind before you were born. I remember rooting around roads like these with my little brothers and finding whiskey and medicine bottles, tractors, rubber tires, abandoned stoves, and little hills of metal junk, all half-buried in the dirt. And, like Dad said, you always found something new to take home. By this time Mom and Dad were divorced, so home meant Mom's house, where scraps of metal or glass arrived carefully hidden in pockets or under our shirts.

Our best find was an old hood from a VW Bug. Dad flipped it over, roped it to the back of his car, and let us ride in it, one at a time, on the dirt back roads of rural Florida. At thirty miles an hour, riding on the back of a VW hood, you are scared and fast, racing like a river down a cataract as decades of old trash rush past you.

So with one last question in my mind, the junk road next to the Big Bend Tunnel invited me for inspection. I drove up as far as I could and then walked when I reached the deep mud. As junk roads go, this was a good one. I saw nothing made of plastic, which, I've learned from my years of Dumpster-diving, originates post-1968. Railroad spikes and sleepers bore rust that dated them from the early sixties. Farther in I found the front fender to a 1950s Ford and skinny rubber tires from the 1940s. The icy winters here would have destroyed paper and wood and eroded tin, brass, and burlap. Within fifteen minutes, I started climbing and put my hands on artifacts made before my time. Sometimes my meanderings took me far off course, but this junk road was leading me right where I wanted to go, straight up over the Big Bend Mountain to the place where the hammering happened.

I knew from contemporary accounts that if the Big Bend Tunnel had been built with the labor of men like John Henry, the work would have started from the top of the mountain. Hammer men drove spikes downward, making three shafts that descended diagonally into the rock, creating a kind of stairway that traced the spine of the mountain. This shaft allowed the broken rock, or "spoil," to be dragged up the steps and out of the hole. As workers carved the tunnels deeper, others dug across in straight lines, blasting in both directions. Acupuncturing a mountain from five directions was costly, but the multiple lines of attack allowed at least five gangs of workers to hammer, blast, and haul simultaneously.

From the top of Big Bend Mountain, I could see where work on the vertical tunnels had begun. The descending shafts had been partly bricked over, but even from here I recognized that they were too small for steam drills to enter them. Instead, little well-shaped structures suggested sites where the tunnels had been drilled by hand. From top to bottom, I had a better sense of the place now, and from both my observations and my maps, I found myself less and less convinced that a steam drill could have made it up here in 1872.

There were many reasons that using steam drills would have been impractical in this spot. Steam drills had never been used in Virginia before,

and few people understood the geology of these mountains. Steam engines
broke down frequently. C. P. Huntington, the man who acquired the C&O
Railroad from the Virginia legislature, had promised to finish the tunneling
before 1872. With ten million in bonds to sell to New York investors and
everything to lose, Huntington would have plotted out the hazards like a
safecracker. The C&O would have established a blacksmith's shop for cast-
ing the drills to be used on any crystalline rock. Nitroglycerin would have
been laid up by the hundredweight, and barrels of gunpowder would have
been stored nearby in case the nitroglycerin failed. There would have been
nothing left to chance in the execution of Huntington's plan. He would have
had telegraphs installed as close as possible to the tunnels. He would have
gotten daily reports. He would have visited the site itself often. He did.[9]

But there were no signs of dense rock in this place, no signs of a massive work camp, and none of the engineering reports I had photocopied
and brought with me suggested that there ever had been. "The heading of
the tunnel at Great Bend," wrote the chief engineer in his report to the
directors, "was opened in May [1872], and the track laid through the tunnel early in the past month. The roof, under the crest of the mountain,
was treacherous, and the cause of some fatal accidents before it could be
secured; this delayed the opening of the tunnel nearly two months."[10] He
made no complaint about the hardness of the rock, though, and no mention of steam drills. Another tunnel on the Virginia–West Virginia border,
one I had sped past on my way to Ronceverte, was in more trouble. In 1871,
the year before the line was supposed to be finished, the engineer was worried that this other tunnel was "not in so forward a condition" and noted
that there "the Burleigh steam drill has been introduced into two of the
headings."[11] Wouldn't he have mentioned the drill if contractors had used it
at Big Bend? According to the myth, somewhere in the hills of West Virginia
John Henry had raced a steam drill to the bottom because Huntington had
paid him to do it. But was this really John Henry's grave?

Thousands of people had come to this place before me, to see the tunnel and to imagine the burlap, paper, and skin left on the bare metal and
rock that stood here. Hundreds of us have tried to draw a line backward in
time, to the fateful day when the world of water and wood confronted the
world of steam and steel, and when a single man fought a machine to the
death. Years of archival work showed me how the C&O came to acquire
John Henry as a steel-driver, and why driving steel would have killed him,
but this tunnel could not help me find him. In my disorganized, obsessive

scouring of the junk roads of West Virginia I was searching for a clue, for the object overlooked, discarded, or misunderstood that might help me put his story together. That day I went home empty-handed. The C&O had not had problems cracking through this mountain, and the top of the mountain did not have vertical shafts wide enough for a steam drill. The tunnel where John Henry died was somewhere else.

2

TO THE WHITE HOUSE

SOME HISTORIES are better hidden than others. This, I suppose, is why I kept worrying over a nineteenth-century medical report from the Virginia Penitentiary. The document was incomplete, and I only half understood it when I found it. But it led me to John Henry, and the tragic story of his death, before I went looking for him.

We learn skepticism in graduate school. At Chapel Hill I worked briefly as a researcher on a documentary about a historic railroad repair shop in Spencer Shops, North Carolina. The producer drove me and another graduate student out to the gritty industrial town of Spencer on weekends to interview retired shop workers. The town controlled the Southern Railway's old shops after the doors had been shut in 1960. White shopmen, mostly old friends, tinkered with the broken locomotives in the engine house while we asked questions about Spencer Shops' history. Their stories about the old days were nostalgic: Workers and foremen all got along in the steam engine days, until the diesel engines started arriving after World War II. The diesels required less maintenance, leading the Southern to eventually close the shops. Questions about racial conflict, politics, and working conditions got us shrugs mostly. But the documents told us a different story. By watching eight-millimeter movies of the shops from the 1940s, we figured out that railway shopmen celebrated their Labor Day on May first—International Workers' Day. Workers closed down the whole town for the Communist Labor Day. This event did not jibe with their stories about all the foremen and shopmen being on the same team.

When I asked shopmen about Communists in the shops, they professed ignorance. On a follow-up trip we spoke to a shopman's wife about the ladies' auxiliaries and only gradually shifted the questions toward politics. She told us that the trainmen's union had been the radical group back in the 1940s and that the place had been torn by bitter strikes. Then the producer located "Hot-Shot." Older than the others, this black railwayman had been in the shops back in the 1930s. In our prefilming interviews, he told us how complicated racial divisions were in the shops between the 1930s and the 1950s. Black and white men worked side by side in the shops, he told me, though black workers were invariably listed as "helpers" no matter what their skills. The white shopmen sat together over lunch, clearly upset about Hot-Shot's answers to our questions.

Looking further back into the railroad's history, I located a nineteenth-century photograph of road construction in the North Carolina State Archives. Newly freed workers stood proudly holding up the wheelbarrows that they had used to "make the grade" for the line. Employment rolls in the

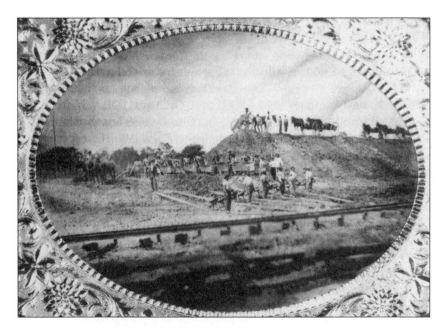

Railway workers making the grade. "Construction of Southern R.R." (North Carolina Division of Archives & History)

archives told me that in slavery days and for decades afterward most of the railroad's employees had been black men. I helped write the script for the documentary. All of us were excited about the film, and how it would demonstrate that repair shops like these had racial divides but not segregation.

By the end of that summer, though, I discovered how people can alter documents. This historic railway shop had an advisory board. One board member, a vice president for the Southern Railway, told the film's director that we had it all wrong. No black men had worked on his railway until he had hired them in 1969, over the objections of the white union. He wanted our section about black workers removed. Most of the still photographs from the archives would be dropped from the script. Interviews with Hot-Shot were off-limits. The vice president put forward the name of an aging black Pullman car porter, who called the Southern Railway a great benefactor. In the final script the Southern Railway appeared, quite improbably, as an institution that had blazed new trails against discrimination. I took my name off the credits.

I learned then why historians view history books, articles, and historical documentaries with such skepticism. They are infected, in later days, by people and power. Southern history has constant erasures, minor revisions, embarrassing facts skipped over. Each generation comes up with simple narratives that cover over a complicated, contested past. These narratives come to us with the hard edges roughed over, easily digestible. This is why historians think of history as hidden. While some stories just do not get told by generations embarrassed about their past, we trust our archives. Archives always await the careful reader, contradicting the official story that our own time and place can impose on them.

Even documents are not reliable, of course, and institutions routinely destroy them, fabricate them, declare them trade secrets, or bury them. At times the erasure is itself a document. Think of the eighteen-and-a-half-minute gap on the Nixon tapes, the erased e-mails in the Iran-Contra scandal, the ink on Martha Stewart's stock worksheet. When people try to erase the past, they often draw attention to it. So it was with John Henry.

History in the archives is not rational inquiry, and it is seldom disinterested. It is disorganized, messy, and obsessive, much like junk-road scavenging. You learn not to read material but to mine it, brushing across hundreds of documents for a nugget, then plunging in and rooting around in unlikely places. Historians scour documentary back roads almost randomly, reconstructing family life from the census or reading business reports for the telling anecdote. We are suspicious of other people's narratives, but we always assemble our own stories out of the flotsam and jetsam we find.

The virtue of a scholarly career is that you can become an expert on things that most people don't really care about, so long as you keep teaching. As I started teaching, I became an expert on nineteenth-century railroad workers in the South. My fascination started about the same time as the documentary project, when I found the letters of a dyspeptic railway worker named Henry Grady.

There is another Henry Grady, the famous editor of the *Atlanta Constitution* in the 1880s, the man who got credit for the term "New South." *That* Henry Grady was a popular public speaker who dreamed of an industrial future for the postwar South. When the Southern Historical Collection at the University of North Carolina bought the Grady papers decades ago, they probably thought they were getting the private letters of the famous Henry Grady. When the archivists found they had bought the papers of a railway carpenter, they must have felt disappointed, to say the least.

But the Grady papers are fascinating. Grady worked between 1882 and 1888 on half-finished railway trestles that reached from Atlanta west through Louisiana swamps into east Texas. He and his crew built a dozen bridges in what would become the western edge of the Southern Railway, a road that paralleled the Chesapeake & Ohio. Grady wrote his older sister Theodosia often. At times he wrote from the back of a moving boxcar, which made his hand shake terribly. These crabbed letters used terrible penmanship and spelling. As Grady moved farther west, his digestion bothered him, and he found none of the traditional remedies like scuppernong grapes available to him in Louisiana.

Grady's address must have bedeviled postmasters, because he often wrote from what railway workers called "end of track," a residence that was always moving. One letter had the return address of "Chattahoochee Bridge"; another was marked "Louisiana Swamps, VSVP Rwy." To me Grady would always be defined by his regrettable choice of writing instrument. A railway carpenter in the 1880s always had one tool at hand: a purple crayon for marking cut lumber. This thick purple crayon was the device with which Grady wrote to his sister. The product of Grady's letters would try anyone's patience. He had a poor hand; his *e*'s looked like *u*'s and his *l*'s looked like *t*'s. He had never learned to spell, but he loved big words. Deciphering Henry Grady's letters took three weeks in the archives.

As Grady built railroad bridges, he moved farther and farther into Louisiana and Texas, places he described as unfamiliar and creepy, and they made his digestion worse. Of Ouachita Parish he wrote, "Everything is covered with long gray moss, it is all very unhealthy, and having chills is the chief employment of the leisure hours of all." He was troubled too by the frightful accidents that he saw on the line, the mangled bodies, and the terrible way people treated railway workers. He mentioned that a contractor nearby, a hunting partner, was using "several hundred state convicts" to raise the roadbeds; like everything there, this seemed to unsettle him. When Grady reached Texas, where the family he boarded with housed him in a tent rather than let him sleep in the house, he decided to leave the Deep South forever.[1] Grady's concerns about the development of this new railroad artery, and the ugliness of railway work there, intrigued me. Hooked by a document, I saw an incomplete narrative that I wanted to fill in.

It was while finishing my book on the Southern Railway in the fall of 1994 that I came across another story in the archives of the Virginia State Library. Back then the library was a cramped little reading room in Richmond that had wonderful material, six-foot-tall windows, and terrible catalogs. In any historical research, finding material consists of diving: asking for help, requesting things indiscriminately, and skimming. Collect names, assemble timelines, order manuscripts, follow hunches. I got a little off track, you might say, but the diversion was worth it.

The reports of the board of the Virginia State Penitentiary, bound in a volume labeled *State Reports*, told a terrible story about railroad work. In 1872, the worst year of its record, the board made a full report on mortality to the state assembly. Forty-eight black convicts died in that year, or nearly 10 percent of the entire penitentiary. The members of the penitentiary board were horrified. To protect their reputation, they asked the penitentiary surgeon to make a thorough mortality report with a chart showing the cause of every death that year. His final report attributed "less than half of the deaths during the year [to] disease contracted in the building." The other deaths, he felt sure, had been caused by railroad work.

Three hundred and eighty black convicts had been leased to the C&O Railroad between September 1871 and September 1872, and these were the men who died. About a third were killed on the railroad, and twenty-four died a few weeks after they returned from work. The surgeon stated that scurvy, dropsy, dysentery, and consumption could mostly be attributed to construction work and tunneling on the C&O.[2]

This document provoked me at the time, but it seemed tangential to my topic, the Southern Railway. Halfheartedly following the story in 1994 produced very little. Aside from the stray mention in the penitentiary minutes, the event seemed elusive. No one mentioned the deaths in the local newspapers, company reports, the private letters of railroad builders, or even the proceedings of the Virginia Assembly, where the penitentiary board had presumably reported its findings.

The absence of discussion was in itself provocative. Many Virginians objected to the fact that the Commonwealth of Virginia had handed over the Chesapeake & Ohio's railway track to C. P. Huntington. The road, which stretched from the Tidewater all the way to the Allegheny Mountains, had cost the commonwealth millions before the war. Competing railroads were so angry about the C&O's threat of capturing trade through the Alleghenies that they bought the newspapers in the city of Richmond—the Norfolk & Western bought the *Richmond Whig,* and the Southern Railway the *Richmond Enquirer*—and used reporters and editors to promote their own railroads and to attack Huntington and the C&O in those years.[3]

So many deaths would seem a perfect story for the Southern Railway or the Norfolk & Western to use against the C&O, but it seemed to escape mention anywhere except in this surgeon's report to the penitentiary board. Without further information, I worried over the report from time to time, trying to find the story there.

Why keep such a document? Do not ask a scavenger, a collector of civilization's lost relics. Documents about black railway workers in the nineteenth century are difficult to find. Letters, diaries, census records, and legal reports help reconstruct daily life, but few documents touch on the lives of these men. We have faint traces. There are a few black railway workers' letters from this period, certainly none as rich as Henry Grady's purple prose. Court testimony occasionally gives us their voices. Some fascinating material can be found in the detective reports of men hired by North Carolina's governor to investigate Klan violence in railroad towns. But there are almost no documents written by trackliners, that gang of perhaps forty thousand black men who built and rebuilt the railroads of the South after the Civil War.

The reason is obvious. Tracklining is the lowest-paid railroad work, paying less than a dollar a day after the Civil War. Most trackliners had been born slaves, and before the Civil War Southern states had outlawed the teaching of slaves and free blacks. Very few trackliners were literate.

Their voices were mostly gone from the official and unofficial records of the postwar South. The men who worked with iron rails—laying, dogging and relining track—had left little behind them but carefully aligned timber and half a million miles of track.

Years later, I began to look at black work songs. Songs are a very different kind of source. Historians routinely use them as book or chapter titles, but songs usually fail our litmus test for a good document. People sing them, update them, misremember and transform them. The passage from event to writing is often long and complex and untraceable. Unlike wills, diaries, census records, and the other documents historians tend to find in archives, songs continue to change long after their creation. Yet African American trackliners' songs were not so different from documents at all. They *had* been passed down, documents without paper.

Of course, these songs were more than documents. The complicated rhythms of tracklining songs were the basis for much of modern music. Blues, jazz, even country music owed a lot to songs about railroads by railroad workers. In fact, the complicated, synchronized work of tracklining may have formed a basis for the complex rapping, tapping, and clapping of the modern "step show" that has become the hallmark of black fraternities and sororities.[4]

Work songs might tell more about the experience of railroad work than the tiny collection of documents in the archives. They might give a sense of workers' everyday conflicts, what they dreamed about, even how they thought about the dense network of rails that bloomed in the South. Planning to use songs as documents, I promised in July 1998 to deliver a paper on railroad work and work songs that November. The conference paper would compare Grady's letters to the railroad songs and consider how the two kinds of narratives overlapped. That summer and between my classes in the fall, I collected.

Four months later, reading and listening to dozens and dozens of work songs had put me, like Grady, at end of track. As documents, work songs are difficult. Most are fragments. For the most part they seemed to be extended complaints about work, not really stories about anything.

> Take this hammer, huh
> Give it to the captain, huh
> Tell him I'm gone, huh
> Tell him I'm gone, huh

And

This old hammer, huh
Killed John Henry, huh
Killed my brother, huh
Won't kill me, huh
Won't kill me, huh

I did figure out a few things. While the songs were not objects, trackliners nonetheless used them as tools, just like a maul, a pick, or a shovel. Gangs of four to twelve workers sang them as they dug up, or "dogged," track. The dog was a railroad pick, and everyone jiggered his dog under the track as he sang a phrase in the song. The *huh* in the song told workers to push their dogs down and lever the rail up. Just as sea shanties told sailors when to pull on the rigging, hammer songs told trackliners when to dog the track. If everyone pulled at once, it helped prevent backaches and muscle strain (both *serious* problems for railroad workers). The tempo of the song set the crew's pace.

Unlike sea shanties, which were long and involved, almost narrative poems, track songs were mostly about hard work and loneliness. Sea shanties were meaty, collectible. Like Henry Grady's letters, they told you something about people's dreams and experiences. Tracklining songs seemed hard and short. What did they suggest besides that trackliners' lives were hard and short? Tragic, certainly, but not very revealing.

I was stuck. I was just a month away from having to deliver the paper about railroad work songs in Chicago. All I could do was keep returning to the songs, rereading them, thinking about the bare stories they told. The one song that drew me, as it drew so many others before me, was the story of John Henry. Unlike most railroad songs, it was long, it told a story, and there were dozens of versions to consider. It was so rich in content that sociology and English professors had compared it to the epic poems of ten centuries ago.[5] They concluded that John Henry must have been a trackliners' hero. Because the song of John Henry was a long, partly improvised ballad, it was easy to collect. Dozens of verses repeated, but every one of the ballads looked different.

When John Henry was a little lad
A-holding of his papa's hand,

Says "If I live until I'm twenty-one,
  I'm goin' to make a steel-driving man."

And Johnny said, when he was a man
  He made his words come true,
He's the best steel-driver on the C&O Road,
  He belongs to the steel-driving crew.

They brought John Henry from the white house
  And took him to the tunnel to drive,
He drove so hard he broke his heart,
  He laid down his hammer and he died.

I heard the walking boss coming,
  Coming down the line;
I thought I heard the walking boss say,
  "Johnny's in tunnel number nine."

John Henry standing on the right hand side,
  The steam drill standing on the left,
He says "I'll beat that steam drill down,
  Or I'll die with my hammer on my breast."

He placed the drill on the top of the rock,
  The steam drill standing by his side,
He beat the steam drill an inch and a half,
  And he laid down his hammer and he died.

Before he died he said to his boss,
  "O bossman! how can it be,
The rock is so hard and the steel is so tough,
  I can feel my muscle giving way?"

Johnny said just before he died,
  "I hope I'll meet you all above,
You take my hammer and wrap it in gold,
  And give it to the girl I love."

When the people heard of poor Johnny's death
   They could not stay at their home,
They all come out on the C&O line,
   Where steel-driving Johnny used to roam.

If I die a railroad man
   Go bury me under the tie,
So I can hear old number four
   As she goes rolling by.
If you won't bury me under the track,
   Bury me under the sand,
With a pick and shovel under my head
   And a nine-pound hammer in my hand.[6]

There are more than fifty John Henry work songs, some sung as hammer songs. These were brief, usually punctuated with the *huh* of the trackliners. Others were sung as ballads to be accompanied by banjo, fiddle, or guitar. The songs about John Henry intrigued me because they seemed to be about a railroad line I knew a lot about—the Chesapeake & Ohio, the Southern Railway's chief competitor.

As I worked on my hammer-songs paper, I couldn't help recalling the story of the railroad workers who had been leased to the C&O by the penitentiary and then died. I suppose that troubling story led me to read the songs a little differently. The songs had been recorded by academics who could not easily annotate or describe their speed, phrasing, or rhythmic accompaniment. All that was saved, for the most part, was the words.

Most interpretations analyzed the words but *heard* the modern versions, which made it a fast and chirpy country song. Those upbeat versions of the song probably predisposed these scholars to interpret John Henry as a hero, a man who had performed an impossible feat. That interpretation didn't fit with what I knew about hammer songs. Most seemed bitter. They cursed hard work, bosses, and unfaithful women. They predicted pain and death.

Cap'n don't you think I ever gets tired,
Cap'n don't you think I ever gets tired,

> Of drivin' steel, Lord
> Tired of drivin' steel
>
> . . .
>
> 'Cause this here old hammer
> Hammer it must be loaded.
> 'Cause this here old hammer
> Hammer it must be loaded.
> With cannon ball, Lord
> With cannon ball.[7]

In fact, the earliest collected lyrics seemed to emphasize the supernatural, suggesting that John Henry died but still lived in the ground, knocking, as though haunting the living. In one hammer song the driver says, "Can you hear me/Knock John Henry/On this hammer?"[8] One folklorist noted that many black workers in the 1930s still refused to go near the C&O tunnels at night, fearing the ghost of John Henry.[9] The supernatural aspect of John Henry recalled West African traditions, particularly Igbo stories about evil spirits that would have been transmitted from Africa by slaves. According to Igbo tradition, those who had died in terrible or surprising circumstances still inhabited the underground. These spirits might possess or haunt the living and needed to be warded off by various means, including singing to keep their souls at bay.[10] Collectors who gathered, recorded, and transcribed these songs in the late 1920s mentioned their creepy, supernatural side, but fewer modern songs sounded this way.[11]

In the context of the traditions around the John Henry story and the hammer songs, this seemed less a story about praise than a chilling song about death—a song that men at work sang to warn themselves about the dangers of overwork.

> Lordy, Lord
> Why did you send dat steam?
> It's caused de boss man to run me,
> Run me like an oxyen team.[12]

Above all, they seemed like exhortations to *slow down*.

> This old hammer
> Killed John Henry,

> Killed my brother,
> Can't kill me.

They were fantasies of escape.

> Take this hammer
> Hammer to the captain
> Tell him I'm gone.[13]

Many hammer songs referred to John Henry, dwelling on his hard work, suffering, and death, not his victory over the steam drill.

> The hammah that John Henry swung,
> It weighed over nine poun',
> He broke a rib in his left hand side,
> And his intrels fell on the groun'.[14]

These were songs about escape or death, not exhortations to work hard like some hero out of the *Iliad*.

So I began to write about how the song "John Henry" fit into the genre of hammer songs that reminded trackliners to slow down. Labor historians talk about how workers managed their labor by setting a "stint," or pace, for it. Men who violated the stint were shunned. In the same way, perhaps, the hammer song and ballad acted as a tool in a second sense. Besides setting a pace, here was a song that told you what happened to men who worked too fast: They died ugly deaths; their entrails fell on the ground. You sang the song slowly, you worked slowly, you guarded your life, or you died.

With this in mind, "John Henry," especially the convict version from Parchman Farm, Mississippi, recorded in 1948, sounded like a dirge, one more in keeping with African American burial songs of decades earlier. The convict version of "John Henry" had many voices, not quite in unison, singing slowly and mournfully.

> John Henry had a little baby
> Well you could hold him in the palm of your hand (yah, yah)
> Well and before that baby was nine days old
> He was drivin' down steel like a man (my lord)
> Well he was drivin' down steel like a man (talk it, talk it, talk it).

John Henry told his captain
Says you'se old enough to know
That they pay more money on that C&G
Than they do on that M&O (well, lord)
Well they do on that M&O

Darlin' who gonna buy your slippers (yes)
Well-a who gonna glove your hand (yah, yah)
Say now who gonna kiss your rosy cheeks
Darlin' who gonna be your man (oh, lord)
Well-a who gonna be your man
Well my brother gonna buy my slippers
And my mother gonna glove my hand
And my mother gonna kiss my rosy cheeks
Well, I ain't gonna have no man (my lord)
Well, I ain't gonna have no man

John Henry went up on the mountain (hah)
And the mountain was so tall
Well the mountain was so tall and John Henry was so small
Well he laid his hammer down and he cried (lord, lord)
Well he laid his hammer down and he cried

John Henry had a little woman
Well her name was Polly Ann
Well John Henry took sick and he had to go to bed
Well and Polly drove steel like a man (well, well)
Well and Polly drove steel like a man

Well they's some said he come from England
Well they's some said he come from Spain (a yah)
Well but I say he musta been a West Virginia man
Cause he died with the hammer in his hand (my lord)
Well he died with the hammer in his hand[15]

I heard the echo of this dirge in three other prison songs I had collected. All were sung plaintively, with a mix of deep bass, falsetto, and tenor voices. The first was "Long John," the story of a man who escapes from a

chain gang—or slave pen—and then hides his tracks by putting heels on
the front of his feet. The song hovers between suggesting he has either
escaped or is long dead.

> Well it's long John
> He's long gone
> Well it's long John
> He's long gone
>   . . .
> Well-a God said
> In the chapter fourteen
> Every man lives
> That he can be seen
>   . . .
> Well it's John John
> Well-a marble-eyed John[16]

If John was alive, then he should be seen. Was he dead, his eyes glazed
over like marbles, or was he invisible? The second song that John Henry
recalled to me, "New Buryin' Ground," was even sadder. It begins

> Come on, come on, let's go to buryin'
> Come on, come on, let's go to buryin'
> Come on, come on, let's go to buryin'
> Well over, over on the new buryin' ground
>
> Well the hammer keep a ringing on somebody's coffin
> Well the hammer keep a ringing on somebody's coffin
> Well the hammer keep a ringing on somebody's coffin
> Well over, over on the new buryin' ground[17]

That song has a tenor lead, and then peculiar falsetto breaks at the beginning of the lines, and a bass voice underneath that becomes loudest at
the end of each line. The harmonies, as in the John Henry work song, are
often accidental, as the person harmonizing climbs up and down the scale.
Here again was the ringing. The man to be buried would not rest but kept
at work underground, refusing to stop.

Finally, John Henry reminded me of the mournful songs about Lazarus.
In "New Burying Ground," the man whose hammer keeps ringing is named

Lazarus. Another song, "Po Laz'rus," which I recalled in my wandering around the tunnel, also had the same dirgelike qualities, with a tenor lead, falsettos, and accidental harmonies. Lazarus was an escaped convict. He either sat or shat upon the commissary counter (depending on the version you read). He then ran off between two mountains.

> Captain to the High Sheriff
> Go and bring me Laz'rus
> He told the High Sheriff
> Go and bring me Laz'rus
> Bring dead or 'live
> Oh, oh, dead or 'live
> He found old Laz'rus
> Waiting in the high Bald mountains
> He found old Laz'rus
> Waiting in the high Bald mountains
> His head hung down
> Lord, lord, his head hung down.[18]

All three songs had pieces that connected: John Henry hammers back, as Lazarus does; John Henry wanders up in the mountains, as Lazarus does; the burying men dig downward, as John Henry does.

The story about the many deaths at the Virginia Penitentiary made me see "John Henry" with different eyes, both as a song about slowing down and a song of mourning or burying. I do not ordinarily see death everywhere, but the song of John Henry seemed more depressing and disturbing than the accounts I read. And while black informants told the song collectors of many deaths on the line, folklorists tended to see the song as upbeat, missing its downbeat. They assumed that if John Henry worked on the C&O he must have been paid for his labor. Some narratives of the life of John Henry told by white folks who lived near the tunnels seemed like flights of fantasy. They described a big strapping black man with a rhinestone belt and his shirt open, a man who traveled around the South as an elite laborer, making dozens of dollars a day. John Henry, it was said, could get work in Alabama, Georgia, or Tennessee, wherever hard work was needed. I knew too much about the conditions of black railroad workers in the postwar South to accept these accounts.[19] As a skeptical historian, I distrusted the story and clung to the documents, to the bitter and mournful songs.

I began by reconsidering the documents that other students of the song had used. Scholars in the 1920s referred to a few newspaper articles, some recollections, and letters by railway officials in the 1920s. Most accounts were second- or thirdhand, from children of observers, children who were not alive during the construction of the tunnels. They focused almost exclusively on the Big Bend Tunnel in West Virginia, though one of the engineers at the site stated flatly that steam drills were not used on that tunnel. Another who had been a waterboy at the tunnel during the 1870s and then became an engineer said the same thing. Researchers did not find the engineering records of the C&O, having been told that the records had been destroyed in a fire.

What these scholars did not have was the song's context. Folklorists needed to hear Henry Grady's fears of tracklaying's many dangers, the painful physical labor involved, the black-and-white interactions in the shops, the almost constant specter of death. Understanding the complicated context allows us to hear "John Henry" as a terrible and beautiful song both.

While surfing the Web in one of those fits of distraction that come upon all researchers, I found a postcard with a picture of the Virginia Penitentiary from the turn of the last century. Why a picture of the Virginia Penitentiary would be on a postcard is a question in itself. There are certainly more interesting landmarks in Richmond to be immortalized in a postcard: the statue of Robert E. Lee, for example, or the falls of the James River. But images of big, institutional buildings, no matter how drab,

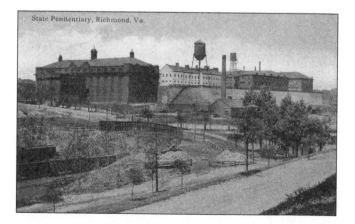

Virginia Penitentiary, circa 1910. (Virginia Commonwealth University Library)

were a perpetual source for postcard photographers between the 1880s and the 1920s. I can imagine the fun that travelers could have had in sending a penitentiary postcard to someone: "Richmond is beautiful, but this place made me think of you" or "We just arrived in Richmond. Wish you were here." As a cure for distraction, the picture itself seemed gnawingly unsettling, like the John Henry song. It had a railroad, the penitentiary, and a kind of finality to it: All roads lead to Richmond.

The image is visually complicated, which made it easy to look at again and again . Visual composition in painting often relies on a single line that draws the viewer's eye in one direction, yet the penitentiary picture has many lines: the horizon, a string of railway cars, a dirt road, a paved walkway, and a fence. The primary line seemed to point to a large white building in the center. I knew from reading an old master's thesis on the penitentiary that this was the main work building, where prisoners made shoes and brooms.

The picture recalled a lyric.

> They took John Henry to the white house,
> And buried him in the san'
> And every locomotive come roarin' by,
> Says there lays that steel drivin' man,
> Says there lays that steel drivin' man.

I suddenly recalled a conversation I had had recently with an archivist and felt a prickly, goosebumpy feeling.

I remembered that close to three hundred skeletons had been discovered back in 1992 when a wrecking company began to tear down the old Virginia Penitentiary buildings. The bones, dug up beside Byrd Street in what was once a poorer suburb of the city, had been given to a local archaeologist who worked for the Commonwealth of Virginia. She set up a dig near where an open field had abutted the fence, next to the old white house in the penitentiary. Penitentiary records had said nothing about bodies there.

I made calls all over Richmond, trying to find the Department of Historic Resources, but some reorganization made them impossible to find. After half a dozen calls and help from a *Washington Post* reporter, I reached Katherine Beidleman, the archaeologist who had examined the site. She had been assigned to analyze the bones and other junk in the ditch next to the penitentiary. She had speculated that this was a black burial ground, not part of the penitentiary at all, but she was puzzled because carbon dating revealed the bodies to be concentrated in the nineteenth century, rather than spread out over centuries. She told me about the objects found with the bodies, objects she had not completely identified. I knew when she described the objects to me that they dated from immediately after the war: a tiny piece of granite, a wartime penny cut into quarters, and a ring made from vulcanized rubber. That, I knew, was an old comb. Prisoners heated them up, wrapping them around metal to make finger rings. These were prisoner's goods.

And where had they found the skeletons? They were right next to the old white house, near the tracks of the Richmond, Fredericksburg & Potomac Railroad. This is not the railroad in the picture but a railroad on the other side of the white house, a railroad that had been torn up before the turn-of-the-century postcard was made. The skeletons and fragments of skeletons were buried in boxes. Sizes ranged from the size of cigar boxes to piano trunks. The small boxes had a few bones; the piano-sized boxes had groups of men. Each box was separated from the other by a small layer of sand. The old RF&P railroad line came down a steep trestle from Gamble's Hill onto the ground near the penitentiary, so that railroads would, in fact, roar by on their way into the city.[20]

I knew then that if John Henry had indeed worked on the C&O railroad, and died from an encounter with a steam engine, then I had found his resting place not fifty minutes from where I lived and worked, and the image of his grave was immortalized in pixels on my computer screen. Beginning on the day I discovered the man I *thought* was John Henry, I set out to confirm the story.

I found the plans to the Virginia Penitentiary in a master's thesis and discovered that the new workshop was built in 1825 out of stone from the old courthouse. It was plastered with lime, giving the building a bright white appearance—a white house. The penitentiary had stood at the top of one of the seven hills of Richmond and would have been visible from a long distance. Later, in 1877, after complaints by the city council about burials on the premises, the penitentiary established a new burying ground for convicts.[21] Where the old convicts were buried was unrecorded.

After years of perseverance at the Library of Virginia, I found an archivist who would let me examine the sealed records of the penitentiary. Using a pencil, she helpfully crossed out the line in the finding aid that declared the records sealed.[22] The records showed an inmate named "John Wm. Henry."

John William Henry c[olored] (#497)
When received: 1866 Nov. 16
Where sentenced: Prince George
Crime: Housebreak & larceny
Term: 10 years
Nativity: US
State or Province: New Jersey
County Dist or city: Elizabeth City
Height: 5 ft 1 ¼
Age: 19
Complexion: Black
Col of Hair: Black
Col of eyes: Black
Marks or other peculiar descriptions: a small scar on left arm above
    elbow. A small one on right arm above wrist.
When Pensioned, discharged, or died: Transferred [in pencil][23]

John Henry was short and had been born in New Jersey! The manuscript census for 1870 listed him as John Henry, a resident of the Virginia Penitentiary. A close comparison of the census page to the prisoner register shows that the census taker simply copied the pages from the register directly into the census. While John Henry's name appeared in the Richmond census, the prison register shows that he was actually contracted out to work on the Chesapeake & Ohio Railroad in 1868, charged to Captain Goodlow, an employee of C. R. Mason, railroad contractor.[24]

I began to search for sources using the names mentioned in versions of the song and by the black informants interviewed in the 1930s. The song mentions Captain Tommy Walters, and contemporaries mentioned C. R. Mason. The company reports of the C&O named H. D. Whitcomb as chief engineer. Contemporary newspaper reports mentioned that the general superintendent of construction was A. H. Perry.[25] Searching for information on these names, I found what previous scholars had declared to be lost forever: the engineering reports made to the chief engineer on the Chesapeake & Ohio Railroad. They were in an unlikely place, the Western Reserve Historical Society in Cleveland, Ohio.[26] These records revealed how convicts and steam drills, working side by side, cut through not the Big Bend Tunnel but the Lewis Tunnel nearby. Just as officials had informed scholars in the 1920s, no steam drills were used in the construction of the

Big Bend Tunnel. But steam drills were pitted against men at the Lewis Tunnel, where nearly all the workers were convicts, leased to railroad contractors by the Virginia Penitentiary. The medical report I had found so many years before revealed how the men who did the hand labor died in the process.

The song of John Henry is beautiful and catchy, and it has resonated with people of all ages. What started as a haunting burial song became a song about many things. John Henry was appropriated to tell the story about the position of black men during Jim Crow, about the joys and pains of the life of tracliners, about the dangers of mining, about blind men robbed of their power to see, about the coming of the machine age, about nostalgia for the past, about the terrors of textile mills, about capitalism, and about the Black Power movement. It has become a story of courage in conflict with power. But it started as a tool, used to dig tunnels and line track, to set a pace that protected railway workers' lives. For that reason it remained available, in regular use, for more than one hundred years. While the ballad of John Henry has been forged, reshaped, and recycled by people who feel an uncontrollable urge to change it, the song is still a document, a kind of black box in an age before jet engines: It carries a message from the supposedly voiceless, illiterate railway workers of the nineteenth century whom no one expected to leave a trace. "John Henry" is a tale of the terrible betrayals of the postwar South, about black workingmen's race to the bottom, and about where the bodies were buried. The rest of this book will tell that story.

The song of John Henry is the path to a history long abandoned. But it is not a pleasant story. When veteran workers told a new man to "take this hammer," it was not to make him hammer away like some black Ulysses. It was to tell him to escape.

3

WISEMAN'S GROCERY

WHAT DID JOHN HENRY DO to warrant ten years in the Virginia Penitentiary? Who put him there, and who controlled his fate? A former mechanical engineer with a hole in his forehead, a second lieutenant from coastal Maine, put him in prison. A Supreme Court ruling turned John Henry over to a county court in Virginia, where he would be tried by a jury of white men under Virginia's black codes. Documentation is scarce, but some traces of John Henry's journey to the penitentiary are scattered around us. He first appears in the court records of Prince George County, Virginia, a county radically altered by the Civil War.

Where the Appomattox River meets the Powhatan River (now called the James), they converge into a wide basin. South of that basin, among the swamps that feed the river, Powhatan and Weanock Indians built a fishing village some ten thousand years ago. At this spot in 1619 a tobacco planter traded food crops for the first enslaved Africans in North America. He made them tobacco laborers on one of the first plantations in Virginia. The tobacco they planted over the next two hundred and fifty years robbed the best soil of nitrogen, turning the land around the oldest houses into little more than baked clay, sand, and swamp. The worn-out land was worthless. In the words of an old country saying, Prince George land was fit for nothing more than holding the world together. By the time of the Revolution, Virginia planters had erected a racetrack here, and planters from up and down the James came to its taverns to wager their tobacco on horses. By 1838, the merchants of nearby Petersburg, stuck on the banks

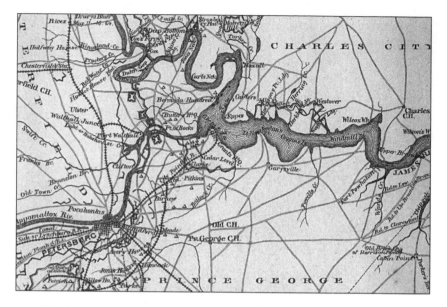

Detail from *Field of War Around Richmond and Petersburg, 1864*. John Henry first appears in court records for an incident at Wiseman's store, which stood one mile east of the Prince George Courthouse at the center of this map. A U.S. Military Railroad line (not pictured) ran near the Prince George Courthouse and Wiseman's Grocery. (Library of Congress)

of the shallow Appomattox, had sent Virginia's first railroad line through the swamps of Prince George County to give them access to the steamboats that plied the deep James River basin.

In 1863 and 1864, the sand and swamps of Prince George County became the seat of war. An instant town, City Point became a Union depot, filled with black Union soldiers. General Ulysses S. Grant, along with dozens of black regiments from General Benjamin Butler's Tenth Army Corps, camped on the eastern edge of the county. They faced forty miles of confederate trenches that had been dug into the swampy soil, surrounding Petersburg. The Union army arrayed itself along the entire line for almost two years. Tens of thousands of its black and white troopers, artillerymen, and soldiers tried again and again to cross the Confederate trenches and make their way into Petersburg. Upwards of twenty thousand died near City Point in that last year. The landscape, once a swamp, was now a ruin.

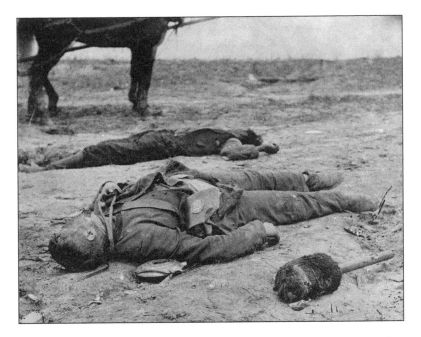

"Confederate and Union Dead Side by Side in the Trenches at Fort Mahone."
This image appears to show an African American soldier with the boots of a
cavalryman, a white soldier with a U.S. Army bag, and an artillery sponge.
(Library of Congress)

In the spring of 1865, Union forces finally crossed the Confederate re-
doubts, forcing the entire Army of Northern Virginia to surrender days later.
As planters and farmers alike now pleaded for mercy, a two-hundred-year
old plantation dynasty dissolved on Petersburg's ramparts. The Union
army, having helped to sow so much destruction, now paid others to reap
the harvest. The army hired thousands of ex-slaves into the U.S. Burial
Corps to gather the corpses, Union and Confederate, which had settled
half-submerged into the swamps. Indeed, corpses proved the county's
greatest harvest in 1866, with more bones, by the pound, pulled from Prince
George County than corn or tobacco. The army's corps of gravediggers
competed with a local fertilizer manufacturer who paid cash for bones
delivered to his door, no questions asked.[1] Thousands of black soldiers
and citizens converged on City Point to do the army's last work.[2] John
Henry was among them.

Black soldiers mustered out of the war also came to City Point, much to the dismay of local white residents. From May 1865 to February 1866, federal steamboats landed thousands of black troops at the wharves in the makeshift town of City Point. After weapons were collected and soldiers received their severance pay, they were free to find their way home. The temporary residents of City Point spent their final paychecks buying food and gifts from the "small dealers," many of them black, who had set up tents and shanties on the wharves.[3] John Henry, if he worked for the army as a sutler or laborer, would have received free passage here then.

The editor of the *Petersburg Daily Index* expressed the anger of many white natives at the arrival of these young, independent-minded black men at the wharves of City Point. They referred to these black men who had seen the collapse of slavery by the derogatory servant name of Cuffee. "Regular streets have been laid out, and walking down them one may see every line of business represented. Bar rooms, of course, are plentiful and brass-buttoned Cuffee patronizes them extensively. There are houses of public entertainment, where music and dancing can be enjoyed with a complaisant partner, upon moderate terms." The paper complained of instant "faro banks, restaurants and clothing stores." Most disturbing was the manner of black soldiers who, in the place where slavery had started, had played a conspicuous part in the revolution that ended it. "The incoming troops strut through this improvised town with an evident air of satisfaction. They feel the importance of having, by their coming, given rise to all this bustle and preparation, and show it in every tone and action."[4]

John Henry first appears in Prince George County records in April 1866. We know from prison records that he was five feet one and a quarter inches tall and born in Elizabeth City, New Jersey, and we know that he turned eighteen in 1865. No John Henry from New Jersey appears in the military records of the U.S. Colored Troops. His youth combined with his small stature had probably prevented him from entering the Union army as a soldier.

So John Henry's arrival at Prince George County is not recorded. He may have cooked for Union soldiers, worked as a day laborer, harvested bones for the Burial Corps, or lined track for the U.S. Military Railroad lines behind the Union trenches. He may have been a stevedore, loading and unloading the James River steamboats that stopped at the federal wharves at City Point.

John Henry and thousands of black men like him had transformed Prince George County, once a sleepy county of woody swamps, ramshackle

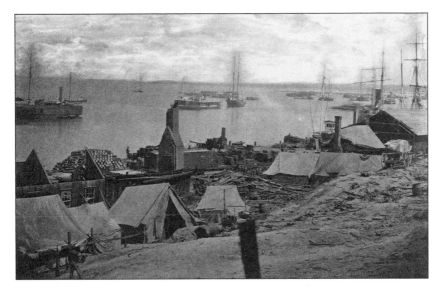

"Wharves After the Explosion of Ordnance Barges on August 4, 1864." This shows the tents and other structures erected at City Point, Prince George County, Virginia, in the last year of the war. By 1865, they had been converted to use as temporary shops. (Library of Congress)

plantations, and wasted soil, into a bustling transportation hub. Whatever his reasons for being there, John Henry was one of the young black men who raised the hackles of local whites. He would have been a free black person who, if he did not have money in his pockets, had the confidence of a conqueror. The photograph on the next page of a man named John Henry can only show us what a young black man, an inch over five feet, might have looked like in a Union camp at the end of the war. No evidence connects this photograph to the steel-driving man who worked alongside the steam drill at Lewis Tunnel.

Direct evidence points a dozen miles south of the clothing stores and restaurants on the docks to a grocery that had weathered many of the changes in Prince George County. Wiseman's Grocery was a place that John Henry knew well. A grocery, in the parlance of the nineteenth-century South, had a general store in the front and a liquor store in the back. City directories confirm that William H. Wiseman did not sell goods by the gross (as "grosseries" were supposed to) but instead ran a small shop

"Beal[e]ton, Va: John Henry, Servant, at Headquarters, 3d Army Corps, Army of the Potomac." This young man, named John Henry, is approximately the same age and height as John Henry, the man arrested in Prince George County and later transported to dig tunnels for the Chesapeake & Ohio Railroad. No direct evidence connects the pictured man with that John Henry, however. (Library of Congress)

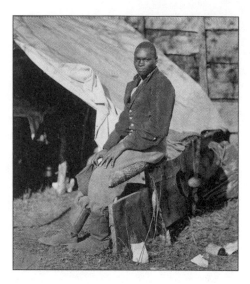

that retailed general goods and liquor. Wiseman, a native of Prussia, had operated the grocery for some time before the war as an adjunct to his forty-six-acre farm on the Blackwater Swamp, just east of the county court-house and close to the temporary military railroad. His neighbors and customers included railway carpenters, stevedores, and steamship captains. These men would have bought tinned food, crackers, pickles, and hams in the front, and whiskey or applejack brandy by the dipperful in the back. On sale days and court days, the front of the store, in the area around the cracker barrel, would have been filled with half-drunk men, black and white. A grocery, particularly in a county that had so recently received independent black workers and soldiers from the North, would have been the scene of intense conflict, including fistfights and general brawls. Young women and children would have been shooed away from the front porch.[5]

John Henry was arrested for a crime reported at Wiseman's Grocery, but the county court records do not show his initial arrest and arraignment. On April 26, 1866, John Henry entered the Richmond jail, where he awaited a trial in May. No arrest records exist for any of the gang of ten men and women who accompanied him to Richmond. His sudden appearance in the Richmond jail at that time, along with the other nine, suggests a great deal. From the end of the war until April 1866, a federal agency called the Freedmen's Bureau managed criminal cases in Virginia. In March, the Freedmen's Bureau was ordered to turn over all criminal cases to county

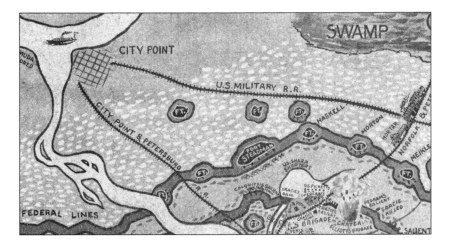

The Seige [sic] of Petersburg, 1907. A postwar historical map showing the temporary U.S. Military Railroad that ran to the wharves at City Point and near Wiseman's Grocery. (Library of Congress)

authorities for trial.[6] John Henry and the nine others would have been arrested first by the assistant commissioner of the Freedmen's Bureau.[7]

At first blush, it appears ironic that a black man would have a conflict with the Freedmen's Bureau. The Union army had established the bureau during the war to act as a sort of relief agency, yet the bureau's powers expanded greatly at war's end. In the power vacuum created by the collapse of Confederate governments, the Freedmen's Bureau became law in many parts of the occupied South. After President Andrew Johnson allowed Southern states to create new governments, Freedmen's Bureau courts continued to operate in criminal cases that touched on black men and women. Whether they were treated fairly depended on the duties and sensibilities of the local bureau officials. John Henry was unlucky enough to have encountered Charles H. Burd, the Union lieutenant who ran the Freedmen's Bureau in Prince George County.

Burd had been born near the seaport town of Belfast, Maine, in 1836, making him eleven years older than John Henry. Burd received an engineering education in or near Boston in the 1850s and briefly settled in the Boston suburb of Roxbury, where he invented and patented a mechanical relay for telegraphs, allowing engineers to stretch a telegraph's range from a few miles to hundreds of miles. As the war began, Burd returned home

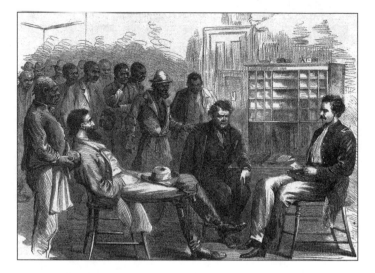

Freedmen's Bureau Court in Memphis, from *Harper's Weekly*, 1866.
(Library of Congress)

to Maine's little coastal port on Penobscot Bay. In May 1861, as his father marched through town with other veterans of the War of 1812, young Charles enlisted as a first lieutenant in the Maine Greys, Company F of the Fourth Maine Volunteers.[8]

Burd's early success as an engineer and inventor did not seem to carry over well into the military. Indeed, Burd may not have been particularly inspiring as an officer in Company F. At the time of their enlistment, Burd and his men had mustered into the Maine *militia,* answering President Lincoln's call to serve for ninety days, but when his company arrived in Washington, the U.S. Army demanded a three-year stint. While the rest of the regiment signed on, most of Burd's men refused to reenlist. The Maine government had to find another fifty willing soldiers. When the regiment finally enlisted, Burd was demoted to second lieutenant. This apparent conflict with his soldiers, not much younger than he, may have embittered the young engineer. But the civil war had even harsher lessons for young Burd.[9]

Company F saw its first fire at the battle of Manassas, or Bull Run, in July 1861. The Fourth Maine was ordered up a steep hill, where they received a barrage from Confederate artillery hidden in the trees. Two hundred and fifty yards away from their enemies, Company F became a

Confederate firing range. The rifled Confederate cannons could easily reach the Union soldiers, but the muskets in the hands of Maine soldiers could not reach half that distance. Burd received a severe and disfiguring wound when a round musket ball smashed into the left side of his frontal lobe. Leaving him for dead, his comrades beat a hasty retreat toward Washington. Confederates found him on the battlefield and transported him to Richmond as a prisoner. In Richmond, Confederate doctors removed the half of the musket ball that had buried itself in his scalp, four inches back from the initial point of impact. Burd then spent seven months in Richmond's prisons with an open wound that freely oozed blood and pus. After Union General Lorenzo Thomas issued a special request for his exchange, Burd entered a U.S. military hospital in eastern Virginia.

Union surgeons became fascinated with this wound that had collapsed part of his skull but had left Burd painfully alive. Days of probing by a military doctor yielded small pieces of the ball deep within his head. Doctors probed further, finding even smaller portions, along with tiny pieces of the inner and outer table of his skull. Burd reported that a tiny piece of his brain fell out with the last incision. The subject of two published medical reports, Burd was pronounced fit for service though he complained of a "fullness and giddiness of the head" that led to "some pain and mental dullness if he took cold."[10] He later rejoined his regiment.

After seven months with a musket ball in his brain, Burd would never be the same. He may have come to sympathize with his captors, who had collected him from the field where his men had left him for dead. Much of his time in Richmond prisons must have been a haze. Lead poisoning from the musket ball would have interfered with his concentration and memory in the short term. He would have suffered from joint pain and irritablity. Over the longer term, he would probably have been infertile. Burd would never patent anything again. Because of the musket ball's trajectory and the larger and larger hole made by surgeons to extract the ball, the wound healed to make an ugly fistula on the left side of his head.[11] Finally, we can only speculate about exactly how Burd received a hole in his head at First Manassas. Let us just say that a musket ball could not easily have traveled two hundred and fifty yards, nor come from the Confederate cannons. It is possible that the musket ball that pierced his forehead came from one of the muskets of the Fourth Maine Infantry—that Burd had been shot by one of his own men.

In April 1865, Burd traveled to Petersburg to become assistant commissioner of the Freedmen's Bureau for Prince George County. He settled at the military base in City Point, where he acted as magistrate, judge, and jury for cases involving freedpeople. Unlike most other bureau officials, Burd could back up his authority with a show of force. Two regiments of soldiers under a Major Putnam awaited his instructions. While most other Freedmen's Bureau officials busied themselves with legalizing the marriages of freedpeople, establishing freedpeople's schools, or distributing rations to the destitute, Burd apparently did none of these things.[12] Where most other commissioners reported conflict over wages between planters and their former slaves, Burd was strangely upbeat: "The feeling between the white citizens and the freedmen is very good, and they seem mutually to understand and appreciate each other's distress."[13]

The Petersburg newspapers saw little mutual understanding between blacks and whites in Prince George County and accused Burd of using his office to turn a profit. They noted that Burd and his superintendent (like their counterparts in eastern North Carolina) owned federally controlled land, which they rented at inflated prices to freedpeople. The assistant commissioners, according to Petersburg's daily, were "indulging in the most extravagant living, and all out of the . . . *illegitimate profits* of—the Bureau!"[14] The Petersburg paper also accused Burd of allowing highwaymen to rob farmers in City Point.[15] We should look on these reports with considerable skepticism. The Petersburg daily would have disliked any interference in local affairs by a Maine Yankee with a hole in his forehead, but there were peculiar things going on in Prince George County.

The peace between the mostly landless black laborers and white property owners in Prince George County seemed to come from Burd's frequent use of the military regiments available to him. For example, Burd had sent soldiers to help a landowner put down a minor revolt by his former slaves, now sharecroppers. Another bureau official later called this landowner "guilty of outrageous conduct toward the freedmen." Acting as provost marshal, Burd had the sharecroppers "confined in the guard house" on the landowner's first complaint.[16]

Farm disputes were not the only place where Burd's police power seemed suspect. Burd justified using nearby regiments in trying to track down black criminals in nearby Petersburg but reported little success in finding them. "The Freedmen from Petersburg and vicinity are very troublesome," he wrote in early 1866. Many were the "thieves" in the area, who "having arms . . . kill the hogs, cows and steal the poultry of the inhabitants of this country."[17] The next month he declared these Petersburg outsiders the source of all of his troubles: "The whole county is harassed by thieves who plunder all, irrespective of sex or color!"[18]

While Burd claimed that all was peace and quiet at home and that only the "thieves" of Petersburg were a problem, black workers in Prince George County might have disagreed. In March, carpenters and blacksmiths at the South-Side Railroad went on strike, after which Burd and his troops apparently paid them a visit. A month later, black farmers struck for higher pay. Burd came to the property himself and later reported to his superiors offhandedly, "On or about the 17th of April, a strike for higher wages occurred, but the freedmen were easily convinced of their folly; and returned cheerfully to their work."[19] When stevedores had struck earlier in April, Burd had not been able to convince them to go back to their jobs, but according to his report, he found them "quiet and peaceable." Burd's little army might have made any strikers quiet and peaceable.[20] After Burd left, his successor suggested what seemed apparent, that Burd had been acting as a policeman for hire, bringing soldiers out to support the highest bidders

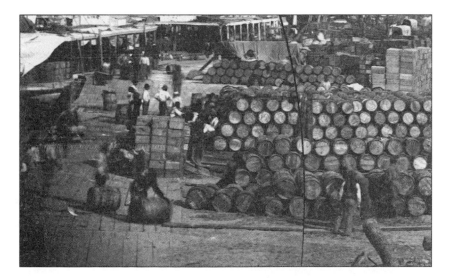

Detail from "City Point, Va., Federal Supplies Deposited on the Landing." This photograph from July 1864 shows stevedores unloading barrels at City Point. (Library of Congress)

against black workers or tenants. While Burd was almost unique in his corruptibility, the nearby soldiers may have proved too strong a temptation. Indeed, in Virginia, unlike most other Southern states, the Freedmen's Bureau's activities were entirely supported by its own operations. The bureau even had to pay for its own rations with payments from landowners.[21] This proved a terrible inducement for anyone in Burd's position.

Whatever his motivations, Lieutenant Burd saw himself as an enforcer of discipline against recalcitrant black workers. Burd ran a county court for cases involving black men and women, and he acted without juries. His supervisor, Captain Barnes, controlled the Freedmen's Bureau's second district, a multicounty area around Petersburg that included City Point and Prince George County. Burd turned over all the "negro prisoners and vagrants" he collected to Barnes, and Barnes sent them to Petersburg for "cleansing the streets."[22] The Petersburg paper noted that one black resident in the city, a former soldier, so objected to the way that the bureau handled freedpeople that he took justice into his own hands. When officials brought arrestees "from one of the upper counties" through Corling Street in Petersburg, "one of their brethren," the paper exclaimed, "jumped into the group and commenced to cutting the thongs with which they were bound, when a police officer interfered and the whole party, eight in number, were lodged in jail."[23]

Burd made no mention of the arrests he made in the spring of 1866, but John Henry must have been among them. Over a period of a week in late April, Burd turned all of the freedmen over to county authorities. John Henry was later tried for burglary. William Wiseman, the grocer of Blackwater Swamp in Prince George County, told the court that John Henry stole something from his place. And John Henry was tried under Virginia's black codes.

Besides some initial concerns about Lieutenant Burd and how he pursued justice in Prince George County, there are reasons to doubt John Henry's guilt. In 1865, the year of John Henry's conviction, the Virginia legislature—elected in that year's white-only election—wanted to stop crime. It defined crime somewhat differently than we do today. Among the objectionable crimes were "vagrancy," the flooding of black men and women into places like City Point, and the "air of satisfaction" (as the Petersburg paper put it) that black people showed about the end of the war. In its first meeting in the winter of 1865–66, Virginia's legislators framed laws to put a halt to the revolution that the war had brought, and to punish those who had brought it. Their first laws were protests against Yankee government. They then voted to repeal the separation of Virginia and West Virginia and petitioned for Confederate General Robert E. Lee to be named their governor. Finally, they passed a series of harsh laws against black people, including a vagrancy law that made it a crime for black men and women to be without employers. Black people were not allowed to testify against whites, and the punishment for property crimes increased drastically. Critics called these new laws "black codes."[24]

Though freedpeople were hardly mentioned in the black codes, enforcement efforts targeted them, especially in and around cities. In some Virginia cities, like Petersburg, the downtown slave pens were reestablished to hold these black "vagrants" until their trials. Men and women without labor contracts could be picked up by police and auctioned off to the highest bidder for three months of labor. Those who tried to escape during their three-month term could be used for an additional three months and be bound with ball and chain. Virginia enabled a "special police," a resurrection of the old slave patrol; if a white person reported that goods were stolen, the special police or Freedmen's Bureau agents were authorized to raid and search black neighborhoods. Black defendants found it difficult to defend themselves because, as under slavery, they could testify against each other but never against whites. In theory Virginia's new codes appeared to be race-neutral: A white woman could be arrested for vagrancy, for example. In practice the courts quickly filled with black men and women.[25]

In the spring of 1866, especially in the counties where a black urban population was emerging, the special police made sweeps to round up these "rogues," as the Petersburg paper called them. Sentencing was especially harsh. The General Assembly increased the sentence for grand larceny (stealing goods valued at more than twenty dollars) from a term of one to five years to a term of five to ten years. Horse thieves could be hanged. Being inside someone's house without invitation was proof of burglary, whether you had goods in your hands or not. In short, Virginia's black codes, like the codes in other Southern states, mandated a special sort of justice for black people. Every county soon held scores of black men and a few black women who faced long criminal sentences. Black or white, Virginians with prison sentences longer than a year would find themselves escorted to Richmond and destined for the penitentiary.[26]

It is ironic that the combination of the black codes and the Freedmen's Bureau would spell danger for John Henry, but Lieutenant Burd's interpretation of Virginia's black codes assured him an ugly fate. He would have been denied most of the rights in the Constitution when Burd first arrested him. Freedmen's Bureau agents were instructed to interpret the existing law, though allowing blacks to testify against their white accusers. Freedpeople in City Point asserted that under Lieutenant Burd's watch, they were not believed.[27] Thus Sarah and Lucy Thomas, both former slaves, complained to the governor that their kinsman Washington Thomas was apprehended by bureau agents and sentenced to fifteen years. The only evidence against him was that when the patrol raided a room he shared with other men, they found goods claimed by a white landowner.[28]

Who should have authority in Prince George County? No one could agree. The Supreme Court disliked the arbitrary power of military courts like Lieutenant Burd's. Republicans in Congress, on the other hand, liked the Freedmen's Bureau in principle but would have agreed that black people should have constitutional rights that Virginia's black codes and Charles Burd ignored: the right to freedom from unlawful search and seizure (Fourth Amendment), right to a grand jury trial (Fifth Amendment), and the right to a trial by jury (Seventh Amendment). Ironically, protection from Lieutenant Burd's authority came from the U.S. Supreme Court.

On April 3, 1866, the Court declared in the landmark case *Ex Parte Milligan* that military courts could not operate while civil courts were in session. The decision was aimed at overturning wartime military prosecutions, but it had sweeping ramifications for John Henry and hundreds of other arrested under the black codes. Prosecutions under the Freedmen's Court and the military tribunals were suddenly unconstitutional, and prisoners had to be turned over to county officials. In an instant, Lieutenant Burd's power over Prince George County had ended.[29] In the last week of April, Burd turned his prisoners over to the county magistrates. "The county is in a bad situation," he wrote. "They have neither constables or police, nor do they seem to have energy to make them. I have referred to the Magistrates of the County for arrest and trial, all criminal cases of Freedmen."[30] At the end of April, at least ten people, including John Henry, were deposited in the Richmond jail to await trials on May 10.[31] John Henry was thus one of the first black men tried under the regular courts of Virginia. But other branches of government still had something to say about how justice was done in the South, in Virginia, and in Prince George County.

On April 9, six days after the high court's ruling and a month before John Henry's trial in county court, Congress also made history, in the process calling all the arrests under the black codes into question. The Civil

Rights Act of 1866, passed over President Johnson's veto, made it a crime for any state official to subject any person "to different punishment, pains, or penalties . . . by reason of his color." Thus sheriffs, deputies, and even judges could be arrested for employing black codes against suspects held in custody. Freedmen's Bureau officials were commanded to attend county and circuit court trials and bring criminal charges against anyone who enforced the suspect codes. Bureau officials would bring countercharges to U.S. district courts, which had a national standing. They would be presided over by federal judges, appointed by the president. The change was potentially momentous. Still, the federal courts could not retry every court case in the South in 1866. Yet the threat existed.

So between John Henry's arrest and his first trial on May 10, the relationship between Southern courts and the federal government appeared to have changed. Twice. The Freedmen's Bureau official who arrested him no longer had jurisdiction, and then the federal government threatened to reach down and investigate state trials, even threatening to arrest judges who failed to act properly. For a brief period, all eyes were on the Southern courts. William Wiseman, owner of the grocery at Blackwater Swamp, testified against John Henry in the county court at Prince George, and the case was sent up to the circuit court, where felonies were tried. The circuit court trial came a week later, on May 17.

In rural Virginia, circuit court was a spectacle that had attracted huge crowds since the time of the Revolution. A superior court judge, a Virginia state official, presided over the circuit court. He traveled a circuit of half a dozen counties and cities, arriving in each venue with great fanfare twice a year. Circuit court might last two weeks or more. Many houses in town took boarders on those days, while some visitors pitched tents on the public grounds. Horse races, fights, and circuses usually followed court days. The sensational jury trials for murders came first, then lesser felonies, followed by the tedious civil trials. The judge always opened with a speech, commenting on the habits of the people and the condition of the country. Justice Edward Chambers, John Henry's judge, arrived in the middle of May, and he was angry.[32]

We do not have Judge Chambers's speech to Prince George County citizens, but he gave a similar speech a week later in Petersburg, which the local newspaper reported. Judge Chambers would have told the assembled crowd that "the people" ought to be congratulated on their condition, but that he could not do so. Chambers had new powers now that *Ex Parte*

Milligan had given his court exclusive authority over black men and women like John Henry. There was a "drawback," however, "on the part of the ultra radicals of the North." He would have railed against the hated Civil Rights Act, which threatened to put him and his officers in jail if they prosecuted under the black codes. And he would have decried the power of the "radical" John Underwood, the U.S. circuit court judge appointed by Lincoln, who allowed *black* men to be used as jurors. Indeed, this federal Judge Underwood could use his sweeping new powers to overturn any decision Judge Chambers might make there. (The Petersburg newspaper echoed these complaints, using every letter in the alphabet to impugn Underwood as an "absurd, blasphemous, cowardly, devilish, empirical, fanatical, ghoulish, horrible, ignorant, jacobinical, knavish, lily-livered, maudlin, nondescript, odious, poisonous, querulous, rascally, sycophantic, traitorous, unrighteous, venal, witless, extravagant, yankeeish zero.") Chambers told the people to stand behind President Johnson in his battle against these radical congressmen and radical judges. At the end of his diatribe, he would have opened the court for criminal proceedings and begun the trial of John Henry.[33]

A simple case of burglary then became anything but simple. The rules of evidence under Virginia's laws were now suspect, and capable of federal review. Under Virginia law, John Henry's alleged burglary could only be a felony if he had taken more than twenty dollars' worth of goods. The trouble was, no one could have walked out of Wiseman's store with twenty dollars' worth of merchandise. In 1871, an auditor put the combined value of the goods in Wiseman's store at fifty dollars, the single most valuable item being the store's clock, valued at two dollars. The two hogs sleeping in the back were worth only five dollars apiece. If the case was burglary, John Henry could only have committed a misdemeanor inside Wiseman's store. And if the crime was a misdemeanor, Judge Chambers would have no business trying it in a circuit court. In addition, Virginia's laws were now suspect. Was the higher penalty for burglary one of Virginia's "black codes"?[34]

The prosecutor then encountered a related obstacle. Stealing goods from a shop in daylight is shoplifting, which is a misdemeanor. To find John Henry guilty of a felony, the prosecutor had to change the store into a house and charge John Henry with housebreaking. Thus, the prosecutor had the court clerk cross out "burglary" on the indictment and replace the charge with "housebreaking and larceny." But housebreaking was a problematic charge. City directories, tax rolls, and census rolls show that

Wiseman's only building on his land was a grocery. Tax records for 1871
show that Wiseman had only one building on the entire property, valued
at one hundred dollars. For John Henry to have broken into a house,
Wiseman's hundred-dollar building must have operated as both a dwelling
and a grocery, perhaps with Wiseman's family living upstairs. Apparently
the prosecutor wasn't sure whether this was the case, so the judge gave
him time to gather more evidence.[35] Chambers ordered the trial "continued until the next term at the Defendant's costs." John Henry would have
to wait in jail for six months, until Judge Chambers came back to Prince
George County.[36]

Standing in the crowd during Judge Chambers's speech, and sitting at
the trial in May 1866, was Lieutenant Burd, the man who had arrested
John Henry. A few days later he blandly declared to his captain: "Four
criminal cases, in which freedmen were defendants, were tried. I am pleased
to state that no feeling against them as colored persons was exhibited[;]
they were tried impartially." Soon Burd faced his own kind of trial. Later
that month Freedmen's Bureau commissioner General O. O. Howard began investigations into charges of corruption and cruelty among the
commissioners and assistant commissioners. Howard declared that officers
accused of "severity and cruelty toward the freedmen on their own part . . .
carelessness in rendering their monthly accounts, and other offenses" might
receive a court-martial. "But the occasions for such trials are to be deprecated," he continued, "and they may be forestalled by a thorough system
of inspection, and a prompt removal of every unfaithful officer." Burd's
supervisor was quickly mustered out of the service in June. Burd was ejected
in August, three months after John Henry's circuit court trial. John Henry
remained in jail for another three months, awaiting his second appearance before Judge Chambers.[37]

The Freedmen's Bureau replaced Burd with a more sympathetic agent,
Lieutenant J. Arnold Yeckley, who arrived in August and watched John
Henry's second circuit court trial that November, as he was expected to
do. The trial was short. Yeckley felt that, in general, Judge Chambers's conduct "seemed to me to be fair towards the freedmen," but one defendant
may not have received justice: "John Wm. Henry, a freed boy, was found
guilty of having committed burglary, and sentenced to the penitentiary
for ten years. The sentence seems a long one," he noted. Yeckley did not
routinely call other black men "boys." John Henry was only nineteen and
at five feet one, may have appeared young for his age. Since Yeckley was

new to the area and had little knowledge of local conditions, he did not feel compelled to interfere with the proceedings. A. P. Rainey read John Henry's verdict: "We of the jury find the defendant guilty and assess the term of his imprisonment in the penitentiary house and public jail at ten years."[38]

The evidence in Prince George County's records suggests that John Henry broke into William Wiseman's store and stole something of value. A misdemeanor in 1864 was a felony in 1865 and afterward, now that Virginia's white legislature had rewritten the law to punish what they perceived as black crime. By turning hundreds of misdemeanors into felonies, Virginia actually invented a crime wave, one that juries felt they had to stop. For the all-white landowners' jury empaneled before Judge Chambers that day, this young black man would have symbolized the black and Yankee invasion of Prince George County begun by Butler's Tenth Army Corps of black and white soldiers. John Henry, from Elizabeth City, New Jersey, was its last and most visible remnant. Another black man, Andrew Heath, was tried on the same day for rape. Heath's sentence was reduced to a year when his former owner testified to his good conduct. In John Henry, the jury saw a young black man and a stranger. He received no supporting testimony. [39]

Lieutenant Burd arrested John Henry at the time of the railroad shop and stevedore strikes that spring, for theft or destruction of property at Wiseman's store. John Henry may have been on strike, he may have stolen food, or he may have taken the cash box in Wiseman's Grocery. We may never know. Whatever John Henry's crime, the punishment for a daylight theft at Wiseman's grocery store was a harsh one, because at the Virginia Penitentiary ten years would be a death sentence.[40]

4

WARD-WELL

WHO WAS RESPONSIBLE for John Henry, and who sent him out west to fight a steam drill? It was a white-haired man from Maine, descended from wizards, himself a political prisoner during the Civil War. He sought to reform the Virginia Penitentiary, but in doing so he loaded the inmates into railway cars and sent them off to die in a railway tunnel.

Radical Reconstruction was brief, but it changed Virginia in lasting ways. We remember it as a period when military commanders controlled Southern states, requiring that the states draft new constitutions, allow black men to vote, and pass the Fourteenth Amendment. But Radical Reconstruction, also called Military Reconstruction, also radically transformed the Virginia Penitentiary and made the C&O Railroad possible. Radical Reconstruction didn't free John Henry. Instead, military government helped turn the penitentiary into a vast source of cheap, transportable labor. Just as the penitentiary opened, Virginia's military commander allowed a cabal of private investors, styling themselves the Chesapeake & Ohio Railroad, to gobble up the Virginia Central and Covington & Ohio railroads, while leaving behind all the contracted debt to the state. The combination of cheap labor, new railroad owners, and new technologies allowed the C&O to create one of the longest vertical tunnels in the world.[1] In three years a black man without friends, convicted by unconstitutional laws, would use his hammer to rewrite the history of the South.

On a Friday in the middle of November 1866, sheriff's deputies from Prince George County transported John Henry to Richmond's Virginia

State Penitentiary. Coming from nearby Prince George County, the prisoner and his captors would have boarded one of the last steamboats coming up the James before the ice set in. Their journey would take them a dozen miles in less than an hour, with John Henry shackled to a rail. If he stood on the decks he would have seen a landscape transformed by war: the immense Union depots at City Point, the Dutch Gap Canal built by Union engineers, the river obstructions erected by Confederates, and the gunboats wrecked by grapeshot and canister. West Richmond was being rebuilt, but it still reeked of smoke. Convict and captors took a route that Abraham Lincoln had taken only nineteen months earlier, when the western half of the city had burned to the ground.

The Confederate government had abandoned the city at the surrender, taking the last train out after Union soldiers broke through the trenches in nearby Petersburg. Retreating Confederates laid torches to the tobacco warehouses, the arsenal, and a flour mill on the banks of the river. The fires jumped from block to block in the neighborhoods south and east of the penitentiary. In the confusion of that April night, when no government existed in Richmond, all the convicts in the penitentiary escaped. Only fifty or so had been recaptured. As John Henry and the deputy entered the newly erected gates, the walls of the penitentiary buildings were still standing. They would have seen a yard, some serviceable outbuildings, and nearly five hundred inmates, most of them newly convicted. John Henry became prisoner number 497.

Upon his arrival, Mr. Pendleton, the receiving clerk at the penitentiary, would have inspected his body carefully. Most white men who entered the penitentiary had tattoos, often of stars or anchors. Every black man listed on Pendleton's prison rolls had a scar. If John Henry did not have a scar when he arrived, Mr. Pendleton would have instructed the gate wardens to give him one. At age nineteen, John Henry had, or shortly received, two: a small one on the left arm above the elbow, and another small one on the right arm above the wrist. He was easy to identify. Shorter than most convicts, he stood five feet one and a quarter inches tall. Though Pendleton and the guards would not have thought of it, the diminutive man before them was the perfect height for tunnel work. After his head was "neatly cropped" he received a cotton undershirt, a uniform with black and white stripes, a straw tick bed, and a blanket. All had been made by convicts, the women, children, and crippled men who worked in the penitentiary shops.[2]

Outside the sprawling twelve-acre grounds of the penitentiary, the ru-ined city of Richmond was filled to bursting with other new arrivals, mostly black men, women, and children from the nearby counties. Young black men roamed the streets in discarded Union uniforms. Men and women scavenged and sometimes stole scrap iron for sale in the pawnshops and "junkers" that sprang up in Richmond's storefronts.[3] Black entrepreneurs, wearing caps with black stars that would have identified them as brothers in secret fraternities, sold lottery tickets for as little as a halfpenny. In the year after the surrender, Richmond had become a black city, and a poor city, overnight.[4]

As a young man, John Henry might have fit in, but prisoners would have seen the young man as a foreigner: The warden listed his birthplace as Eliza-beth City, New Jersey. He was the only man from New Jersey in the peniten-tiary, and one of just ten black men from New Jersey in the entire state.[5]

He entered the grounds of the penitentiary on November 16, just as President Andrew Johnson declared the twenty-ninth of November a "day of thanksgiving and praise." The president suggested that the provisional state governments he had created should all shut their doors on that day. Reconciliation was the watchword. In an act of Thanksgiving mercy, Gov-ernor Francis H. Pierpoint pardoned a white convict named James Artes of Southampton County, ending his two-year sentence for housebreaking and larceny. President Johnson believed that the war's bitter recrimina-tions were at an end and that Southern states need only abolish slavery and petition to rejoin the Union. John Henry and hundreds of other black men and women, convicted under the black codes, would have doubted that the bitter recriminations of civil war were over.

For those black men and women in the penitentiary, the Civil Rights Act passed by Congress in 1866 had not guaranteed justice. To perma-nently invalidate the black codes that had convicted them, Congress radi-cally and permanently transformed the relationship between state and national government. Back in the summer, while John Henry waited for his second circuit court trial, Congress had passed and forwarded to the states a proposed amendment to the Constitution. This Fourteenth Amend-ment declared that all people born in the United States were citizens of the United States. No longer would states decide who was and who was not a citizen. Just as important, neither states nor state laws could deny a person equal protection of the laws. Black people would be guaranteed all the rights in the Constitution, rights that would invalidate Virginia's black codes, one by one.

The conflict over state and federal power might have ended there, but Southern legislatures fiercely resisted this federal intervention. For a constitutional amendment to be passed, three-fourths of the states had to ratify it. Southern states, and a few Northern ones, flatly refused to accept either equal treatment for blacks and whites or federal interference in state law. A mile away from the penitentiary, when John Henry was in his third month of captivity, the Virginia Assembly rejected this proposed Fourteenth Amendment, 74 to 1 in the House, 27 to 0 in the Senate. The *Richmond Dispatch* was frank about the case. Yes, the editors wrote, the United States guaranteed to each state a republican form of government. But was this "intended to guarantee any rights of any sort to the negro race? We answer unhesitatingly, No . . . we are astonished that any one should seriously question the correctness of our original assertion."[6]

The American public in the North was inclined to disagree. As the winter settled over the nation at the end of 1866, public opinion about the South had shifted decisively, and it showed in the November elections from Maine to Missouri. Perhaps it was President Johnson's veto of the federal legislation that continued the Freedmen's Bureau. Perhaps it was his drunken speech on Washington's Birthday suggesting that Republicans Thaddeus Stevens and Charles Sumner were as guilty of treason as Jefferson Davis! Perhaps it was the black codes throughout the South, or the fact that Southern states had sent Confederate officers to Washington, ready to take their seats in Congress. Did Republicans "wave the bloody shirt," recalling the Union soldiers buried in shallow trenches at Andersonville Prison Camp? They certainly did. When Congress returned in December 1866, the halls were filled with Radicals: Republican majorities in both houses. Justice would be done in the South.[7]

John Henry might have had his doubts. As Radical Reconstruction began in January 1867, John Henry saw the weather turn cooler outside the gates of the penitentiary. In that season, Congress declared that the new postwar governments that President Johnson had set up were illegitimate. Any Southern state that failed to pass the Fourteenth Amendment would be treated like a federal territory and remain outside of the Union. The South would be divided into five military districts, with Virginia becoming Military District Number 1. New constitutions would have to be written by the states, and black and white voters together would elect the men who would draft these constitutions.

John Henry and the hundreds of other black men arrested under the black codes would not participate in this egalitarian process of re-forming the state. Nor did the new states created by Radical Reconstruction invalidate the convictions of black Southerners tried under the black codes. Indeed, the mass arrests of black men (and some women) continued through the spring of 1867. In October 1866, before John Henry arrived in Richmond, black inmates outnumbered whites in the facility by three to two. By January 1867, shortly after he had arrived, black prisoners would exceed whites there by nearly ten to one. The vast majority, nearly 80 percent, were imprisoned for property crimes.[8] John Henry would have had two roommates when he arrived at the penitentiary's grounds in November. By 1867 he would have shared a cell with a fourth man.

By then the penitentiary, which had once supported itself by the sale of goods manufactured in prison, was in a financial crisis. With Richmond so impoverished, the penitentiary could no longer generate income from items manufactured by prisoners in the shoe shops or weaving rooms. Tax money was not available either, as taxes could hardly be collected in a state that had seen so much war. Yet the number of prisoners kept increasing. Formally at least, the black codes had been eliminated. The federal government had invalidated special police raids and limits to black testimony. But the whipping post and ten-year sentences for minor property crimes remained in force. In that sense the black codes in Virginia never ended. Dozens of prisoners, convicted of minor crimes, came streaming in from the counties to serve terms alongside the murderers and rapists for whom the penitentiary had been intended.

Radical Reconstruction had come to Virginia, but it did not enter the Virginia Penitentiary right away. Because John Henry was black, he could be forced to do labor on contract. Spring and fall would have entailed outdoor work with shovel and pick at one of the firms chosen by the governor. When John Henry took up residence in the penitentiary, other black prisoners were digging out coal at Major Claiborne R. Mason's mines in Chesterfield County, or working under the watchful eye of J. W. Ezelle at the Maiden Voyage Dam on the James River and Kanawha Canal. John Henry and his fellow inmates would work on projects to reconstruct the city, but they would not benefit from its political reforms.[9]

Military Reconstruction came to Virginia in the unlikely person of its district commander, General John M. Schofield. Schofield was a lifelong Democrat, as suspicious of Radical Republicans after the war as he was when they had attacked slavery before the war. A Northern Democrat raised in Freeport, Illinois, Schofield learned of original sin from his father, a

Baptist minister of the old school. From his roommates at West Point, two planters' sons, he learned how white Southerners viewed New England Yankees. Schofield was a "Western man," and therefore safe in their eyes. He remained that way throughout the war and afterward.

Schofield never forgot his lessons or his friends. Before the war came, Schofield owed his rapid promotion to his Southern friends and a family acquaintance with then–Secretary of War Jefferson Davis. When the war came, Schofield stood by the Union and became a decorated general. Now, after the war, a trifle plumper and prematurely balding, the military commander in charge of Virginia's reconstruction was suspicious of Radical Republican plans to reshape the South. Like many in the army, he would have believed the conventional wisdom that blamed the war on New Englanders who meddled in the domestic affairs of the South.

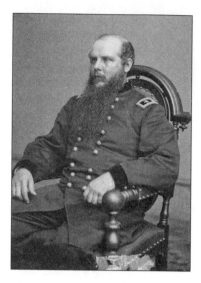

General John M. Schofield. (Library of Congress)

As a career army officer, Schofield was considered a competent general and an astute political operator. Machiavelli would have marveled at the man who convinced Louis Napoleon to remove his troops from Mexico in 1866. Schofield was also well liked by white conservatives, who saw him as a Republican they could live with.[10]

Military Reconstruction gave Schofield the power to appoint a new governor. Sniffing the political wind, Schofield chose a seemingly moderate Republican friend in April 1866, Brevet Brigadier General Henry Horatio Wells. Wells had become famous in his management of the investigation into the Lincoln assassination. Wells's men had captured John Wilkes Booth, and Wells was currently the country's assistant counsel in the trial of Jefferson Davis. Governor Wells, in consultation with Schofield, would appoint moderate Republicans to office and try to prevent the Radicals from coming to power.[11]

Yet a few Radicals slipped through. Burnham Wardwell was the most famous of these, a man whose family had seen prisons from the inside. Wardwell was a small, unassuming, white-haired man, descended from Quakers in Maine. But Burnham Wardwell had ice in his blood. He was no moderate.

He was a proud descendant of generations of religious dissenters who had paid dearly for their faith. Wardwell's father, now dead, had been named after their well-known ancestor Eliakim Wardwell. *That* Eliakim had been raised a Quaker in Salem, Massachusetts. It was dangerous to be a Quaker in Salem. In the days of the Salem witchcraft trials, Quakers like the Wardwells were despised and feared. And Eliakim's father's faith was tested. In 1692, when Eliakim was five, all of his adult relatives—father, mother, sister, and half sister—were arrested as "witches." When his father refused to admit to demonic possession, the town of Salem hanged him as a wizard. Five-year-old Eliakim was bound off to a neighboring town as a laborer. Years later, when he and his wife had their first child, both were stripped and publicly whipped for "fornication," that is, for not marrying in the Puritan church. From his first years in cold and rocky Maine, Burnham Wardwell would have learned about unjust trials, persecution, and a state's capacity to enslave and murder its own citizens.[12]

Wardwell did not just learn this lesson secondhand. He had come to Richmond in the 1840s as an ice merchant, had raised two children there, and had made the dangerous decision to support the Union during the Civil War. When the Confederate government advised foreigners to leave Richmond, Wardwell stayed to watch over his successful ice business. Then in 1862 the Confederacy had declared martial law in the city and imprisoned its most prominent Unionists. Those who refused to take an oath of allegiance to the Confederate government were jailed as possible spies. Along with eighteen other citizens, mostly lawyers and merchants, Wardwell entered Castle Godwin. He was later transferred to one of the Confederacy's most terrible prisons, nicknamed Castle Thunder.[13] After the war, military investigators declared the prison commandant "harsh, inhuman, tyrannical, and dishonest."[14]

Burnham Wardwell remained a prisoner of the Confederate government for much of the rest of the war. His young sons, captured with him, traveled more freely in the city. They often visited Union officers held in Libby Prison, where the soldiers gave them military buttons from their jackets, according to their mother.[15] Wardwell was released only after Union officials arrested Confederate sympathizers in Alexandria and held them hostage for the release of Wardwell and others. After the fall of the Confederacy, Wardwell returned to the wasted city that had incarcerated him.

Wardwell shortly became a Radical Republican and supported the right of black men, literate or not, to vote in general elections and rewrite their state constitutions. The white Richmond elite feared that Wardwell sought to punish them and circulated rumors that he had joined a secret society called the Ferrets. This group allegedly ferreted out old Confederates in postwar Richmond society, notifying Union officials if an ex-Confederate sought political office. After more than two years in Confederate prisons, Wardwell might have had little concern for the snubs of polite Richmond society.

Governor Wells, as assistant prosecutor for Jefferson Davis, would have seen Wardwell in action a few months before. In May 1866, Wardwell had been empaneled on a federal jury in Virginia for the trial of Jefferson Davis, for treason. While John Henry's jury was all white, Jefferson Davis would have looked over, to his horror, at the first interracial jury in Virginia. Burnham Wardwell was proud to have been called. When a photographer came in to take a picture of the jury, Wardwell, unembarrassed, posed with a brotherly hand on the shoulder of his fellow juror, a former slave. In a strange coincidence, John Henry's trial and Jefferson Davis's began on exactly the same day. John Henry faced trial for theft and was imprisoned for ten years. Jefferson Davis faced a trial for treason, piracy, and the intentional murder of five hundred soldiers at Andersonville, but Judge Underwood suspended the trial indefinitely, and it ended without prosecution.[16]

When Radical Reconstruction put General John Schofield in charge of the administration of Virginia in March 1867, Colonel Orlando Brown of the Freedmen's Bureau suggested that Burnham Wardwell, once a captive of the Confederate state, was a troublemaker. Appoint him, said Brown, to a government position where he would "keep still."[17]

Perhaps Schofield saw some humor in appointing a man named "Wardwell" as the warden of a penitentiary. Making a former prisoner of Confederates into a warden himself may have seemed peculiarly fitting. But even as a warden, Wardwell did not "keep still." He was horrified, though perhaps not surprised, at what he saw when he arrived in April 1868, a year and a half into John Henry's term. In a report to Governor Wells, he declared the cells in "bad condition generally, very dirty, not to say (in every case) absolutely filthy—many of them being badly ventilated." He set the prisoners immediately into "the work of fumigation, whitewashing & ventilating."

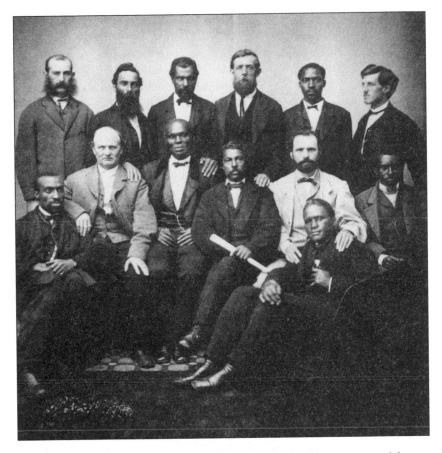

Petit jury for the trial of Jefferson Davis. Burnham Wardwell is seated second from the left. (Valentine Richmond History Center)

Inside the cells, conditions seemed even worse. Blankets for the coming winter were so "worn, torn, patched and dirty" that, while some could be boiled in salt water, most of the rest were so infested with lice that they had to be burned. No religious tracts or services were available for prisoners, and few could read. Wardwell contacted a prison reform society in Philadelphia about the conditions there. They sent an elderly Quaker reformer to Richmond to establish a day school inside the prison.[18] Wardwell worried that the many metal nails and files lying around the prison could be used for escape or for violence against other prisoners. He had them replaced with wooden pegs.

Wardwell was most surprised by the punishments meted out by the guards. While Virginia's penitentiary officials had declared the "dungeon" a barbaric relic as early as the 1820s, when Wardwell arrived, prison rules still allowed prisoners to be sealed in a covered hole in the floor. Wardwell also discovered that the penitentiary had a rack of equipment designed to torment its inmates, including "the lash, whipping-post, gagging irons and other instruments of torture."[19] Wardwell concluded his report to Governor Wells by wondering whether it was not "rather late in the nineteenth century to resort to such punishments as shaving a portion of the head, gagging, or, even, ducking."[20] Wardwell removed Mr. Pendleton, the receiving clerk who would have issued John Henry his scars, and began replacing the guards.

Wardwell's solution to his prison's financial woes relied on a massive expansion of the prewar convict program. Whereas previously workers had been sent out seasonally to dig canals, work in mines, or break land and lay track, Wardwell imagined a system in which workers would be leased year-round to railroad contractors in the mountains of Virginia. In exchange for providing safe and well-guarded barracks, and twenty-five cents per day per prisoner, contractors would get access to the hundreds of men who were filling his penitentiary.[21]

The next month, May 1868, Wardwell took a train to the western edge of the state, where a few prisoners were already at work under the new system of year-long contracts. Compared to the penitentiary, the Covington & Ohio railroad works under Joseph Shultz and his son seemed bucolic. "I visited the quarters of the prisoners. These were comfortable, as well as secure, being well provided with bunks, straw and blankets." Shultz and Wardwell both agreed that some of the prisoners were confined for crimes "too trivial for such punishment." Shultz even asked that three prisoners be released. The food, Wardwell noted, was much better than prison fare. "The Messrs. Shultz, the Guard and myself dined on the same kind of food furnished the convicts," Wardwell wrote to the governor, "and I observed it was not only plentiful but good and well cooked."[22]

Seeing the splendid example set in western Virginia, Wardwell instituted the year-round convict lease. He saw the lease as a reform, a cure for the many ills of the Virginia Penitentiary system. Between September 1868 and January 1869, he signed over more than 225 men to the Covington & Ohio Railroad for the continuation of the western section of the line. John

Henry left on December 1 with fourteen other men, fifteen blankets, and thirty rations. Although his age was listed as nineteen, that was his age at incarceration. He would have been twenty-one at the time. Other black men were voting for the first time in their lives; John Henry would never see the outside of Virginia's prison pens. He had not been outside of prison since before his nineteenth birthday.[23] Because it had been over two years since his arrest, even if John Henry could have afforded a lawyer, state law declared his case beyond appeal.[24]

Eighteen years later, after John Henry died, Wardwell, still a prison reformer and warden in Boston, would change his mind about the convict lease system that he had helped to expand. In a speech to the Constitution Club in Boston he declared that the convict system "injured honest workers outside" because it forced day laborers to compete with the low cost per day of convict laborers. Meanwhile, said Wardwell, the convict lease "was often death to those inside," because convicts forced into dangerous working conditions could not quit.[25] But in 1868, Wardwell had not yet seen the horrible things that the convict lease could do to men like John Henry. As Wardwell considered year-round leases to the railroads, a new corporation was emerging, determined to bore a path through the Appalachian Mountains and hungry for the inmates of Wardwell's penitentiary.

Indeed the Covington & Ohio that Wardwell visited would not remain the Covington & Ohio for long. As Radical Reconstruction moved forward, Congress and the president tussled over who would be war secretary, the man who appointed the military commanders in the South. In the summer of 1867, President Johnson had tried to remove Lincoln's wartime appointee, Edwin Stanton, putting Ulysses S. Grant in his place. When Congress reconvened, it demanded that Stanton be reinstated. Grant resigned, and from January until June 1868, President Johnson had no secretary of war, leaving military commanders to informally take orders from Grant as the Commander of the Armies of the United States. The year 1868 would see all the South's state-supported railroads move into private hands.

By June 1868, John M. Schofield had become the architect of Military Reconstruction, at the rudder of the Southern states. At first, when President Johnson faced congressional impeachment for having fired Stanton, he seemed almost powerless. But after surviving his impeachment vote in May, Johnson found a kindred spirit in Schofield, Virginia's military commander, and saw him as cabinet material. When Schofield joined Johnson's cabinet on June 1 as the next secretary of war, he still had one last thing on his to-do list: the privatization of Virginia's public railroad system.

Schofield had always disliked Virginia's policy of buying 30 percent or more of the stock in each of the state's railroads, and he understood that voting control over the railroads gave Southern governors tremendous power. The Virginia governor's appointees to the Board of Public Works voted all of the state's stocks, and thus effectively chose the railroads' presidents. Railroad presidents in turn made excellent candidates for political office, allowing a sharp-eyed governor to groom his own successor in a railroad president's office. In October 1868, Schofield's replacement as military commander, General George Stoneman, wrote privately that he had discovered a plot by railroad baron Collis Potter Huntington and others to persuade Virginia's Board of Public Works to vote its shares in favor of a tool, Confederate General Williams C. Wickham. This man who knew nothing of railroads would turn over the Virginia Central railroad system, along with the Covington & Ohio, to Huntington and his men. What, Stoneman wrote Schofield, should I do?

The newly minted secretary of war shot back to Stoneman that giving away public railroads to private interests was a very good thing. "Indeed," he wrote, "the whole system of internal improvement there was built up and maintained through political influence and for political purposes." He suggested that Stoneman might safely let political influence pursue its course in this particular case and allow the Covington & Ohio to land in the laps of the men who wanted it.[26]

Thus, without objection from Stoneman, and with the direct support of Governor Wells, C. P. Huntington received his windfall. Huntington got a state-funded system of railroads that stretched from Richmond to the Allegheny Mountains, nearly all the convicts in the Virginia Penitentiary, and railroad land that extended through West Virginia to the Ohio River. The giveaway would cripple the commonwealth for decades because while the company assumed control of the railroad line, it left Virginia with tens of millions of dollars of debt that had been contracted to build it. The General Assembly only demanded that this new railroad company— named the Chesapeake & Ohio Railway—complete the Virginia system through the Appalachian Mountains and all the way to the Ohio River in six years. Huntington laid out the town of Huntington, West Virginia, on the banks of the Ohio River and got to work.[27]

The many political opponents of this sell-off may have held their tongues after the final deal was reached on the floor of the Virginia Assembly. Surely this was an impossible task: What superman could build a railroad from eastern Virginia to the Ohio River in six years? The state had already assumed millions of dollars in debt to blast through the smaller Blue Ridge Mountains. Previous engineering estimates suggested a cost of more than fifty million to reach the Ohio River.

But Huntington had learned of a new way to blast through mountains that would let him complete the railroad in time and gain control of the lucrative state line. His secret instrument, probably unknown to the legislature of Virginia or its military commander, was an oily, almost clear liquid called nitroglycerin. The old method for making railroad tunnels required that miners drill a half dozen mouse-sized holes a foot deep into the side of a mountain. These holes would be filled with gunpowder and then exploded to blast a round hole. Muckers would then clear the "spoil," or exploded rock, for the next round of drilling and blasting. Progress was measured in inches per day.

Nitroglycerin packed considerably more punch in a hole than gunpowder did, roughly ten times the force. Huntington had used the new explosive successfully during the war in the building of the Central Pacific, though he had run into some snags. Many of the Irish workers on the road refused to work around it, considering the process too dangerous. Soon Huntington found that Chinese immigrants, indentured to the Central Pacific through independent contractors, would put up with the dangers of nitroglycerin blasts without going on strike.[28]

Transporting nitroglycerin was a problem, to be sure. Just after the war a leaking container of nitroglycerin, en route to the Central Pacific, was stopped in San Francisco. Agents refused to accept the damaged container. When porters pried open the box with hammers and a chisel, a number of downtown blocks exploded.[29] But by the latter part of the 1860s, experimenters in Europe and America, most famously Alfred Nobel, had developed vessels for the safe transportation of nitroglycerin. They discovered that by very carefully mixing nitroglycerin with gunpowder or clay they could make a solid block that was relatively stable. Nobel called his mix of clay and nitroglycerin by the trade name of dynamite; a competitor called his blend of sawdust, potassium nitrate, and nitroglycerin by the trade name of dualin. Huntington bought both.[30]

Nitroglycerin in its many transportable forms radically reshaped tunneling, making blasts more powerful and tunneling much cheaper. Men could pierce the especially difficult slates and shales that were at the base of the largest mountains in the world. These tough minerals, which had melted and cooled in the Precambrian era, had been nearly impossible to crack.

As blasting became more powerful, that part of the process speeded up considerably. The use of railway cars to clear away blasted rock shortened the time between blasts. Soon, hand-drilling the blast holes became the bottleneck in the process. One civil engineer in 1867 called hand drilling the "the most difficult portion of the labor and that which consumes the most time."[31] On the major tunnels of the late nineteenth century—the Mount Cenis and the Hoosac—miners would drill for hours at a time, while the blasting crew worked perhaps an hour. Speeding up the drilling process became critical. Huntington cared not just about efficiency but about time. At least three tunnels had to be made through the Appalachian Mountains to finish the C&O in the six years he had been allotted.

That was where convicts and steam drills came in.

5

MAN VERSUS MOUNTAIN

HOW DID JOHN HENRY DIE? A barrel-chested Yankee from California dreamed of steam drills, machines that would make instant holes for nitroglycerin charges, allowing a railroad to puncture the Allegheny Mountains. When free workers balked at the danger and the pay, Huntington turned to John Henry and hundreds of other prisoners in the hands of Virginia. John Henry hammered, as he and dozens of other men in chains learned to drill alongside new steam drills. As the drills kept failing, the convicts did wonders. But soon dozens died, then more.

Once Collis Potter Huntington had nitroglycerin to blast holes into mountains, he recognized that making the pilot holes would become the bottleneck, just as it had been on the Central Pacific Railroad. Huntington's solution to that bottleneck was the steam drill. The power of steam engines had been the marvel of the last two centuries, but it was difficult to transfer that power to something other than a piston or wheel. A steam engine typically consisted of two parts: a boiler that heated water and an engine that acted as a piston. The two devices, boiler and engine, had to be side by side for the boiler steam to move the engine's piston. While the piston might act as a drill, miners found it difficult to push both boiler and engine into man-sized tunnels and then pull them both away for a blast.

In an age before the practical transmission of electricity, engineers and mechanics discovered that one way to transfer steam power over a distance was to transfer *pressure* over a distance. In what came to be called the pneumatic system, engineers connected powerful steam engines to long

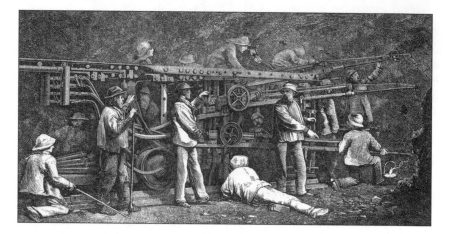

Steel engraving of the steam drill used on the Mount Cenis Tunnel. Tubes on the left and in the middle transferred power to percussive drills on the right. As many as five drills worked simultaneously. (Swem Library, College of William and Mary)

vacuum pipes. An automatic valve at the rock face could then release pressure four times a minute or so. Whether the drill was directly harnessed to the boiler or operated over a distance using compressed air, the mechanical force from a boiler pushed a steel chisel into rock, emulating the hand labor of miners.[1]

A competing steam drill, sometimes called a Leschot or diamond drill, was also in development. This drill had been developed in Switzerland, as a by-product of watchmaking. In the nineteenth century when a watchmaker received a packet of white and yellow diamonds for decorating watches, it always included many valueless black diamonds. Georges-Auguste Leschot, the son of a Swiss watchmaker, had collected these black diamonds and forged them around a steam-powered drill. The drill was the engine, driven by the steam of the boiler. The diamonds mounted around the rotating drill burned their way inside a small pilot hole, pushing rapidly into the most difficult rock. This rotating motion worked best in softer rock or rock that was crumbly. It was simple, elegant, and clean. In fact, modern oil drilling still relies on the rotating force of a diamond-tipped drill.

In 1868, both drills were experimental. Huntington contacted both percussive and rotating drill manufacturers and had them contact his contractors to run tests on the tunnels. With dynamite and steam drills Huntington was confident that he could tunnel through the Alleghenies by 1872.[2]

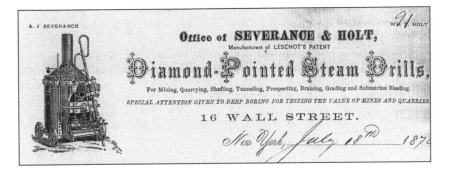

Image of Leschot's rotary diamond drill, 1870. (Western Reserve Historical Society)

Both steam drills, however, were what engineers today would call kluges—fiendishly complex devices designed to solve a basic problem.[3] In the years that John Henry spent in the Allegheny Mountains, contractors tried both drills, and neither worked consistently. The pipes for the steam drill broke down frequently, and the diamond drill often broke at the sharp end.

Both kinds of drills lacked the flexibility found in the skilled two-man hammer teams that had been tunneling through mountains for centuries. The hammer man swung a sledgehammer down onto the chisel. The shaker shifted the drill between blows to improve the drill's bite. A good shaker had a supple wrist and could adjust the drill in the two or three seconds before the next blow came. Rocking, rolling, and feeding, as a mechanical engineer described the process in 1867, were the actions that steam drills mimicked. In rocking, the shaker rocked the drill back and forth to clear away bits of broken rock. In rolling, he twisted the drill to improve the bite. In feeding, he pushed the drill farther into where the hole was progressing.[4]

Song coordinated the movements. White observers in the 1840s noted the presence of singing deep underground in the Chesterfield mines, though they declared black miners tuneless.[5] The descendants of these singing miners became the skilled men on the C&O tunneling sites, men who would have supervised the unskilled workers, free and convict. They would have taught the unskilled workers how to use song to manage drilling.[6] Tunnelers sang humorous songs, sad songs, religious songs, all rhythm and meter and intonation but without an obvious melody—phrases, really. A driller learned to sing them all day, and every day they were slightly

different, changing with the condition of the rocks. Like the rocks, these
little songs were chipped down by regular use, repeated with tiny variations, until they took the shape of black America's folk poetry.

> Hikin' Jerry,
> Hikin' on the main line Southern
> Dead on time, lord lord
> dead on time.
>
> Look yonder,
> standin' in the head of a tunnel,
> Standin' in the head of a tunnel,
> with a head rag on.
>
> Here comes the walker,
> comin' down the line,
> With a forty-five, lord lord
> with a forty-five.
>
> The walker
> hit my woman this mornin'
> And now she's gone, lord lord,
> now she's gone.[7]

The breaks between the lines of these hammer songs coordinated the
complex movements of drilling. The hammer came down at the end of the
line, forming what would decades later be called a backbeat. Sometimes it
was the hammer man who sang, telling his partner with his rhythm and
lyrics when the next blow would come. Other times a third man would sing
for hammer man and shaker. Between blows the shaker would work his
magic, either rocking or rolling. Many hammer songs echoed the work process, describing the rolling that the partner, or "buddy," did with the drill:

> Roll on buddy, don't you roll so slow,
> Baby how can I roll when my wheel won't go?

Here in the mines and work camps of Southern railroads the phrase
"rock and roll" was born.[8] A group of men swinging hammers, twisting

drills, moving to the beat of a terrible, rhythmic song, formed out of their own bodies a complex machine. Theirs was a finely tuned instrument that a manufactured steam drill could not match. Huntington imagined that a steam drill could replace the skilled labor of miners, that he could work without their rock and roll. He was wrong.

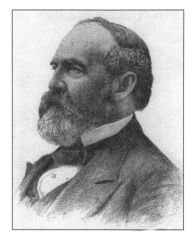

John Henry and the dozens of others shipped to the mountains would have begun as unskilled laborers for the C&O. They worked as "muckers," loading the broken rock and muck onto railway cars. They dumped the rock and muck down the mile-deep ravines between the mountains. They pulled scrapers along the

Collis Potter Huntington. (Library of Congress)

ground to make the roadbed flat. Problems with the construction would gradually draw them into the mouth of the Lewis Tunnel.

Prisoners' contracts dictated very little about the work they would do. When Virginia's Governor Wells and prison superintendent Wardwell designed contracts for the lease of these men, Wardwell would have had in mind his visit to Joseph Shultz and his father the previous year. On that visit the convicts had "bunks, straw, and blankets," Mr. Shultz had agreed that prisoners were convicted of trivial crimes, and Wardwell and the Shultzes had a dinner prepared by prisoners that was "good and well cooked."[9] But the men who received the convicts were not Shultz and his son. Instead Wardwell gave the men to Claiborne R. Mason, who was much more closely tied to the future of the C&O Railroad and would drive more than a hundred men to their deaths as he finished the tunnels.

Mason's connection to the railroad went back to the 1840s, when it was mostly state owned. He was a self-taught railroad contractor who had first bossed slaves and free blacks in his coal mines in Chesterfield County, just south of Richmond. As railroads first came to Virginia, he had used slaves and convicts to grade and lay track, earning himself stock in the railroad. He also had a long connection to the penitentiary. In the winter season, when coal prices increased, he leased black convicts from the penitentiary to work in his coal mines. A reporter described him as "a short, stout, firmly built man, with a head like a Senator's, plain of dress, direct and brief of speech, with that undeniable air of ease that comes to a man who has acquired all he knows from experience."[10]

During the war Mason controlled thousands of drafted slaves, rebuilding bridges for Stonewall Jackson. Many Southerners hated and feared Mason for what he did to stop Confederate desertion. In the last two years of the Civil War, General Robert E. Lee had given Mason broad orders to hunt deserters in Albemarle County in western Virginia near Charlottesville. Mason had dutifully captured dozens of soldiers absent without leave, as well as those who had given them aid. He then brought them to the nearest town, posted notice of their execution, and hanged them. In the mountains, bitterness against Claiborne Mason lasted for decades. This resourceful but hard-hearted man oversaw most of the prisoners who worked on the Chesapeake & Ohio.[11]

Claiborne Mason was an insider, and when he saw the C&O created under Huntington's control he had almost exclusive access to the penitentiary's convicts. On December 1, 1868, when W. C. Wickham took over the state's railroads in order to turn them over to Huntington, John Henry was loaded, along with fourteen other men, onto cars at the Richmond penitentiary. Dozens of other convicts were already at work on the line, signed over to Claiborne Mason or one of his men.[12] As Mason picked up contracts to lay track leading to the tunnels on the West Virginia border, he brought the free black coal miners who had worked for him in prewar days, along with dozens of black men with closely shaved heads and chains on their ankles.

A peculiar wrinkle added to the contract on December 1 ensured that John Henry and the other convicts hired by Mason would be forever tied to the city of Richmond. Months earlier, some convicts on long-term lease escaped from custody, leading Governor Wells to worry about further escapes.[13] Thus just before John Henry departed the prison walls, Governor Wells added a new provision to the contract between the state and the C&O. Contractors like Mason would have to post a bond that guaranteed the safe return of prisoners and pay all the expenses for the state's attempts at recapture, should it be necessary. Governor Wells wrote that contracts have "stipulated damages of one hundred dollars for each *prisoner not returned*."[14] This way Mason and other contractors could not claim that a prisoner had died when he had escaped.

To avoid the hundred-dollar fee, Mason and his lieutenant would have to send the corpses of the many prisoners who died in the coming years back to Richmond. One hundred dollars was a small fortune in 1868, more than a year's labor by a convict. This contract was the reason John Henry's body would be shipped back to the white house and buried in the sand. His resting place would be the grounds of the Richmond penitentiary.

The frenzied construction of the mountain sections of the C&O line started in December 1868, after C. P. Huntington acquired the company. Engineers inspected the site while the contractors tunneled, bridged, graded, and tracked. The engineers dutifully gathered the gossip that traveled up and down the line. They reported monthly on the contractors who got drunk, those who abandoned their contracts, and those who seemed to be failing—a common occurrence. As contractors faced problems with supplies or labor, they quickly went bankrupt. In less than a month, county sheriffs would arrive to seize contractors' mules, scrapers, and shanties. Every bankruptcy pushed the C&O further and further toward the use of convict labor.

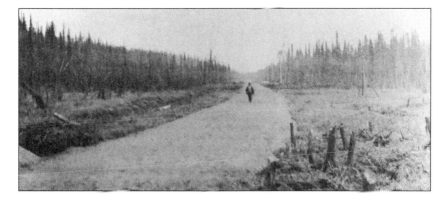

The roadbed for a new railway, circa 1900–1905. (Library of Congress)

When it came to tunneling, black men with experience in the Chesterfield County mines seemed the perfect candidates. Claiborne Mason had grown up there and had bossed slaves, free blacks, and convicts in his coal beds, most of which were less than ten miles from the Richmond market. Mason's convicts from the penitentiary would have only acted as muckers at first, taking out rock generated by gunpowder and nitroglycerin blasts. In the everyday course of work, convicts would have combined songs they had learned on plantations with songs sung by black miners whose grandfathers had mined coal beside the muddy waters of the James River.[15]

Miners also brought a strong tradition of whiskey drinking, though the tracklayers, brick masons, and day laborers may have been able to meet them cup for cup. All the line's workers drank their liquor and had their fights in the ordinaries and public houses that cropped up weeks after tracklaying began. Shanties popped up everywhere, and county sheriffs hardly knew where to find them. A division engineer named Wildman may have privately established the first of these "whiskey shops" on the top of nearby Tunnel Hill. For every legitimate and licensed establishment, like Claiborne Mason's own grogshop at the foot of the Lewis Tunnel, there were two or three crossroads shanties run by Irishmen with names like Finn and Fox. Sheriffs hauled them to court for selling ardent spirits without a license, but apparently with little effect.[16]

The whiskey shops were places where music would have been shared between the black colliers of Chesterfield County, the Irish American brick masons from up the Ohio River, and the black carpenters and blacksmiths who hailed from plantations downstate. The convicts from Richmond would have bought liquor with the extra money they received for skilled work. Contractors called the coins or scrip paid to convicts an "overstint," or pay for the work they did beyond the stint of a common laborer. But convicts would have been sharply restricted in their movements and could have only spent their dimes in Claiborne Mason's grogshop.[17]

Between 1868 and 1872, the Lewis Tunnel and the Big Bend Tunnel consumed the attention of President Huntington and his chief engineer, a former Unionist spy named Henry D. Whitcomb. Henry Whitcomb had come to Richmond before the Civil War as a young man, a graduate of Maine's prestigious Bowdoin College. He acted first as a construction engineer for the C&O's predecessor in the Shenandoah Valley. The war stopped all railway construction, forcing Whitcomb to make temporary quarters in Richmond and act as the railroad's general superintendent. His temporary position allowed him frequent travel outside of Richmond and gave him the opportunity to spy for the Union's Army of the Potomac.[18] Whitcomb emerged from the war a wealthy man with good connections. In July 1869, he and others from the C&O Railway accompanied Huntington on a survey of the entire line. Shortly afterward Huntington came to rely entirely on the former spy as his official mouthpiece at the company, appointing him chief engineer of construction.[19]

The central obstacle for Whitcomb, his division engineers, and more than two dozen contractors was the eastern edge of the Allegheny Mountains. Lewis Mountain stood most prominently in their way, blocking access to West Virginia. With a proposed length of 4,300 feet, the Lewis Tunnel on the Virginia–West Virginia border would be the second-longest tunnel of the route. That mountain would also be the hardest. Forty-two and a half miles west, the Big Bend Tunnel promised to burrow a mile into the Big Bend Mountain. That tunnel would eliminate the need for track along the snake-like bend that the Greenbrier River had etched around Big Bend Mountain. In piercing this mountain, the railroad would head straight through to the Ohio River. As division engineer C. A. Sharp put it to Whitcomb, "If you want a monument, let this Big Bend Tunnel serve to carry your name down to posterity."[20] But no one remembers Henry D. Whitcomb. The Big Bend Tunnel carried only John Henry's name down to posterity.

The Big Bend Tunnel, however, never used steam drills. The contractor in charge of the Big Bend was Captain William R. Johnson Jr., who used mostly free workers to build his tunnel, though he took thirty Virginia prisoners from Wardwell in 1868 and another fourteen in 1869. Johnson, like Mason, had gotten his start bossing slaves in the Confederacy's engineering corps.[21] Johnson distrusted steam drills. He contracted to dig three shafts the old-fashioned way, with hammer men, after which he would tunnel laterally from the shafts and the ends. Despite its length, work on the Big Bend Tunnel was much easier than on the Lewis Tunnel. Steam engines did provide support for the operation at Big Bend, but only for ventilation, lifting, and pumping water.[22]

The Lewis Tunnel proved more difficult. Huntington had contractors grade and lay track to Lewis Mountain. Temporary track ran over the mountain while construction was in progress. Concerned about the harder rock, Huntington immediately sought out steam drills. He had Whitcomb contact John Tilsby, an agent for Burleigh rock drills, who outlined how the Burleigh drills worked. While hand labor made about fifty feet per month, he bragged that in the Hoosac Tunnel in Massachusetts his drill made "as much as 7 feet per day" and allowed blasts that made tunnels wider and taller than could be made by human hands.[23] By October 1869, Tilsby's associate had brought in a man who had superintended "tunnels through the Sierra Nevada on the CPRR."[24] This must have reassured Huntington, since he made his first fortune when the Central Pacific passed through the Sierra Nevada Mountains near the California border. Everything seemed to be falling into place.

By March 1870, contracts went out for drilling, and contractor C. P. Durham received the bid for the Lewis Tunnel. "We expect to use the Burleigh drills," Durham wrote Whitcomb. His hope was not to drill shafts down from the top of the mountain at all. Hand tunneling required multiple shafts; otherwise the work would take too long. But Durham felt that the miraculous speed of the steam drill would allow him to drill straight across and "progress with more rapidity than by going down the shafts and doing the work by hand."[25] The Burleigh drills would require a boiler to produce steam that would be forced through a pipe the size of a drainspout. The chamber that received the steam had a metal drill inside. A valve action pushed the drill forward into the rock with a percussive force that, it was hoped, would far exceed that of a man with a hammer.

Through most of 1870, free workers apparently tunneled while convicts did support tasks. In March, for example, Mason's convicts dug out pits east of the Lewis Tunnel. There they mined the rock that would be used for bridges. Convicts also built shanties in nearby Millboro as the initial drilling proceeded.[26]

But the percussive drills were failing. Boilers to generate air pressure could not be easily transported to the site, and the agents bickered with the contractors about prices. Initial demonstrations in New York and Richmond were not as promising as Whitcomb had hoped, and just a week later he sought out agents for Leschot's rotating diamond drill.[27] The Severance & Holt Diamond Drilling Company sent its diamond drills out to the site after a brief demonstration in Richmond. With the same technological exuberance as the Burleigh agent, William Holt gushed about his diamond drills.

> Our firm would make very liberal arrangements with your co. to furnish all the drilling apparatus for the *entire work* and wd. *guarantee* its entire success, enabling yr. contractors to do their work far more *quickly* & *cheaply* than they can possibly do it with any other machine. Our machines are especially adapted to *through cuts* and *tunnels*—boring in the latter 3 to 5 holes simultaneously at steady rate of eight to ten feet *per hour* in *each hole*. The extreme simplicity of our drilling apparatus enables it to be operated by cheap labor, and renders repairing unnecessary.[28]

Durham declared that he would try his best to use these new drills but that he lacked iron to lay track to the tunnel. By the summer of 1870, things had progressed from bad to worse. Water flooded the tunnel's western end, making steam drilling impossible, and more steam engines were required to pump it out. Moreover, five of Mason's convicts had escaped from nearby Millboro and were at large in the mountains. Neither steam drill was working reliably. Huntington determined that Durham and company had not really made a fair test of the drills and that Durham's contract should be dropped. The C&O kept the drills on lease, however, for a fairer test.[29]

Labor troubles proliferated along the line. The assistant engineer issued a circular requiring contractors to pay no more than "one dollar and board per day for ordinary laborers." He also set the hours of labor at "six o'clock AM till sunset allowing one hour for dinner."[30] Tunnel workers balked about the pay. In response, Huntington threatened to bring impoverished Irishmen from the slums of New York. Though some Irish workers were brought in to work on the western end of the line, most of the men who dug out the tunnels were former slaves.[31]

Then, on the Big Bend Tunnel, the men went on strike in the spring. Miners, black and white, declared that the tunnels had "bad air" and marched out, demanding two dollars a day and a resolution of the problem.[32] On the Lewis Tunnel, Durham had proved unable to get enough laborers at the prescribed rate of a dollar a day.[33] More ominously, the division engineer noted that the Lewis Tunnel appeared to be composed not of shale but of "slate or shaly sandstone."[34]

The workers were right: Drilling in sandstone produced deadly clouds of tiny silica particles. Less than sixty years later and seventy miles away, Union Carbide contracted to build a tunnel in West Virginia that would divert the New River under Gauley Mountain. Black workers by the hundreds volunteered for the work, attracted to cash wages there, but experienced miners stayed away. Drills deep underground produced clouds of silica dust that, over the space of three years, killed more than three hundred, with perhaps seven hundred total dead within five years. It has been called America's worst industrial disaster.[35] Had anyone heard the truth about what happened to the convicts at the Lewis Tunnel between 1870 and 1871, the Hawk's Nest Disaster of 1927 might never have occurred.

By 1870, Huntington was upset about the delays at the Lewis Tunnel. He proposed turning over the contract to an old associate, J. J. Gordon, who offered to "bring Chinese laborers from California immediately." Back in 1862, Irish workers on the Central Pacific had refused to work near nitroglycerin and had struck for higher pay numerous times. Chinese workers, who were often bound to contractors by debt, had submitted to the dangerous blasts in California with fewer conflicts. They too had died by the dozens. In Huntington's mind, no doubt, Chinese laborers were little more than slaves.[36] "I would probably consent to pay him a small advance on the rates agreed upon with Durham," Huntington wrote, "in consideration of the good effect it would have upon other labor."[37]

But by the summer of 1870, Huntington came to understand that "coolie labor" would not do the drilling for him. His contractor told him that Chinese workers from California were unavailable, and to get them from China, he would have to contract them almost a year in advance. In any case, the Franco-Prussian War in Europe greatly unsettled the bond markets, which meant that he could not gather the funds to import Chinese workers.[38]

Thus Huntington had to find cheap, pliable labor closer to home, labor that would work next to the steam drills if a fair test were made. Virginia's overloaded penal system supplied the solution. In 1870 alone, more than two thousand black men had come to the Virginia Penitentiary to serve long sentences for small crimes, so many that the state could not house

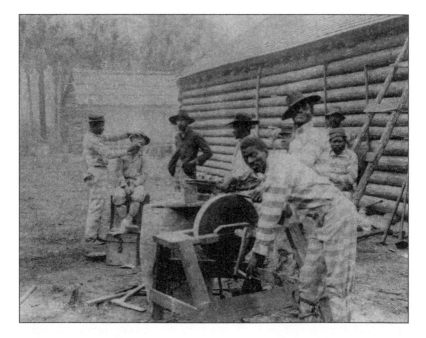

A Southern chain gang, 1898, photographed by Carl Weis. (Library of Congress)

them. Burnham Wardwell, the former prisoner and humanitarian warden who had instituted year-round labor contracts, fed convicts, and cared for them, had just left office in February.[39] Wardwell's replacement, George F. Strother, was much less conscientious but equally eager to remove convicts from the penitentiary.

George Strother estimated that Wardwell had sent only seventy-five convicts to the Chesapeake & Ohio. (Wardwell had actually sent more than two hundred.) Strother complained, "The rest were lounging about the [prison] yard, and spent all their time in idleness."[40] Strother vastly increased the number of prisoners he sent to Mason and did not require that the new prisoners be signed for. His reports to the governor dwelt on his great ability to cut costs and mentioned nothing about conditions.[41] So Whitcomb met with Claiborne Mason in August of 1870, and the deal was struck around this time. Experienced with steam drills and coolie laborers, J. J. Gordon would take over the tunnel. He would try the steam drills underground alongside a few free workers (who understood drilling) and Mason's convicts, who could neither strike nor demand higher wages. Mason and his agents at the time controlled more than two hundred and fifty prisoners.[42] Convicts remembered Mason and "captains" like him in bitter verses.

> Some cap'n give you nickel
> Some cap'n give you dime
> My cap'n give me nothin' 'cept work
> And cussin' you out all the time
>
> I tell you how this man think
> Black man just like Betsy mule
> You got to beat him everyday
> To make you know that he the rule.
>
> I tell you how this man do
> Black man under his command
> Short time, double lifer same
> You never leave that Devil's land[43]

The real contest between steam drills and convicts began, then, in August 1870. As Mason finished grading and filling outside the tunnel, he brought two hundred convicts directly to the site.[44] Gordon built up a whole town to support his drills. Unlike his predecessor, C. P. Durham, he knew that both vertical and horizontal shafts would be necessary to complete the tunnel. No opportunity to drill was ignored, and Durham had teams of convicts drilling alongside his steam drills, whether they liked it or not. A correspondent described the Lewis Tunnel and the temporary track that ran over it, adding that Gordon had assembled entire "machineshops . . . at which a locomotive might be built." To a man who traveled over the tunnel, the activity that transpired beneath him was remarkable:

> 150 feet beneath him are nearly 200 toilers boring through the earth, and showing by patient and persevering labor the triumphs of man over seemingly insurmountable obstacles. Besides the approaches to the tunnel, there are three shafts, measuring in depth 70, 125 and 145 feet respectively. One hundred and twenty men are at work inside constantly, night and day. The difficulty in working Lewis tunnel, as is doubtless known, is the almost unprecedented hardness of the material through which it has been worked. It has the appearance of blue granite, and is so hard that it almost resists the ordinary drill.[45]

Convicts who worked alongside the drill were housed near the tunnel itself and occasionally escaped.[46]

In May 1871, the C&O invited fifty-eight reporters from New York, New Jersey and Pennsylvania on an excursion along the line as the tunneling was well under way. They stopped the train briefly to explore the Lewis Tunnel.[47] They were drawn to what they called "the magnitude of the work and the modus operandi of blasting the hard rock." They described the tunnel construction in some detail: "Shafts were sunk at three different points, and the drilling machines were worked by steam power. A large body of men, mostly convicts from the State penitentiary, were at work in the various shafts and at both ends of the tunnel, in blasting the rock and removing the debris to neighboring ravines."[48]

If it is true that John Henry drove fourteen feet and the steam drill only made nine, then John Henry and the steam drill would probably have been drilling on a shaft working downward from the top of the Lewis Mountain. For blasting at either end of the tunnel, pilot holes needed to be only five to six feet into the rock. When blasting downward, however, holes had to be ten feet deep or more.[49] In the race to the bottom, John

Henry's hole would have been deep enough at the end, but the steam drill's would have required more drilling to make a blast.

> John Henry went upon a mountain
> And came down on the side
> The mountain was so tall, John Henry was so small,
> That he laid down hammah and he cried, "O lord."
>
> John Henry told his captain,
> "Captain, go to town
> And bring me back two twenty pound hammers,
> And I'll sure beat your steam drill down."
>
> John Henry told the people,
> "You know that I am a man.
> I can beat all the traps that have ever been laid,
> Or I'll die with my hammer in my hand,
> Die with a hammer in my hand."[50]

Neither the steam drills nor the convicts worked as planned. Gordon's partner told a correspondent for the *Richmond Dispatch* that he was happy enough with the convict laborers, "despite many drawbacks."[51] One of the principal drawbacks was price. Gordon was paid by the cubic foot, but he would have paid Mason and his partner for the convicts by the day. If no drilling got done, Gordon would have to pay for an entire crew of workers anyway.

While he liked his steam drill well enough, Gordon could not meet his contract. Though Gordon gave them a fair test, the steam drills failed again and again. He had thought that the Sierra Nevada Mountains near the California border were remote, but he had never been to the edge of the Alleghenies. Gordon continually faced engine problems, probably from the dust generated by the drills themselves. He found he could not get replacement boilers to compress the air to drive them. "I am very anxious to get that boiler to run Burleigh Drill in East approach," he wrote Whitcomb in October 1871. "If you have done anything in regards the furnishing it please inform me, if not I will have to double on it with hammers."[52]

The phrase "double on it with hammers" is telling. Gordon would have been drilling two sets of holes on the rock face of the east approach, one with convicts, one with the Burleigh drill. If the steam drill failed that day, he would have to do the work with two teams of hammer men. Before the boiler failed, Gordon would have run a steam drill on one side and a hammer team on the other.

The last time a steam drill was used on the Lewis Tunnel would have been the summer of 1871, when the boiler failed on the eastern approach. Until then, possibly at many of the approaches, men and drills worked side by side.

> The steam drill set on the right hand side,
> John Henry was on the left.
> He said, "I will beat that steam drill down
> Or hammer my fool self to death."

> The men that made that steam drill,
> Thought it was mighty fine;
> John Henry sunk a fourteen-foot hole
> And the steam drill only made nine.[53]

By October, Gordon had run out of steam. The western tunneling expert who "thought his drill was mighty fine" was hemorrhaging money by hiring workers from Mason. Gordon asked to be excused from the contract by the middle of the month.[54]

Once Gordon abandoned his contract, Mason and his partner, Mr. Gooch, did the work entirely with convicts, for whom they paid just twenty-five cents a day. Because Mason and his partner had not bid on the price of drilling, the convict owners and C&O officials haggled over prices. As Peyton Randolph told the chief engineer in October, "The rock is hard but drills and blasts well and I consider $4 [per foot] an outside price for it. Yesterday Gooch talked about $5 but I laughed at him."[55] Randolph knew that Mason and Gooch got their convicts for twenty-five cents a day, and had hundreds of them to spare.

It was sometime during or immediately after Gordon's trials that John Henry died, for he disappears from prison records after 1873, presumably when his corpse arrived at the penitentiary.[56]

> John Henry, O, John Henry!
> Blood am runnin' red!

Falls right down with his hammah to th' groun',
Says, "I've beat him to th' bottom but I'm dead, -
Lawd, - Lawd, -
I've beat him to th' bottom but I'm dead."

John Henry kissed his hammah;
Kissed it with a groan;
Sighed a sigh and closed his weary eyes,
Now po' Lucy has no man to call huh own, -
Lawd, - Lawd, -
Po' Lucy has no man to call huh own.[57]

Despite the seemingly heroic tale of John Henry's death, he was just one of many convicts who died with their hammers in their hands. The Virginia Penitentiary workers died at the rate of approximately 10 percent per year through the entire decade of the 1870s. Even after the survivors were transferred back to the relatively safer work of constructing the James River and Kanawha Canal near Richmond, they continued to die, their lungs still filled with the silica dust they had inhaled in the tunnel. As early as 1880 most of the convicts who worked on the tunnel would have been gone and unable to tell the story of what happened to John Henry underneath Lewis Mountain.[58]

Few would have lived to tell their story. It was up to free workers on the nearby Big Bend Tunnel to report what had happened. One man, an African American roundhouse cook named Cal Evans, traveled from the Lewis Tunnel to the Big Bend Tunnel in 1875. As he cooked for workers at the Big Bend, he told many stories of the exploits of John Henry. When the story of John Henry became popular in the 1920s, interviewers passed Evans by, believing that since he had not been at the Big Bend Tunnel between 1870 and 1872, "he got no opportunity, therefore, to see John Henry drive steel." Yet the interviewer noted something peculiar. Cal Evans had many stories about John Henry, "and his practice of telling them is a matter of general knowledge in the community."[59] He and others immortalized John Henry in an old-fashioned ballad, one that miners and railway workers alike sang as they tunneled and laid track for C. P. Huntington, Henry D. Whitcomb, and Claiborne Mason, the men who killed John Henry.

In retrospect, no one can say exactly how John Henry and over one hundred other convicts died building the Lewis Tunnel. The surgeon's report for the penitentiary listed the names of the men who died in prison but only gave the total number of men who died on the C&O Railroad. The Virginia Penitentiary's board of directors reported that from 1871 to 1873 death rates were increasing rapidly, but that their penitentiary was not to blame. "Less than half of the deaths during the year were caused by disease contracted in the building," the surgeon reported. "All the cases of scurvy we have had in this institution were contracted while the men were at work on the Chesapeake & Ohio railroad. They were returned on account of the disease." Scurvy, what we know now is vitamin C deficiency, was understood then to be the result of malnutrition. The surgeon also noted three cases of "dropsy," the swelling of organ tissue because of excess fluid. This, he felt sure was also "the result of scurvy." The single greatest cause of death the prison surgeon saw was "consumption," the nineteenth-century shorthand for death that originated in a wasting away of the lungs. The prison surgeon marked half of the prisoners who died in the penitentiary in 1872 as "Died of dis.[ease] con[tracte]'d while at w'k on R. R."[60] Others returned to the penitentiary as corpses.

The fact that the Lewis Tunnel was composed of "slate or shaly sandstone" may be the key. While many cases of consumption can be attributed to the tuberculosis bacterium (discovered in 1882), miners knew that in certain kinds of rock, the mines themselves could destroy men's lungs. Agricola, the founder of geology, noted in *De Re Metallica* (1555) that "there were women in the Carpathian mountains who had married seven husbands, all of whom had died from consumption."[61] Miners' consumption was not caused by bacteria or close confinement but by the silica loosed by blasting rock, particularly sandstone. The men who went on strike at the Big Bend Tunnel understood that "bad air" put dust in your lungs that could kill you. These miners demanded that tunnels be washed down or ventilated before workers entered them. But convicts could not strike.

The use of steam drills on the sandstone in the Lewis Tunnel, mentioned repeatedly by division engineers and observers, probably killed every worker in the tunnel in the space of a few years. The "bad air" that Big Bend workers noticed would have been generated in much larger quantities by the combination of hand drills and steam drills in the Lewis Tunnel. This was in part because steam drills worked both faster and *less* efficiently than hand drillers. A drilling team could make a hole cleanly with relatively little dust; a steam drill jabbered crazily on rock, spitting crystalline dust in every direction.[62] Contractor Durham had the drillers work right next to the steam drills. As Claiborne Mason pushed the convicts harder and harder in the last year of tunneling, he would have driven them back into the tunnels immediately after the nitroglycerin blasts, to meet his schedule. And because no one knew about the Lewis Tunnel disaster, a similar tragedy followed less than sixty years after it, at the New River under Gauley Mountain. Union Carbide kept workers near the drills without wetting them down and pushed workers back into the tunnel right after nitroglycerin blasts.[63]

What was in those clouds of sand, generated by drill and dynamite? Freshly ground silica between five and ten microns wide, silica that floated through men's nostrils and directly into their lungs. While Big Bend workers left their site when they saw dust, convicts at the Lewis Tunnel could not. Even a single day's exposure to freshly ground silica can cause acute silicosis and early death. In a process that is still not well understood, these microscopic particles of silica get caught in the alveoli, or air sacs. The lungs have microphages, white blood cells that ordinarily ingest bacteria. When these microphages ingest freshly ground silica, they die. Other microphages rush to the site, also dying. Pus fills the air sacs, providing a breeding ground for tuberculosis and pneumonia, as well as constricting air supply. Those not killed by tuberculosis and pneumonia will die anyway, because acute silicosis is almost always fatal within a year or two. In 1969, nearly one hundred years after John Henry and his fellow workers died, the Coal Act mandated that powered drills have collars to prevent silica from shooting out, that workers wear masks near them, and that drills be wet.[64]

The Lewis Tunnel steam drills left the tunnel by the end of October 1871. The race was over. Nearly two hundred men, mostly convicts, now finished the tunnel for C. P. Huntington. Thousands of free laborers graded, laid track, and finished the surfacing of the other tunnels. Men had triumphed over machines, but at a terrible cost. For two years, between the last month of steam drill operation and the completion of the tunnel—in September 1873—close to one hundred convicts died from a variety of diseases, most of them associated with lung impairments. Forensic anthropologists at the Smithsonian Institution, who received the corpses buried at the penitentiary, noted that approximately 80 percent of the corpses they examined were black men in their early twenties. One anthropologist wrote me that of the skeletons she examined, "several had evidence of rib lesions indicative of some sort of chronic disease infecting the lungs."[65]

Some prisoners escaped, and some were killed by guards for what the railroad labeled "mutiny," but the remainder entered tunnels where tiny bits of microscopic rock floated in the air, entered their lungs, and over a period of six months to three years, strangled them. These prisoners died gasping for air.[66] By contract, they had to be returned to the Virginia Penitentiary in Richmond, "the white house." If they were not sent back, the C&O faced a one-hundred-dollar fine per man. Nearly one hundred men came back between 1871 and 1873, most of them dead. More than two dozen more died in the next year.[67]

John Henry did not die inside the Virginia prison, because his name is not listed in the surgeon's report. He does, however, disappear from prison records by 1874, with no mention of pardon, parole, or release. Along with nearly one hundred other prisoners, he is marked transferred, in pencil. His corpse, then, was one of the counted but unnamed bodies shipped back to the penitentiary by rail. Other men returned from the Lewis Tunnel to the penitentiary with advanced cases of consumption and died in the hospital ward. John Henry, if he lived past the contest, might have died on the way back to the penitentiary. Otherwise, he would have died in a prison shanty outside the Lewis Tunnel, asking for a cool drink of water before he died.

> John Henry hammered in the mountains
> Till the hammer caught on fire.
> Very last words I heard him say,
> "Cool drink of water 'fore I die,
> Cool drink of water 'fore I die."[68]

John Wm. Henry, prisoner and railroad man, raced a steam drill at the Lewis Tunnel in the late summer of 1871. He beat the steam drill, but he and dozens of other railroad men died doing it. And so the harsh sentences meted out by Virginia's Reconstruction courts became death sentences in the Appalachian Mountains. The biggest problem, as the superintendent saw it, was what to do with the bodies. They were taken to the white house that lay along the track of the Richmond, Fredericksburg & Potomac Railroad and buried in the sand, and no one was the wiser. Only a song, stubbornly sung by railroad men, convicts, and miners, kept the story alive.

6

THE SOUTHERN RAILWAY OCTOPUS

FOR ABOUT THIRTY-FIVE YEARS, from the early 1870s until 1909, the story of John Henry was transmitted orally, apparently without written record. It traveled along the route of the railway system that John Henry's hammer had made possible. Reconstruction ended as railroad corporations effectively took control over much of the modern South. The embarrassing story of a man killed by a railroad company was effectively buried at the time, but through this period at least three distinct versions of the song emerged, sung in different contexts, all by the men whose labor made the railroads' fortune. Coal miners framed it in a familiar ballad tradition, convicts made it an early blues song, and trackliners turned it into a bragging song, while carrying the legend everywhere in the South. After 1909, when folklorists discovered the song, they reunited the different versions into a single coherent tune with many variations. They also turned John Henry's story from a cautionary tale into a legend in the mold of Homeric myth.

John Henry was not exactly a hero who single-handedly built a railroad tunnel to the west. But by 1873, his hammer had nonetheless changed the shape of the South. His labor proved Huntington's boast that a private corporation could penetrate the Allegheny Mountains. A man, a drill, and nitroglycerin had erased the barrier that separated Kentucky, Tennessee, and West Virginia from Virginia and the Carolinas. He had joined East and West.

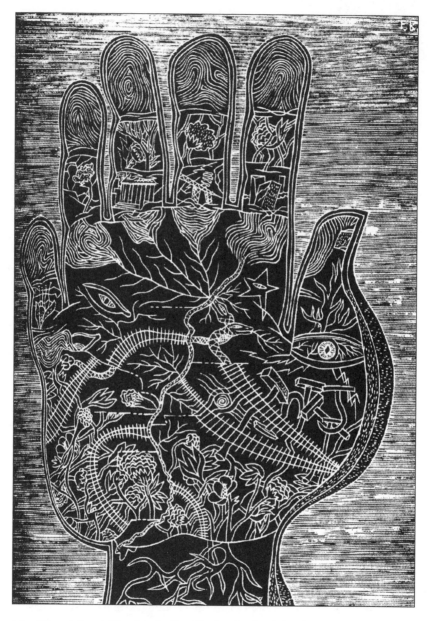

John Henry's hand. Woodcut by Fred Becker for the Federal Art Project of the
Works Progress Administration. (Swem Library, College of William and Mary)

John Henry died on a Tuesday,
It looked very much like rain;
The station was crowded with women and men,
They were waiting on that east bound train.

They took John Henry to the white house,
They put his remains in the sand;
Some from the east and some from the west
Came to see this steel-driving man.[1]

After 1873, an "east bound train" in the Midwest, one "crowded with women and men," would have passed through John Henry's tunnel to reach Richmond, Charlotte, or Raleigh.[2] His labor made it possible for women and men to reach the white house in Richmond from a railway station in Chicago.

Despite the new express line, the old folkways remained in the land where John Henry died. Slavery had ended, but thousand-acre plantations still dominated the South, having etched the landscape with plantation roads, fields, pastures, and dependent buildings. Former slaves abandoned the old slave quarters at slavery's end, but they could not move far. Tens of thousands of black families hammered together the windowless houses that represented freedom, but the houses still stood within hollering distance of the big house.

In societies where everyday life is closely regulated, language goes underground. Coded language carries a heavy burden, and it can change from code to jargon back to code again, becoming mangled and transformed, while growing stronger and more richly metaphorical. Songs moved from mouth to ear to mouth again, for many who sang could read neither lyrics nor musical notes. People sang in groups, repeating the lines for emphasis, to aid memory, and to recycle old stories for new purposes.

They sang in churches, where attendance in the singing congregations—the AME Zion, Baptist, and Holiness churches—skyrocketed between 1865 and 1920.[3] They sang at work, in cotton fields and tobacco factories. They sang to mules, cows, and pigs to get their attention and to tell them what to do. They sang at night, in crowded roadhouses between sips of apple-jack brandy, and they sang to put their children to sleep. Children sang as they walked, in high and warbling tones, to make their presence known to parents and neighbors. You heard "field hollers" in the evening, when work

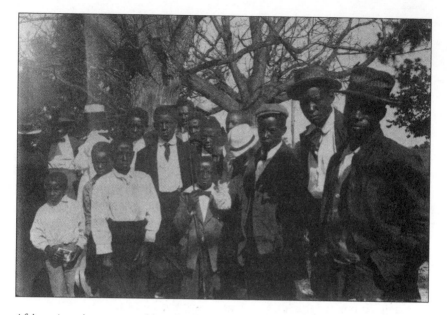

African American men and boys in the South, circa 1900. (Library of Congress)

was ending. The field holler was a supper bell, a doorbell, a telephone, and a call to the dogs to shut up. Song blended into regular talk and stretched into praise. It was omnipresent.

For former slaves, their only capital was labor, their own and their children's, along with a few mules, cows, and the chickens cooped nearby. Most farmers cropped a dozen or so acres, paying it off with a percentage of the corn, cotton, and tobacco they tended. Former slaves received a weekly allotment of food and necessities at a commissary counter, paying the planters at the end of the year out of their own portion of the crop.[4] Escaping from your sharecrop contract was dangerous:

> Oh bad Lazrus, shat[?] upon the commissary counter
> Oh bad Lazrus, shat[?] upon the commissary counter
> He walked away, Lord Lord, he walked away
>
> The Deputy told him, go and bring me Lazrus
> The Deputy told him, go and bring me Lazrus
> Dead or 'live, Lord Lord, dead or 'live

And then wondered, where in the world could he find him
And then wondered, where in the world could he find him
Says I don't know, Lord Lord, I don't know

And then he spied him, walking in between two mountains
And then he spied him, walking in between two mountains
His head hung down, Lord Lord, his head down

And then he told him, Lazrus I come here to 'rrest you
And then he told him, Lazrus I come here to 'rrest you
Here today, Lord Lord, here today

Well Lazrus told him, Sheriff I never been arrested
Well Lazrus told him, Sheriff I never been arrested
By no one man, Lord Lord, by no one man

And then he shot him, shot him with a great big number
And then he shot him, shot him with a great big number
A forty-four, Lord Lord, a forty-four

And Lazrus mother she come screamin' and a hollerin'
And Lazrus mother she come screamin' and a hollerin'
My son dead, Lord Lord, my son dead

And Lazrus sister she couldn't go to the buryin'
And Lazrus sister she couldn't go to the buryin'
Sit home and cry, Lord Lord, sit home and cry.[5]

The power of the planters, the plantation, and the commissary counter was not exercised over former slaves alone. Poorer white families left failing farms throughout the South in the 1870s, only to fall into the orbit of the same plantations. Soon thousands of white farmers had become tenants as well. While black and white tenants generally farmed food in their own patches, only those who produced the old slave crops of cotton and tobacco could secure the funds to rent land and buy the plows, seed, and fertilizer they needed. While "stations were crowded with women and men" from time to time, most trains bound east or west were filled with plantation staples.[6]

Radical Reconstruction in 1867 and 1868 had briefly promised to make the South into something other than a plantation society dominated by planters. While John Henry worked at mucking and filling outside the Lewis Tunnel, his brothers and sisters had made dramatic plans to change the South. For the first time, black men had elected their own representatives to the state legislature and to Congress. As legislators these new men tried to strike down what they called the "Jim Crow" segregation of streetcars. Throughout the South these same black legislators abolished the whipping post and fought against a poll tax. They pleaded the case of convicts in the penitentiaries.

For former slaves, in and out of the legislature, the convict lease system held a particular terror. Workers in chains, abused by guards, threatened with rifles: All were chilling reminders of slavery days. In the Virginia Assembly one afternoon in 1873, William Gilliam, a black legislator from Prince George County, stood up to describe the terrors of the whipping post and asked if the commonwealth could stand such a stain on its reputation. The entire hall grew quiet. Reconstruction was a revolutionary time. Black men served on juries. Black families voted, built their own churches, made their marriages legal, used the court system, and lived their lives as national citizens. They held on to some of these rights, but were stripped of others before John Henry had even entered the Lewis Tunnel.[7]

In 1867, a group of capitalist adventurers like C. P. Huntington, men with tight connections to the War Department, acquired, for nearly nothing, most of the state-supported railway systems in the South. Tom Scott got the Southern; William Mahone the Norfolk & Western; Huntington the C&O. In the same year, the War Department's military governors allowed the largest landholders back into politics, then turned their backs while these Democrats used fraud and violence to regain political control of Southern states. White Democrats took over the statehouses from black and white Unionists, calling the trade a fair one: loss of all Southern state railroads for planters' return to power. Only a few states—South Carolina, Louisiana, and Florida—maintained widespread black voting and Republican dominance until 1877, and their control grew increasingly precarious. Then, as part of the so-called Compromise of 1877, Rutherford B. Hayes received the presidency and the federal government ordered Union troops to leave the statehouses of those three states. Democratic rifle clubs, after hurried negotiations, quickly seized the Republican-controlled statehouses, ending Reconstruction in the South. Democrats called their seizure of power Redemption.[8]

Few had forgotten the trade: an armed white revolution in exchange for the South's state railroads. Traces of the bargain were visible everywhere. A newly Redeemed South became home to the first national, multidivisional corporations in the world: the Southern Railway, the Norfolk & Western, and the Chesapeake & Ohio. White Democrats who reclaimed the South found that they had little power over them. The new corporations lay at the spine of the South, serving as the region's imperial centers. Critics called the new railway system "the Octopus."[9]

For forty years, one could not get elected governor in a Southern state (or a Western one) without a free railway pass signed by the vice president of a major railway. Most newspapers in capital cities were owned or controlled by the major railway firms. No important piece of legislation could be read on the floor of a state assembly without a copy arriving in the Pullman car of a railway vice president. Although those cars could travel anywhere, newspaper editors, governors, and congressmen always came hat in hand to visit the offices of the octopus instead, awaiting decisions about matters large and small.[10] The stenciled logos of the cars were everywhere: SR, N&W, C&O. During Reconstruction, John Henry and thousands of other black workers had stitched the beasts together, fusing the state-managed railroads, threading them through the mountains, and extending their tentacles north and south, east and west. Western mountaineers and Eastern planters were finally linked. But while the railway octopus seemed to have the power to control the dissemination of information through newspapers and legislators, its power was never complete, and its control of information was undermined from within. Even though no newspaper reported on the Lewis Tunnel disaster or John Henry's feat of strength, its own employees carried on the message. These men sang the story of John Henry, telling everyone about the terrible costs of a South revolutionized by armed force, and by the building of a railroad tunnel.

> If I could drive steel like John Henry,
> I'd go home, Baby, I'd go home.

> This ole Hammer killed John Henry,
> Drivin' steel, Baby, drivin' steel.

> If I had forty-one dollars,
> I'd go home, Baby, I'd go home.

I'm goin' home, en' tell little Annie
Uv my triuls, Baby, uv my triuls.[11]

At first, Democrats praised the railways for helping to bind the South together and to bring an end to "Negro rule."[12] But every trade costs something: While the railway systems blossomed, Southern states withered on the vine. Since before the war, the states had printed millions in state bonds to build railroads, and states kept those debts when they gave the railroads away. As the bonds started coming due in the 1880s, the Democrats returning to power fussed and fumed, calling railways like the Southern "the hydra headed monster" with an "iron heel on the industries and trade" of the state. Others called the Southern "the vampire that is feeding on the life blood of our industries and trade."[13] Some repudiated a part of their debts, though that destroyed the bond rating of North Carolina, for instance, as well as Georgia and Alabama. In the end, Southern Democrats called for "retrenchment." They would cut funding to every public enterprise to pay the railroad debt. If state funding for other enterprises was slashed, states could pay off the bonds and bring taxes back to prewar levels.

Public schools, most erected after the war, were quickly impoverished. White students in primary schools used the family's Montgomery Ward catalogs as textbooks. Black primary schools, most built entirely with the labor of parents, were crowded with young students, but they often lacked floors, not to mention chalkboards and chalk. Every state institution shrank to pay the railroad debt and keep state taxes low, pulling black and white Southerners in a downward spiral. Penitentiaries filled to the bursting point. Public schools were not mandatory, and literacy was low. State health boards hardly existed. Thus after the South's revolution, the old folkways reemerged. Mules, chickens, and bare feet tracked bacteria into houses; hookworm and pellagra thrived in the guts of Southerners, black and white, leaving children chronically undernourished.[14]

While the South in the Redemption period was locked into old folkways, it nonetheless changed a great deal. Miners, convicts, and tracklayers who worked on the railway octopus saw the South changing and changed the story of John Henry as well.

Miners were the first to see the South change, and they sang about it often. As pokeweed and wildflowers grew over the unmarked graves at the Virginia Penitentiary, steam engines improved, replacing the muscle of man and machine in more and more enterprises. And steam engines required coal. The board of the Chesapeake & Ohio Railroad knew this well.

While the C&O board told investors and bondholders that the line would increase through traffic to the West, Huntington, his board members, and railway contractors quietly bought up coal lands to lease at high prices to private mining companies. With the mountains punctured, West Virginia could be mined for its burnable wealth. As early as 1875, little chunks of the state entered coal cars, bit by bit. They were bound, like the railway passengers who heard about John Henry's death, for the East and the West.[15]

Coal miners, black and white, traveled through the mountains to do the profitable work of digging West Virginia up. Their lives were very different from the lives of workers trapped on plantations. Black coal miners from Chesterfield County had gone to the mountains to oversee the work that John Henry and others did. They stayed to mine West Virginia's coal.

Miners carefully limited their time in the tunnels. They also controlled their hourly pace at work, and they did so with song. Contemporaries were somewhat baffled by the slow and mournful songs that miners sang as they burrowed through mountains. As one tunnel engineer in 1897 noted of black miners: "Their chief characteristic was to strike in time. Their accompaniment of weird and monotonous chant (sometimes pitched in a minor key) to the sound of clinking steel made an impression on the sensitive ear not soon to be forgotten."[16]

Miners did not really *sing* the song of John Henry in the way that contemporaries would have recognized. They crafted the story as a plaintive chant, broken up by hammer blows and structured inside a much older ballad tradition. Black coal miners would have heard Anglo-American ballads for a century, stretching back to the time that Welsh miners first introduced coal mining to Chesterfield County. These Welshmen, called "badgers" for the way they dug through hills, hammered to the accompaniment of ballads like "The Lass of Loch Royal" and "The Ship Carpenter." The old ballads remained in the Southern mountains for hundreds of years after their passing. Such ballads had a distinctive content: They tended to focus on spectacular deaths, crime and punishment, or the tragic fate of lovers. In most ballads, the characters foretold their death again and again, heightening the dread.[17]

John Henry's story fit snugly into the envelope of the mining ballad. Many of the most familiar lines in the ballad emphasize John Henry's premonitions of his death. John Henry predicts his death at every point in the song: at birth when he says that his hammer will kill him, when he first sees how high the mountain is and cries, when he tells his shaker to be careful or he will die from a hammer blow, when he hears the tunnel rumbling and the captain fears for his life. The miners' tale of John Henry's death has elaborate endings that emphasize his burial in the ground they dig in. Perhaps because miners really did end up entombed in their workplaces, they turned the details of John Henry's death into the sort of tragedy familiar to them.

> John Henry was buried,
> He was buried with each hammer in his hand.
> It was written on his tomb just as solid as a doom,
> "Here lies our steel drivin' man."

> or

> About nine o'clock in the morning
> That walking boss came walking down the line
> I think I heard that walking boss say,
> "John Henry is in tunnel number nine."

> The white folks in the mountain,
> And the negroes in the dread.
> John Henry in the tunnel lying dead. [18]

As the song was assembled its composer or composers borrowed phrases from much older Anglo-American ballads. The most familiar tune for the John Henry ballad derives from the British ballad "Earl Brand," from the 1560s. And many versions of the John Henry ballad include these very old lines:

> Darlin' who gonna buy your slippers (yes)
> Well-a who gonna glove your hand (yah, yah)
> Say now who gonna kiss your rosy cheeks
> Darlin' who gonna be your man (oh, lord)
> Well-a who gonna be your man[19]

The phrases come from "The Lass of Loch Royal," a song written down by ballad hawkers four centuries earlier, when movable type first arrived in England:

> Oh, who will shoe your pretty little feet?
> Who will glove your hand?
> And who will kiss your sweet little lips,
> While I'm in a foreign land?[20]

Another phrase about John Henry "sittin' on his Mama's knee" and predicting his death comes from the Scottish ballad "Mary Hamilton," about a mistress of Lord Bothwell who was hanged for killing her child in 1563 by Mary, Queen of Scots.[21]

The first person to transcribe the John Henry ballad as it was sung by the South's black coal miners was Natalie Curtis-Burlin. She had become famous for transcribing Native American songs in the 1890s and was asked in 1910 by professors at Hampton University to come to Hampton, Virginia, to look through their collection of "Work and Play Songs," which faculty members had been collecting from students since 1893.[22] Around 1917, Curtis-Burlin and another professor approached a student, George Alston, who recited hammer songs he had learned in the mines of Virginia, including this one:

> Mom' an' Pop-per
> Keeps on writ-in'
> Thinks I'm dade
> Thinks I'm dade
>
> Ef I could hammer
> Like John Henry
> I'd be gone
> I'd be gone
>
> Nine pound hammer
> Killed John Henry
> Can't kill me
> Can't kill me[23]

Each verse was finished by a *huh*, as the hammer came down.

How had the song been transmitted from the mountains of western Virginia back to eastern Virginia? Apparently by the same route that miners took back every Christmas since 1868. The census puts the black Alstons in Amelia and Nottoway counties, immediately south and west of the mines in Chesterfield County. George Alston would have heard the song at second or third hand from miners who had previously worked on the C&O's tunnels. Curtis-Burlin said that these miners claimed John Henry as one of their own. He "was evidently one of the best workmen, and [his] death must have made a deep impression."[24]

But the song was not just known among black coal miners. Miners in all-white communities knew the ballad and the hammer song. Many white miners had come from farms and pastures in the mountains to find work in the mines of William R. Johnson III, the grandson of railway tunnel contractor William R. Johnson.[25] They would have learned the song as it passed from miner to miner as a work song, and as a ballad sung to children. In 1933, Louis Watson Chappell, a West Virginia University English professor, published his study of the ballad. With a few exceptions, the thirty versions he found came from white coal-mining regions like Magoffin County, Kentucky; Coatesville, Pennsylvania; and Evington, Virginia. These versions of the song had picked up the jargon of miners, like "John Henry left the white house, went out on the heading to drive, The heading caught on fire with that light, little blaze,"[26] and "The scraper and the sprayers was all getting scared."[27] Similarly,

> John Henry walked in the tunnel
> Had his cap'n by his side
> The rousters held John Henry so long
> That he laid down his hammer and cried.[28]

For miners, the story of a man killed in a tunnel marked a real event. His experience would be repeated with every rockslide and cave-in, his death foretold in the hollow sound of every coal miner's cough.

Miners were not the only men to have remembered John Henry's death. Prisoners also kept the song alive and spread it far beyond the world of tunnels and mines. To them, a man "buried in the sand" was a reminder not only of the shortness of life but of the danger of dying unremembered. Southern prisons between 1873 and 1909 remained as deadly as John Henry's tunnel. In the 1870s, after the State of North Carolina tried and failed to build a tunnel near Asheville, the Southern Railway acquired the contract, but not before ensuring that the company received all the available convicts in North Carolina to build it. Between 1880 and 1882, less than a decade after John Henry died, hundreds of North Carolina

convicts repeated his experience at the Swannanoa Tunnel. Convicts dug
the pilot holes for nitroglycerin blasts while entire steam engines disappeared in the mud nearby. A cave-in killed more than twenty prisoners;
dozens more died from "consumption." The scandal damaged the reputation of the state-appointed physician, though it did little harm to the Southern Railway.[29] For convicts in North Carolina, apparently, the story of John
Henry's death was still a living memory. The song "Swannanoa Tunnel"
connected North Carolina convicts' deaths to the steel-driving man:

> I'm going back to the Swannanoa Tunnel
> That's my home, baby, that's my home
>
> Asheville Junction, Swannanoa Tunnel
> All caved in, baby, all caved in
>
> Last December I remember
> The wind blowed cold, baby, the wind blowed cold
>
> When you hear my watchdog howling
> Somebody around, baby, somebody around
>
> When you hear that hoot owl squalling
> Somebody dying, baby, somebody dying
>
> Hammer falling from my shoulder
> All day long, baby, all day long
>
> Ain't no hammer in this mountain
> Out rings mine, baby, out rings mine
>
> This old hammer it killed John Henry
> It didn't kill me, baby, couldn't kill me.[30]

For convicts in North Carolina, the prison stockades erected at the
Swannanoa Tunnel had become their home and their grave. As the railways of the South penetrated the mountains again and again, John Henry's
story became emblematic of hundreds of unmourned deaths.

The first published description of the performance of the original
John Henry ballad came from a prisoner, though not in the hills of North

Carolina. Rather, a convict called "Bad Bill," was discovered in the hills of Kentucky in 1915 by William Aspenwall Bradley. Bradley was a dabbler in music, poetry, and popular printing who came to Berea, Kentucky, to deliver a lecture. He was impressed by the intimate relationship between blacks and whites in Berea: In fact, Berea College had been for many years the only integrated college in the South until the state outlawed the practice in 1904. Here black and white musical practices seemed to slip back and forth quite easily, even among prisoners. Bradley overheard the song in front of a city jail:

> There a group of village boys would congregate, pick the banjo, sing, and execute the infinitely varied steps of the "hoe-down," while the other boys behind the bars would look out through the narrow windows and join in all the jokes and laughter. Sometimes the banjo would be on the inside instead of on the outside, and there was one youth, "Bad Bill," a favorite performer, who was certain on such occasions to respond to the clamorous request, "Sang Bill, now *you* sang!" with an exceedingly popular composition entitled "John Henry," or "The Steam Drill."[31]

As the miners had done, the convicts imposed their own experiences on the lyrics. Not surprisingly, their versions tended to emphasize John Henry's separation from his absent lover, who appears as Polly Ann in many of the printed lyrics. Many prison songs talked about absent lovers and expressed the men's fears of their lovers' infidelity. Thus

> John Henry had a little woman,
> Just as pretty as she could be;
> They's just one objection I's got to her:
> She want every man she see.[32]

John Henry's woman was tested by the long absence of the prisoner and the presence of so many other men nearer by.

> John Henry had a little wife,
> And the dress she wore was red;
> The last thing before he died,
> He said, "Be true to me when I'm dead,
> Oh, be true to me when I'm dead."[33]

The story of a good man who died and left his lover alone is one that struck prisoners with particular power.

For convicts in the stockades of the South, the John Henry song would also have been sung collectively as a work song. To them, the song of John Henry may have seemed an allegory for crime and punishment in the Redemption South. The song allowed them to talk directly about the strength of black men in a South grown obsessed with and fearful of them. Whites in Southern towns seemed to teeter between admiration of black men's physical strength and fear of their adult bodies. Lynching followed from rumors of rape, many of them fanciful. The ballad of John Henry raised up the image of a fabulously strong black man's body and seemed to suggest that John Henry carried the hope of a people with him. By the end of the song, though, John Henry was dead—separated from the world of the living like so many other black men who had been hanged, disfranchised, or locked up. And Polly Ann, Sarah Anne, Mary Magdalene would carry the work forward. The story of a hammering woman seemed to speak a fundamental truth about black life in the South. As fewer and fewer black men could vote in the years after Reconstruction, black women carried on "race work" in female institutions and clubs. They hammered away when it was dangerous for black men to do so.[34]

Thus while John Henry was at home in the mining camps at the heart of the railway octopus, he was equally at home in the construction camps at the octopus's fringes, where railways still needed convicts to dig their tunnels. At every mile marker of Southern railways stood a chorus prepared to take the song up. That some forty thousand men on railroad gangs sang songs at work, and sometimes sang ballads at night, seemed neither interesting nor odd. In the years before radio, trackliners carried local songs and stories across the South, carrying them hundreds of miles from their source of origin, tucked under their caps.

Regular railroad gangs sang at work and at dusk returned to shanties that stood behind the road boss's house. The forty thousand black men in railroad gangs made up the largest industrial workforce in the South in those years.[35] Road bosses were white, and they maintained the public face of the railroad at the railroad house, with picture windows and all. Trackliners' shanties, built of railway ties and shantlings, stood in the back. These too were the property of the railway.

There were many attractions to the job of trackliner. Railroads were the nerve centers of the South: They took cash for travel and paid cash to

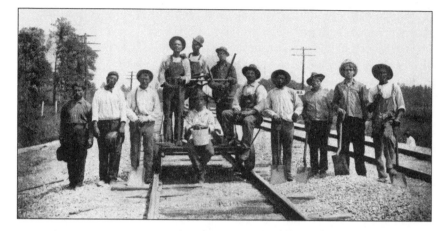

"Peter Delio and Gang Members of Independence Lodge No. 343." Peter Delio was a member of the Brotherhood of Maintenance of Way Employees, a union of trackliner foremen. He is probably the man seated on the right on the handcar. This mixed-race gang of twelve would have worked a stretch of twelve to twenty-four miles near Independence, Missouri. June 1911. (Center for Research Libraries)

workers, often weekly. Sharecroppers or mill hands got paid in scrip, accepted only at the local commissary, but a railroad man could spend his change anywhere. To black workers, the boss provided bacon and bread, either prepared as meals or delivered raw as rations. A railway man could stay in one place for years, working the five or ten miles of track allotted to the road boss.

William Holtzclaw described his father's time as a trackliner on the Western Railway of Alabama in the 1880s, fifty miles from their home in Randolph County. "He would remain away from home three months at a time," Holtzclaw wrote, "working for the handsome sum of a dollar a day . . . I remember how mother and we children would sit in our dark little cabin many nights looking for him to come at any moment, and sometimes it would be nearly a week after we would begin to look for him before he would come." As a man with a large family, Holtzclaw's father found that he could only do the work of tracklayer for a few seasons.[36]

A railway man without a family would move around more, because road bosses everywhere were always prowling roadhouses, city squares, and cockfights for strong, young men. A recurring phrase in the John Henry song provides the trackliner's announcement of his skills as he traveled from job to job:

> I can ball a jack
> I can line a track
> I can pick and shovel too

To "ball the jack" was to work hard and fast, like a railroad engine.[37] Indeed, only strong young men were trackliners. Pictures of gangs in road-boss magazines showed boys as young as fifteen and men as old as thirty. Advertisements in these magazines sold the equipment that trackliners and their bosses needed: construction manuals, pocket watches, work shoes, and hard, leather gloves. They also sold patent cures for backache, lumbago, and damaged kidneys. The physical strain on bodies meant that, while road bosses could work into their sixties, tracklining men had to be young.

In those years road bosses found a new technology for improving work, one discovered and promoted by the young Sigmund Freud in Vienna. That technology, a crystalline alkaloid derived from wild plants in Central America, was called cocaine. Freud and others considered the drug an anesthetic, believing that it interrupted the conduction of nerve impulses. In fact, cocaine is a stimulant that prevents dopamine, a chemical messenger for pleasure, from being reabsorbed by the body. For railway workers, the pleasurable sensation of cocaine seemed to dull the pain that radiated from back, shoulders, and neck. It made hard work easier and allowed workers to extend their days at heavy labor. By the early twentieth century, cocaine, like the song of John Henry, had been transmitted through urban and rural black communities, South and North. By then, the addictive properties of cocaine were better understood. For road bosses, addiction may have been an added inducement, for it kept men from leaving the gang. For black men's health, cocaine was terrible.[38] Whether they used cocaine or not, trackliners accumulated physical pains by the time they reached their mid-thirties. They usually turned to farming or janitorial work when the pains overwhelmed them, or they slowed down.

The elite of road crews were called "extra gangs," though on some roads extra gangs were recruited seasonally from track hands on the line. The pay was better, because extra gangs traveled extensively. When the roadmaster determined that some stretch of track needed major rebuilding or

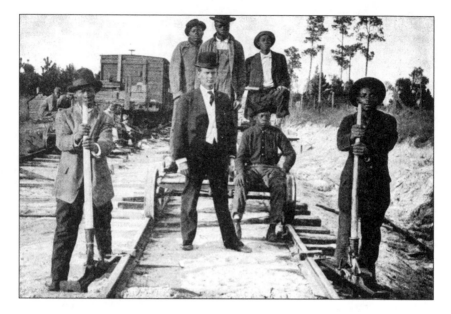

L. P. Puckett's gang demonstrates his patented tie spacer, a specialized spacing jack. Atlantic Coast Line Railway, Jesup, Georgia, 1914. An extra gang watches from the left background. (Center for Research Libraries)

double-tracking, or required reconstruction because of accident or natural disaster, an extra gang of twenty men or more came down to rebuild the line. Rather than use a little hand truck with some picks and mauls, as the smaller track gangs did, the extra gang had a locomotive and a railway car filled with tools. These men worked sometimes day and night, and they slept in tents in open fields or on bunk cars.

Song and story finally ended the day at the mess tent, and it was here that the legend of John Henry the five-foot-one-and-a-quarter-inch convict became John Henry the giant. This John Henry wielded a huge hammer. He was, he shouted in the song, "throwin' thirty pounds from my head on down." Leon R. Harris, who had been a day laborer since 1909, described how the story was transmitted from old-timers to young workers. By then, "John Henry" was not a cautionary tale but a story of great strength and an admonition to work harder.

> John Henry had a hammah;
> Weighed nigh fo'ty poun';
> Eb'ry time John made a strike
> He seen his steel go 'bout two inches down, -
> Lawd, - Lawd, -
> He seen his steel go 'bout two inches down.
> . . .
> One day Cap' Tommy told him
> How he'd bet a man;
> Bet John Henry'd beat a steam-drill down,
> Jes' cause he was th' best in th' lan', -
> Lawd, - Lawd, -
> 'Cause he was th' best in th' lan.
> . . .
> John Henry kissed his hammah;
> White Man turned on steam;
> Li'l Bill held John Henry's trusty steel, -
> 'Twas th' biggest race th' worl' had ever seen, -
> Lawd, - Lawd, -
> Th' biggest race th' worl' had ever seen.[39]

Men who lived on the road would gather in groups at night, often competing in feats of strength, wrestling, or even pissing contests. They also
told tall tales about men like themselves. For cowboys, Pecos Bill became a
man big and strong enough to rope a tornado. For lumbermen, Paul
Bunyan became a giant who dug the Mississippi River single-handedly.
Among extra gang workers still awake in their mess tents, John Henry
grew taller and more heroic. The race was the biggest, John Henry the
best, a man who could drive steel down two inches with every strike. The
story and song grew in a distinctive way among railroad workers, and John
Henry became a working-class hero. Thus one version of the song that
certainly came from the C&O near the Big Bend Tunnel had a powerful,
bragging John Henry. In this version John Henry does not say "A man
ain't nothing but a man." Instead he says "You know I am a man" and "I
can beat all the traps that have ever been made,/Or I'll die with my hammer in my hand."[40] Seldom do versions acquired from railroad men show
a man who "laid down his hammer and cried."

John Henry was an early bragging song among African American men, structured as a ballad that could be spoken, shouted out at a worksite, or even sung with a guitar. In such songs the men described were free, powerful, and angry. In slavery days, stories and songs were much more heavily coded. Thus Br'er Rabbit was the trickster who outsmarted other animals, and John tales told of a slave who lied, cheated, and stole from his master but almost always fooled him. After slavery, as the historian Lawrence Levine has shown, stories of physically powerful, sometimes desperate men became common currency.[41] "Stagolee" was a rhymed song about a "bad man" who killed other men indiscriminately with his pistols.

> It was on a hustle in B joint
> On a Mississippi run
> Stagolee shot Billy de Lyons
> With a smokin' 41
>
> He was a bad man
> That mean old Stagolee.
>
> Stagolee shot Billy de Lyons
> What do you think about that?
> Shot him down in cold blood
> Because he stole his Stetson hat;
>
> He was a bad man
> That mean old Stagolee[42]

"John Hardy," sung as a ballad, told of a bad man who killed men and foretold his own death. The structure of the song was almost identical to the structure of the John Henry ballad. But John Hardy was a desperate murderer who bragged about his exploits and foretold his hanging.

Songs about Stagolee, John Hardy, and John Henry appealed to trackliners, physically strong men, often without families, who could leave everything behind and move on to the next worksite. In slavery days black workers had been owned by railroads or rented out by nearby owners. After slavery a trackliner could be a wanderer, not bound to community and local traditions. It was a circumstance workers found both exhilarating and unsettling. Their heroes might be bad men, like John Hardy or Stagolee, or they might be strong and earnest men, like John Henry. But for these heroes—as for trackliners—the candle burned quickly. Good or bad, they died at the end of the song.

If songs about physically powerful men closed the trackliners' evening, song also woke trackliners up again. The shack rouster, axe handle in hand, called workers out in the morning:

> All right boys let's go back,
> Let's go back boys to the double track
>
> The work ain't hard,
> The man ain't mean
>
> Cook ain't nasty,
> But the grub ain't clean
>
> You sleep on the good beds,
> And you call 'em bunks
>
> You eat my good rations,
> And you call it junk
>
> So now let's go back[43]

Shack rousters used more than songs when calling out the extra gang. They could also be violent. To roust means to lift, and shack rousters were said to lift the shacks of the extra gang to force workers out in the morning. By the 1920s, shack rousters had traded axe handles for whips and pistols to wake workers and get them on the job.[44] A trackliner's day started with song, but not joyous song.

By the 1880s, extra gangs were the first to see new, powerful tools that did the work of men. The most sophisticated tools were increasingly used to lay rather than reline track: steel trusses for bridges, jackhammers for breaking rock, packaged dynamite for blasting. Yet until World War I none of these tools could match the power and portability of a half dozen young men with sharp tools. Tracklaying machinery had made inroads, but until World War I the tools for road maintenance hardly changed.

Still, road bosses were always experimenting—trying new tools to save labor costs. L. P. Puckett's tie spacer was a new kind of jack, one that promised to perfectly set the space between ties. It proved simple enough to become popular. Realigning ties stuck in gravel or clay was backbreaking work, and no one could curse a tool that eased this labor. But workers also understood what laborsaving tools threatened: either replacement or a deadly contest, a race to the bottom. Thus while the song of John Henry seemed to describe a particular time and place—the early 1870s, when steam drills were weak and inflexible—it also described a continuing contest between hammer men and steam-powered steel implements.

In song, this was a battle that workers always won. They lived in a segregated South where blacks and poor whites were denied the vote, where planters controlled sharecroppers as peons and then used violence to get their way. For white workers too, life was often nasty, brutish, and short. "John Henry" may have expressed a utopian possibility. It seemed to suggest that the men who aligned and adjusted the railway octopus were vital and indispensable. It was a dream that laborers, whom no machine could imitate, stood outside the undemocratic, Jim Crow South. It was crucial that John Henry win, just as trackliners knew that they had to wake up strong every morning. If machines arrived to make tracklining easy, that would be a fateful day for black workers in the South.

Ben Lewis, a drayman (or wagonmaster) from Mississippi, described the future of laboring black men in the South by 1936.

> For years I was a drayman an' worked for F. A. Dicksen Co. till they moved to New Orleans. Now I'se too old an' feeble to do heavy liftin', so I cain't run a dray. Besides the dray business is dyin' out. Our Drayman's Association is in a terrible fix. Soon they won't be no more dump carts an' mules. Just a little while back the Geisenberger Drug Company traded they mule an' cart in on a brand new truck. For forty years or more that dray done all the haulin' for that firm. Now I sits on the corner with my friends, all of 'em draymen, an' they is waitin' for calls that never come.[45]

Among trackliners who lived by their strength, the song of John Henry found its home as a story of heroism, one tinged with anxiety about the future. Men traveled from gang to gang, carrying local tracklining songs with them. Extra gangs, composed of men who had done their time on a regular gang, could carry the song for hundreds of miles. And wanderers who lit out from one state to another brought with them a carpetbag of coffee, tobacco, lumbago medicine, a little cocaine, and a half dozen songs in their heads. Leon R. Harris, who had wandered in this way at the turn of the century put it bluntly. "The ballad [of John Henry], by special right belongs to the railroad builders," he wrote. "It belongs to the pick-and-shovel men,—to the scraper and wheeler men,—to the skinners,—and to the steel-drivers."[46]

Finally, after the turn of the century had seen the song of John Henry preserved among miners, convicts, and trackliners, the ballad appeared to scholars. Folklore scholars first noticed the song in the mountains in 1909, when Louise Rand Bascom, a Wellesley student home for the summer in Highlands, North Carolina, published in a folklore journal a couplet of a song that she had heard about. As an aspiring playwright, she had been searching for colloquial songs and mountain expressions to use in her writing. She said she had heard of a particular popular fiddle tune and ballad but had only a phrase of it: "Johnie Henry was a hard-workin' man,/He died with a hammer in his hand."[47] Fiddlers played local songs at yearly conventions in the mountains of southwestern North Carolina, and Bascom had asked a few people about it but had not yet learned more than this phrase.

A brief examination of Bascom's own life suggests that she may have heard of the fiddle tune from the family's white maid, whose two sons were mountain fiddlers. Bascom quipped then that a song about hard work could not really be native to the mountains of North Carolina.[48] Four years later, in 1913, Eber Carle Perrow, a University of Louisville English professor and lover of folk songs, picked up the trail. He transcribed from memory a brief John Henry song he had heard in east Tennessee in 1905, when he was a twenty-five-year-old graduate student in English philology at Harvard, presumably also home for the summer. He also reported a longer version he had acquired in 1912 from someone in the Kentucky mountains.

Perrow suggested that while the song was sung in the mountains, it had strongest currency among trackliners. "Among the workmen on the railroads in the South," he wrote, "there has been formed a considerable body of verse about John Henry, a famous steel-driving man."[49] After Perrow's discovery, a flood of longer versions came from Kentucky folklorist Josiah Combs, the University of Texas's John Lomax, Hampton University's Natalie Curtis-Burlin, Duke University's Frank C. Brown, and the University of North Carolina's Howard Odum and Guy Johnson, both sociologists.[50]

The ballad of John Henry was transmitted and transcribed but never copyrighted between 1870 and 1922, when W. C. Handy copyrighted the first sheet music version. Yet between 1909 and 1912, English and sociology professors at colleges throughout the South found that they were only minutes away from workers who could recite the song from memory. Black men in Mississippi, "mountain whites" in Kentucky, black coal miners in eastern Virginia, and trackliners on the Chesapeake & Ohio Railroad all could render a song with as many as a dozen verses, most of which had the structure of a ballad.[51] Perrow had been the first to recover a separate group of "hammer songs," two-stanza or three-stanza songs sung to the accompaniment of a sledgehammer, which referred to the death of John Henry from overwork.[52] These hammer songs did not have a ballad structure, and only mentioned John Henry rather than telling his story. For English professors and enthusiasts like Bascom, the allure of folksongs was their unique phrasing. Thus they generally collected the words and had little interest in describing how they were performed or transmitted.

While these folklorists did not much care to interview those who sang the songs, they felt free to speculate on what the songs meant. Sociologists Howard Odum and Guy Johnson, smitten with the image of a powerful black man in the tracklaying versions of the song, saw "John Henry" not as a cautionary tale but as the song of a hero. Calling John Henry a "Rambling Black Ulysses," they helped to build up the legend of John Henry as a hero in the tradition of the Greek epic. The scholarship of the 1920s had only recently suggested that the story of Ulysses in the *Odyssey* was not a single work by a man named Homer but a collection of ballads composed sometime between 1200 B.C. and the early Christian era.

For Odum and Johnson, the songs about John Henry seemed to fit perfectly into the mold of the *Odyssey* of ancient legend—if you ignore the considerable changes in time, history, and place. The story of John Henry as a "Negro epic" led Odum to create a collection of fictionalized narratives that he published as a book. The best known of these came out in 1928, *Rainbow Round My Shoulder: The Blue Trail of Black Ulysses*. Odum started with the songs and stories of a one-armed laborer named John Wesley "Left Wing" Gordon. The idea of a tribe of black men who wandered from job to job without a home became a powerful image for Odum, leading him to impose it on black workers everywhere. It led Odum to a view of black laborers that was both romanticized and racist: that black men were feckless wanderers. It was soon imposed on black workers everywhere by modern sociologists.[53]

The song of John Henry flowed along many courses from its source at the tunnels of the C&O Railroad. It traveled along the route of the Southern railway octopus, and it changed as the men and women who sang it commented on the world that John Henry's hammer had made. John Henry had connected the South to the West, and as he dropped his hammer for the last time, the experiment of Reconstruction ended, along with the hopes of four million black men and women in the South. A world both new and hauntingly familiar grew up in the South around them: the Redeemed South. Just as the death of John Henry predicted, steam engines emerged to replace waterwheels in factories, and to replace the labor of horses and men. Yet steam engines, hungry for coal, relied on the Allegheny Mountains that John Henry had penetrated.

The story of his death was carefully folded into the familiar and disturbing horrors of the ballad tradition. Coal miners, black and white, made John Henry one of their own. John Henry became the man whose hammer started large-scale mining in West Virginia, as well as the man who died as Reconstruction was ending: a Moses who gave the South the Promised Land of the West, but could not live to see it. For prisoners, the song suggested the questions about loved ones: Would they be true, and would prisoners ever live to see them again? The terror of Southern justice was the terror John Henry actually faced, that a sentence in prison was a sentence of death. For trackliners, the song of John Henry became a boastful story that nonetheless suggested the gnawing fear that all trackliners faced: of becoming too slow or too old to work again. Trackliners had to be mighty men and so made John Henry in their own image. When English professors and sociologists discovered the complex and unsettling story of John Henry, they glibly turned him into a hero on the model of Ulysses. This was not a complex and bitter story, they suggested, a horrifying ballad of a man killed by a machine, but a fabulous, impossible legend. So by 1909 the song of John Henry reached many lips. Especially dear to the men on the railway octopus, its miners, convicts, and tracklayers, the song traveled through the surging, boiling, diabolical heart of the New South. Within a few years, future generations would take up the song, preparing John Henry for the age of radio, records, and beyond.

7

SONGS PEOPLE HAVE SUNG: 1900-1930

BACK IN THE DAYS of the railway octopus, an individual performance of the ballad of John Henry was a rare thing. Men and women hummed it, called it. They sang it in pairs or groups. They accompanied the song with a hammer, axe, or hoe, not a banjo, guitar, or fiddle. They talked it as much as sang it; it was an everyday thing. But by the turn of the century, individual musicians began to perform it in specific places. John Henry, as a song, had grown up. An individual performer staged the song, using it to suggest a place and a time far away. By the twentieth century, the ballad of John Henry became a historical commentary, its performance carefully calibrated to recall a bygone era. A blind minstrel outside a church, a troubadour at a rent party, a blues woman at a cabaret, a "folk" singer at a downtown lecture, or a "country" singer on the steps of a Southern courthouse, each summoned the ghost of John Henry to tell an assembled audience about the past. Performers sang in dialect, with old instruments, and with a timbre in their voices that suggested that they were using John Henry to tell a history.

In each case, individual musicians performed the song to talk about the new machine age that engulfed them, as if the song could rescue its listeners from their surroundings and return them someplace else. The world was changing at what many people thought an impossible pace. In John Henry's day, the professions of mechanical engineering and industrial chemistry had brought steam drills and portable nitroglycerin. These new devices had fused the world together, annihilating distance. In the same year that John Henry pierced the Lewis Tunnel, contractors with drills and dynamite penetrated the Berkshires in Massachusetts and bored through the Alps in southeastern France. New transmontane tunnels, along with steel-plated steamships, drastically cheapened transportation across land and oceans. Soon, immigrants from Prague, Budapest, Warsaw, and beyond could cross underneath the Alps, over the Atlantic, and underneath the Appalachian Mountains to anywhere on the North American continent. After the tunnels were complete, millions of tons of cheap American goods flowed back along the same route, directly into Europe, realigning the world economy.

These chemical and mechanical discoveries did not stop remaking the world. From the 1870s forward, Germany and the United States became particularly adept at the frenzied round of discovery, invention, and application that reshaped agriculture, mining, and manufacturing. Fertilizers dug out of the South Carolina coast could be sprinkled on arid fields in Kansas. Thousands of industrial workers could tunnel miles underground, extracting coal, iron, copper, and lead. Iron and coke were refined into inexpensive steel. Railways became cheap, and railways cheapened the movement of goods. While John Henry lay buried in the sands in Richmond, the steel-ribbed railway corridors beside his grave sent branches that linked every town and borough around a cluster of cities, powered by chemical and industrial discoveries.

As chemical discoveries created new materials and new sources of power, these massive cities soon dwarfed the landscape around them: Bonn, Berlin, and Dresden in Germany competed with Chicago, Pittsburgh, and Cleveland as monster cities. Cities, not steam drills, became the wonders of the world after 1871. With steel-reinforced skyscrapers and coal-powered railroads, cities choked with tens of millions of people became distribution points for a proliferating body of industrial and agricultural commodities. As industrial centers, Germany and the United States had, in the forty years between 1871 and 1921, displaced the old industrial powers of England and France. Workers streamed in from the countryside, feeding a vast industrial complex.

The pace of change, and the need for rescue, only increased as war came. War, in outsized steam-powered countries like these, looked vastly different from the set battles of cavalry, infantry, and artillery of John Henry's day. Industrial war would be shocking in its efficient brutality, turning battles into long, semipermanent firing ranges, like the trenches of Petersburg, only deadlier. Gas canisters strangled and burned soldiers on the field. Long-range rifles forced soldiers on both sides into trenches, where they awaited hails of supersonic shrapnel that could be fired with terrifying precision from miles away. John Henry's fateful battle with a steam-powered machine would seem quaint, yet hauntingly familiar.

Performances by individual musicians may have seemed like a relic from a lost age to the busy secretaries, bank cashiers, and farmers who walked through twentieth-century cities rebuilt by steel. Yet traveling soloists abounded in this new machine age, bringing John Henry into its cities and deep into America's heartland. African American traveling singers calling themselves "musicianers" or "songsters" sang and played on improvised instruments on the sidewalks of machine-age cities and towns.[1] Their profession went back to the 1840s at least, when "musician" was the largest profession among free blacks in Northern cities, accounting for nearly 20 percent of professional black men.[2]

Oddly, perhaps, black musicianers and songsters became one of the entering wedges for the sale of chemical products, pushing all manner of goods into the most remote rural regions in the South. Of course, circuses had always employed songsters to draw a crowd so that a barker could sell tickets to the big show. But by the 1890s, sellers of patent medicines found black songs and black singers to be the best way to draw customers, black and white, under the tent. When they had captured their prey, the "tout," or salesman, would sell Indian tonics, Kickapoo Joy Juice, and phony cancer cures. In the 1920s, a black college student from Southern University in Louisiana heard a "Negro comedian named Jake" sing the ballad of John Henry to a milling crowd outside Baton Rouge. Soon a "medicine seller known as Doctor Moon" came in to close the deal.[3]

Itinerant comedians and musicians like Jake brought the story and song of John Henry to appreciative crowds who may have known about America's industrial mines only by word of mouth. In Jake's version of the song, John Henry does the impossible work of tunneling deep into mountains. To do so he must leave his father and his small town behind.

> John Henry said to his papa,
> "It's come my time to go;
> I'll get me a ten pound hammer, dad,
> And go to the mountain, you know, (this day)
> I'll go to the mountain, you know."

John Henry went to the mountain,
The mountain looked so tall;
He laid down his hammer by his side,
Said, "A ten pounder is too small, (on the job)
A ten pounder is too small."[4]

Comedians like Jake told men and women about the marvels of the
new machine age with its impossible feats like the hollowing out of mountains. John Henry symbolized the work of thousands, and the work was so
hard that a ten-pound hammer was too small to match a steam drill.

By World War I the practical transmission of music and spoken sound
was possible, though cheap and easy distribution proved difficult. Comedians and musicians still remained the most reliable transmitters of new
sounds from the city. Later, when "John Henry" was first recorded, it was
by these itinerant musicians. The first recording credit (in March 1924)
went to white performer Fiddlin' John Carson; the second recording (in
August) came from an itinerant black street musician named Sam Jones.
A one-man band, Jones had performed on the streets of Cleveland for
years with a kazoo, a harmonica, a guitar, and a stovepipe that "created a
tone somewhere between a wax-papered comb and a sweetly distorted
tuba."[5] Sam Jones seemed to defy the new sounds of the city he heard,
using handmade objects that would have instantly drawn a crowd. Among
his favorite songs were "A Chicken Can Waltz the Gravy Around" and
"Cripple Creek and Sourwood Mountain." His stovepipe became his trademark, and he recorded "John Henry" under the name of Stovepipe No. 1,
at a session in Columbia studios in New York in August. In those years
Columbia recorded many more songs than it released, and Sam Jones's
version was never cut as a record. Jones's other recorded works were among
the first of what would become known as the blues, or country blues.

Sam Jones's strong Southern drawl, his handmade instruments, and
his slow style became a trademark of many black performers in the early
years of the twentieth century. His ensemble seemed a defiant razz in the
face of the machine age, even though machines immortalized his voice
and his instruments. Jones later went on to record one of the first gospel
songs, "Lord Don't You Know I Have No Friend Like You." According to
the musicologist Paul Oliver, Jones may have been a jackleg preacher—a
street-corner preacher with no congregation. [6] Before records or radio,
these comic and preaching performers brought the song of John Henry

out of coalfields and trackliners' shanties onto street corners and stoops in every city and town in the country.

In the United States in the early twentieth century, among black comedians, minstrels, and street performers, blind musicians proved the most popular. For some, blindness had necessitated extraordinary aural memory that assisted musical peformance. Blind Tom, for example, was known for his ability to mimic any music he heard. Among his feats was the ability to hear a new composition once and instantly repeat it on the piano. The black poet James D. Corrothers described a performance.

> Long, long ago I saw Blind Tom.
> The noisy audience became calm,
> And a hush fell o'er the whispering din,
> When the blind musician was led in.
> A moment vacantly he stood,
> 'Till, moved by some mysterious mood,
> The while the inspiration burned,
> He, to the harp that waited, turned,
> And, seated there at graceful ease,
> He swept his hands along the keys,
> Awaking sound so soft and clear
> That Silence bent with eager ear
> Its faintest whisperings to hear.
> He clapped his hands like a little child,
> And sang in accents low and mild:
>> "Dem a gates ajar I'm boun' to see,
>> Dem a gates ajar I'm boun' to see,
>> Dem a gates ajar I'm boun' to see,
>> O, sinner, fare you well."[7]

Indeed, blind performers like Blind Lemon Jefferson, born in 1897, could be relied upon to retain extraordinarily detailed versions of old songs that had been forgotten in the rush of twentieth-century America. Blind musicians' perfect recall of overheard songs made them carriers of a region's musical memory before recording became widespread.

While Blind Tom's performances attracted thousands of black and white listeners, other blind musicians lived closer to poverty. Some sustained themselves by selling "ballets" that acted as primitive recordings of their performances. These performers approached job printers to print copies of songs in their repertoire. Some they learned, others they composed, and others were some combination of the two. After performing they sold these printed "ballets" to customers who wanted to remember the song as it was performed. [8] The third recording of "John Henry," in September 1924, was made by a blind North Carolina minstrel named Ernest Thompson. [9]

Just as miners, convicts, and railroad trackliners had adapted the song to their own circumstances, blind street performers linked it to the story of the blinded hero of the Old Testament, Samson. Like John Henry, Samson was a strong man whose very strength doomed him. The phrase "natural man," used to describe both John Henry and Samson, make the connection most explicit. In many versions John Henry calls himself a "natural man," as in the version that came from Doctor Moon's medicine show:

> John Henry said to the captain,
> I'm nothing but a natural man.
> Before I'll let your steam drill beat me down,
> I will die with my hammer in my hand. [10]

The expression "natural man" comes from the Bible, namely Paul's sermons in First Corinthians. After describing how "man's wisdom" cannot reach God, Paul continues, declaring, "The natural man receiveth not the things of the spirit of God: for they are foolishness unto him." The natural man, unlike the spiritual man, is separated from God. Baptists and Methodists frequently quoted the line as evidence that the pretensions of "men of learning" were useless, that their wisdom amounted to nothing. [11] John Wesley, the founder of Methodism, described the natural man, in one of his most famous and frequently used sermons, as "under the spirit of bondage and fear." [12]

In African American religious lore, there was a strong connection between the natural man and bondage. The best example of the natural man is Samson, who by letting Delilah cut his hair became separated from God. A familiar gospel song suggests the connection between Samson and the natural man, who was spiritually weak. [13] As the Golden Gate Quartet put it in the gospel song they sang at camp meetings:

> They tell me that strength was never found out
> But Samson's wife she said one evening
> Samson tell me where your strength might be

> Samson's wife, she talked so fast
> Samson told her but to cut his hair
> She shaved my head and raise my hand
> And your strength gonna come like a natural man

> Wasn't that another witness for my lord.[14]

Samson's wife, a Philistine, betrayed him, making him a "natural man," so that the Philistines could enslave him. This familiar story of feminine betrayal and male weakness may explain why John Henry's wife—Polly Ann, Sally Ann, or Mary Magdalene—was such an important part of the song. After John Henry dies, she tells him, "John Henry I've been true to you,"[15] thus declaring that his death did not come from betrayal, as Samson's had come from Delilah's.

Other parallels between the story of Samson and the story of John Henry crop up in some unique versions of the John Henry ballad, suggesting that performers saw in John Henry's story a retelling of Samson's. One version declared:

> John Henry had a little hammer,
> The handle was made of bone.
> Every time he hit the drill on the head,
> He thought of regions far beyond.[16]

In this version John Henry's hammer made of bone evokes Samson's biblical tool, the jawbone of an ass. After Samson kills thousands of Philistines with it, he asks God for a drink, which God provides by making water come out of the jawbone. The request for water also has important biblical significance. Throughout the book of Judges, God's chosen men ask for a drink of water, and are usually given milk, suggesting that God favors them, exceeding their wishes. John Henry, in some versions, asks either his mother or Polly Ann for a "cool drink of water Before the death of me."[17]

Samson's final feat of strength also seems to parallel John Henry's death. After Samson loses his strength, he is enslaved by the Philistines who had previously feared him. John Henry's captain, in many versions, fears that walls will cave in on him as John Henry hammers. John Henry reassures him that the rumbling he hears is "my hammer fallin' in the wind."[18] Of course, Samson's own death came after the Philistines had blinded him and God had sapped his strength, turning Samson into a "natural man" for the rest of his life. To kill his cruel masters, Samson prayed to God to restore his great strength one last time, then pushed against the pillars of the Philistine amphitheater where he was chained. His pushing caused the walls to cave in, finally killing all the Philistines inside, and Samson too.

John Henry was not simply a modern Samson; professional songsters and musicianers would have pulled names and expressions from other familiar biblical stories and sermons to fill in verses. The story of Samson's strength, the cruelty of his tormentors, and his martyrdom would have sprung to mind, especially among blind performers. These men may have found in the unfamiliar story of John Henry echoes of the biblical story of a blind strongman who was made into a natural man but who died bringing down holy judgment. As blind and comic performers performed the song of John Henry in circus tents, on street corners, and on stoops outside of churches, they turned it into a personal story that echoed their own lives and lore. At the same time, railway workers and black families were carrying the song far outside of the South, making it into a song about movement, and about loss.

These individual performers, whether blind balladeers, minstrels, or jackleg preachers, moved easily in and out of the South, carrying musical traditions along the routes of a growing black migration. The trailblazers were African American trackliners and construction workers, whose gang-labor songs would be transformed into individual songs, to be sung as blues, folk, and country music.

The first arrivals came as long ago as the 1880s, to line track and drive steel around the largest cities. They dug tunnels for subways, carved out trenches for water and gas lines, and reconstructed railways in the Northeast and Midwest. "Many of them are scantily clothed," wrote the *New York Times* of trackliners working upstate in 1881, "working with bare feet and bare heads. It is a curious sight to see the brawny blacks bending over their work busily plying shovel and pick." The *Times* reporter made the same mistake that sociologists Odum and Johnson did, of mistaking work songs for cheerfulness. "A more cheerful company of laborers it would be difficult to find anywhere," he continued. "There are no dissensions among them, and all day long they join their melodious voices in some refrain."[19] Another observer in Chicago saw steel-driving black tunnel workers in 1894 as they dug tunnels for a subway. "One sits flat on the rock, holding a rock drill [between his legs]. The other two stand to the right and left of him and strike the drill with their sledges." This observer could not identify the strange song he heard the hammer man singing, calling it "a comical darky song" by which "the hammers keep time with the music." Again mistaking performance for play, he continued: "The singer will occasionally roll his big eyes up at the people on the bank to see if any one is watching him, and then if he gets a responsive smile he will chuckle to himself and sing louder than ever."[20]

These workers literally laid the foundations for the modern industrial city, though they were excluded from most of the skilled positions in its factories, slaughterhouses, and warehouses. Despite exclusion, hundreds of thousands of African Americans followed the siren song of trackliners and tunnel workers, following them out of the South during World War I in a movement called the Great Migration. While at first nearly all Northern workplaces were segregated, when the war began in 1914, change crept onto the shop floors. As the European combatants made the Atlantic Ocean a war zone, liable to attack by warships, European countries closed their borders and the flow of immigrant workers into the United States suddenly stopped. Factory owners panicked.

The end of European immigration threatened to close down a new automated factory system that had been growing in America's large cities. It had relied on tens of thousands of immigrants—Czechs, Italians, Hungarians, and Slavs—to work in electrically powered urban factories with a precise division of labor. Beginning in the early 1910s, the steam age appeared to be giving ground to the machine age. Henry Ford's auto plant in Highland Park, Michigan, became a model of this new "assembly line" production. Professional engineers designed these new factories from the ground up. Some Ford plants produced taillights; others produced just dashboards or steering columns. The components were assembled into cars on a constantly moving track inside the plant.

The new factory system, staffed largely by immigrant workers, promised to change everything. For the skilled and unskilled workers of the machine age, work followed the pace of the machines that stood around them. Each worker did one small chore, and people's jobs in these plants become simple, machine-like activities. Assemblers, trained in less than a week, replaced skilled autoworkers who had previously worked in small groups assembling a whole car themselves. Now, workers saw only a tiny part of the production process. As the scale of production increased, prices plummeted, making automobiles and other assembly-line products—camera film, wristwatches, and radios—cheap and popular.

But now, with the collapse of European immigration and the need for semi-skilled labor, men like Henry Ford were in a panic. In the middle of the war, Ford—a notorious racist and a supporter of the German kaiser—nonetheless made the radical decision to accept black workers in his plants in Michigan.[21] Dodge, Chrysler, Chevrolet, and Packard soon followed.[22]

Other industries starved for immigrant workers, especially mines and packinghouses, began to employ black workers by the thousands. Sometimes black workers applied and were accepted at newer plants. At other times, when white workers struck for higher wages, black workers would be shipped in from Southern cities to replace them as strikebreakers. Their opportunities for advancement were limited; only whites were allowed to become mechanics or millwrights, for example. But the appeal of factory wages was hard to resist. A black man traveling north could double his wages; women could earn nearly three times the prevailing wage in the South. Thus as German submarines and warships moved into the Atlantic and immigration slowed to a crawl, opportunities abounded for black migrants.[23]

Some industries even courted black laborers, sending agents to the South to attract young men with offers of cash wages. Black newspapers in the North, surreptitiously brought south by Pullman porters and trackliners, promised higher wages, better schools, the opportunity to vote, and a social freedom unknown in Mississippi, Louisiana, Alabama, and Georgia. Of course, Chicago, Detroit, New York, and Cleveland still had segregated housing and intense racism, but inside these cities a thrilling, largely black world beckoned. The new machine-age Northern cities looked radically different from the rural South, with electric lights, indoor toilets and steam heat. Half a million black men and women came north between 1915 and 1918. Some rode as passengers; others caught freight trains or rode in the blinds, the fabric folds that separated the cars on passenger trains.[24]

Vocalists like Trixie Smith sang in the black "cabarets," basement clubs for "jazzed" music that sprang up in Northern cities during the Great Migration. She told the story of how hundreds of thousands in the South thought about migration with a mixture of hope, anger, and regret. Speaking with the jargon of railway workers, she conjured up a scene in the Deep South. She sang about how much easier it was for a man to go north than a woman. Singing as a woman who has stayed in the South, she tells a tale with a slow, drawn-out, self-consciously Southern drawl:

> I hate to hear that engine blow boo hoo
> Every time I hear it blowing, I feel like riding too
> Got the freight train blues, got boxcars on my mind
> I'm going to leave this town, because my man is so unkind
> I'm going away, just to wear you off my mind
> And I may be gone honey, for a doggone long long time
> I asked the brakeman, to let me ride the blinds
> The brakeman said little girlie, you know this train ain't mine
> When a woman gets the blues, she goes to her room and hides
> But when a man gets them, he catches a freight train and rides.[25]

Trixie Smith pointed out the dilemma that all migrants faced, of leaving to wander but leaving things behind. Beyond the Great Migration was the war itself, and it too changed the lives of black men who traveled to Europe. The new kind of machine-age war required millions of soldiers. The U.S. Army called on black volunteers, then on draftees, promising that some segregated black regiments would have black officers. Training of black and white soldiers took place side by side, though black men almost never got training in the machine-age positions of artilleryman or engineer. Big Bill Broonzy, a black soldier in Mississippi, recalled running into Northern white soldiers at stores and in training camps. At first the blacks and whites were mutually suspicious, but Broonzy recalled that self-deprecating humor could often break the ice with Northern whites, and some Northern-born white soldiers would play dice and drink with black soldiers on the base.[26]

If camp life lowered a few barriers, the war in France brought even more significant changes. The two hundred thousand black soldiers who arrived in Europe in 1918 found that Europe, especially France, had few of the race prejudices that seemed so entrenched in the South. Because many black and white soldiers were billeted in French homes rather than in barracks, they came into close contact with French families. Black soldiers and stevedores flirted with French women, drank in European cafés, and ate at the same tables as Allied soldiers. When reports appeared of white army officers discriminating against black soldiers, the French National Assembly banned discrimination on French soil, even if it took place inside a U.S. Army barracks.[27] Many black troopers returned convinced that their time as soldiers would change matters at home.

The Great Migration and black wartime experience helped alter the racial hierarchy that John Henry had seen in Prince George County, in the Virginia Penitentiary, and up in the mountains along the Virginia–West Virginia border. The Jim Crow South seemed to be crumbling, at least for those who went north. Southern Blacks in the North, segregated but also partly insulated from the constant danger of white reprisals, used song to carve out cultural markers that showed them their new place in the world, and the world they had left behind. A new music called "the blues" symbolized both new and old worlds to people who had migrated out of the South. Blues songs were simple and repetitive tunes that told of lost lovers, loneliness, and the lure of the road. They borrowed their structure—as well as taking countless "floating verses," or endlessly repeated phrases—from trackliners' songs.[28] Thus the tracklining phrase

> I got a girl (huh)
> She works in the yard (huh)
> She brings me meat (huh)
> She brings me lard (huh)

became the blues song "Drop that Sack" by Papa Charlie Jackson. Blues singers like Jackson replaced the trackliners' *huh* with an unvoiced gap in the middle of the blues phrase. Literary scholars of the blues call this the caesura and represent it with a colon.[29] Thus in "Drop that Sack," Jackson describes a craps game at a roadhouse that goes awry:

> Now I got a gal : works in the yard
> She brings me meat : she brings me lard
> Only thing : that keep me barred
> People she works for : don't allow me in the yard
> Going to tell you one thing : it's a natural fact
> Want you to come on home : and drop that sack
> Now I got a gal : she lives on the hill
> Took our corn : to the sugar mill
> Still I know : I wouldn't take no salt
> I'll grind your corn : into sweet jellyroll
> I asked for one : she brought me two
> Down to the crap game : me and you
> Got two dollars : my point was nine

Police come a-running : and the chips went flying
Said I went to the Gypsy : to get me a hand
See my gal walking : with another man
I said you may go : you'll come back
If you ever come back : you got to drop that sack

For individual singers of the blues, these floating verses would not be sung by a group of workers, of course, but by a single man or woman, accompanied by an instrument. For women who sang with a band, a hammer blow might be replaced by a plink on the piano, as it was in Trixie Smith's "Freight Train Blues." For a man playing solo, the smack of a hammer was replaced by a thumb-thump on the body of the guitar.

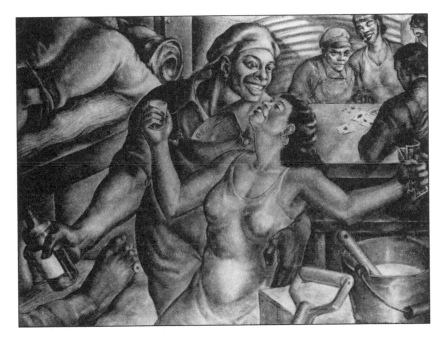

Elmer William Brown, *Gandy Dancer's Gal.* 24 x 32 inches, oil on canvas, 1941. African American muralist Elmer Brown shows a trackliner and girlfriend in a railroad bunkhouse. "Gandy dancer" was a common term used for trackliners, apparently named after the dancing step workers performed to tamp down ties using equipment manufactured by the Gandy Manufacturing Company of Chicago. (Western Reserve Historical Society)

The roadhouses and juke joints of railway workers were the earliest venues for these early blues performers.[30] Beginning around World War I, these individual performers appeared in Northern cities at rent parties: A renter who had fallen behind in payments would send out invitations to friends and relations. People paid at the door, and then again for food provided by the host, usually Southern delicacies like moonshine, fried chicken, and chitterlings. Performers, many from down South, performed on guitar—sometimes singing, sometimes not.

The ballad of John Henry was one of the most popular blues tunes sung by the rent party troubadours. It was the song that Big Bill Broonzy recalled as his most popular at rent parties and cabarets. He performed it and sang it his own unique way, starting the song with a trilling, bouncing guitar solo that sounded like a steam engine preparing a head of steam as it began to pull out of the station. Broonzy's lyrics emphasize his sexual prowess as well as his strength. This John Henry sings, and rings, and then dies as he tries to leave.

> John Henry said to his captain
> Now man Oh don't you sing
> I'm shaking twelve pounds from my hips on down
> Don't you hear that cold steel ring?
> Don't you hear that cold steel ring?
> . . .
> John Henry went down that railroad track
> With his twelve pound hammer by his side
> Went down the track but he never looked back
> Because he laid down his hammer and he died
> Yes he laid down his hammer and he died. [31]

The appeal of the blues was and is complicated, but it had a great deal to do with the hopes and regrets of those who left on the Great Migration. Musician W. Astor Morgan, who had booked many blues singers in the late 1910s, argued that the blues represented nostalgia for the world that migrants lost when they moved north. "In the blues," he wrote in 1924, "we find [a woman] longing to return to an alley in a town in Tennessee because of circumstances in her material life."[32] These were, Morgan suggested, simple songs of heartbreak and depression.

In the early days, blues audiences were almost exclusively black and working class. One black trade unionist pointed out how universal blues songs were among black men by the early twenties: "One who saunters around a building where Jews, Italian, German and Russian mechanics are working, will constantly hear them humming selections from operas. Likewise, one will hear Negro mechanics quite as continuously humming the 'blues.' "[33]

The geography of black life after the Great Migration was critical for the development of blues music. Down south, American dance, even for African Americans had depended on the formalized movement of bodies in a large space like a barn or a field. Actions were "shouted" by a caller who also played a hornpipe or fiddle. But blues music facilitated an intimate, unstructured dance that fit into tiny apartments.[34] When the former soldier Big Bill Broonzy left the army, he became an itinerant performer in these small venues. He brought a guitar to Chicago and performed music that he had heard his father and brother play down south in the 1890s. He remembered that his first blues song was "Jo Turner Blues," a song about a slave trader. In Chicago and New York, singers constantly improvised the lyrics to suit the audience and the mood, but in all cases, blues songs were sung very slowly, at a "blues tempo."

Whether the music was fast or slow, African Americans created a suggestive, close-up dancing that may have started in the roadhouses and juke joints of the South a decade earlier. Dancers bent arms and knees and followed few of the traditions of Western dance. White dancing societies used elaborate diagrams, with lots of arrows and pictures, to describe the unstructured dance of roadhouses, rent parties, and basement cabarets, teaching it to generations of white Americans. The departures from Western dance were considered scandalous in their day. Daring white teenagers in the early days of the twentieth century learned to emulate the rocking, rolling, shimmying styles of black men and women, inventing a succession of new dances, called the turkey trot, the Texas Tommy, the Maxixe, ballin' the jack, the fox-trot, walkin' the dog, the shimmy, and the Charleston.[35] Blues and jazz music accompanied these new steps, first in black cabarets during and after World War I, and then in white clubs.

Music and dance exploded in the black sections of Northern cities. First brought by itinerant railway workers and their partners, then by black migrants and blues musicians, they spread farther and farther outward. Jazz and the blues spread across Britain and Continental Europe during the war, in the wake of black soldiers, sailors, and stevedores. Throughout Europe, avant-garde bars and tearooms sought out performers who could bring this new music with them. By 1922, black performers of jazz and blues had become so popular in France that they displaced the old string bands that had performed classical music in cafés, tearooms, and theaters. To stop the threat of African American performers from displacing their own musicians, the French National Assembly outlawed orchestras with more than 10 percent foreigners, including in restaurants and cabarets. "It seems that while the French people can dance to a 'T' by jazz music," quipped a black newspaper, "the French musicians cannot produce it."[36]

Black music became, especially in France, a symbolic treasure for European radicals searching for a culture that was different from the supposedly high national cultures of Austria, Germany, France, and Italy. As the monarchs of Europe battled one another, a music that was surprising, modern, and divorced from the ancient traditions of Europe seemed attractive to liberals, radicals, and socialists. Indeed, during the war the music traveled back and forth over the lines of battle. German bands quickly imitated the sound and tempo of black jazz bands and became a sensation in Europe. The music had become so popular after the war that Amsterdam musicians staged a protest in 1922, marching through the heart of the city with placards that read "Down with British Jazz Bands from Germany!"[37] In the space of a few years, the black ballads and sorrow songs that had followed migrants from the Deep South to Chicago swept across the Atlantic, to be reinterpreted by British and German musicians. Internationalists, left-wing and otherwise, spread the message of jazz and the blues from Normandy to Berlin by the middle of the 1920s.

While black socialists like W.E.B. Du Bois and A. Philip Randolph disliked the blues music that was so popular with black workers, a few white socialists in America became fascinated with it, particularly its stories of protest and struggle. One of the first people to see a radical spark in the African American tradition of music was the poet Carl Sandburg. He found in the John Henry ballad a style of self-presentation that let Sandburg pose as a sentimental man who defied mechanical innovation. Sandburg became America's first "folk singer," bringing John Henry's legend to millions of white listeners.

Sandburg had been born in 1878 in Illinois, the son of a railroad blacksmith's apprentice. At an early age he dreamed of becoming a great public orator. After high school in the late 1890s, he traveled as a tramp. He worked as a railroad section hand and at other odd jobs throughout the Midwest, learning a variety of American songs and stories: Jewish, Polish, Hungarian, and African American. After a brief stint as a soldier in the Spanish-American War, he became a radical and dropped out of school to become a poet and newspaper reporter. By 1910, the young, handsome Swede sought to create a radical, modern poetry that would express socialist principles in the language of common workers. With his friend John Lomax, another would-be poet, Sandburg traded the cowboy, frontier, and "Negro" songs that they had learned. These became raw material for Sandburg's poetry.

Sandburg's breakthrough as a national poet came in 1916, when he published *Chicago Poems,* a surprising blend of lyrical descriptions of architecture with the daily speech of street preachers, police reporters, ice handlers, and day laborers. Describing African American muckers digging up a new gas main, he wrote.

> Wiping sweat off their faces
> With red bandanas
> The muckers work on .. pausing .. to pull
> Their boots out of suckholes where they slosh.

> Of the twenty looking on
> Ten murmer, "O, its a hell of a job,"
> Ten others, "Jesus, I wish I had the job."

Sandburg wrote rhapsodically about the black migrants and European immigrants who made up the city of Chicago. Jazz and blues, the music of street corners and street preachers, became raw material for his art.

Gradually, as Sandburg sought to advertise his work, his performance of folk expressions and everyday songs became as important as his poetry. He continued to perform as a public lecturer, a common method writers used to reach a large audience. Sandburg had worked for years on his public lecturing skills but had never quite broken into the popular lecture circuit that was dominated by famous philosophers, politicians, and historians. He hoped to fuse the styles of philosopher, poet, and historian, but by the time World War I began, he was still unhappy with his public performances. His repertoire featured historical and literary appreciations of Abraham Lincoln and Walt Whitman, but he fretted that the topics had little of the drama he was hoping for.[38]

Shortly after *Chicago Poems* came out in 1916, Sandburg began to improvise. As a Chicago reporter with a beat in working-class black neighborhoods, Sandburg had seen and heard blues and jazz performers like

Big Bill Broonzy. From the beginning, he appears to have appropriated and transformed the style of the solitary blues singer in his attempt to find his voice as a public performer. After one reading, perhaps as early as 1917, Sandburg reportedly pulled a guitar from behind the rostrum and told his audience: "I will now sing a few folk-songs that somehow tie into the folk-quality I have tried to get into my verse. They are all authentic songs people have sung for years. If you don't care for them and want to leave the hall, it will be all right with me. I'll only be doing what I'd be doing if I were home anyway."[39]

Sandburg performed a mix of railroad ballads, drinking songs, and levee camp hollers. He knew then that folklore scholars did not consider any of these to be "folk songs." By the official definition set forth at Harvard, folk songs had to be anonymous, orally transmitted songs that preceded the arrival of print. In England this meant songs composed before 1475. A folk song was "The Rantin' Laddie" or "The Earl of Mar's Daughter." Sandburg's favorites, like "The Buffalo Skinners" and "John Henry," did not count. Sandburg thus qualified the term "folk songs," calling them "songs people have sung." An early compiler of popular songs for the men's magazine *Adventure* also called them "Songs Men Have Sung," recognizing that these songs could paint a picture of a time and place in America's own recent past.

Carl Sandburg had been perfecting this hayseed style for years, with its mixture of apology, ad hoc delivery, and professional unprofessionalism. By the early 1920s, the effect on the audience was electric. A contemporary described one performance in 1925 before the novelist and playwright Sinclair Lewis, who had just returned from Europe:

> Somebody brought a guitar and the iron-jawed Swede stood up and, in that soft, don't-give-a-damn way of his, sang "The Buffalo Skinners."
>
> Everything got quiet as a church, for it's a great rough song, all about starvation, blood, fleas, hides, entrails, thirst, and Indian-devils, and men being cheated out of their wages and killing their employers to get even—a novel, an epic novel boiled down to simple words set to queer music that rises and falls like the winds on Western plains. I've heard the discoverer of the song, John Lomax, of Texas, sing it, but never like Carl sang it this night. It was like a funeral song to the pioneer America that had gone, and when Carl was done Sinclair Lewis spoke up, his face streaked with tears, "That's the America I came home to. That's it."[40]

Sandburg was not a professional singer, and most critics agreed that he could barely carry a tune and only knew a few chords on the guitar. He usually preceded each song with a little story, describing the time and place where he heard it, or where it would have been first performed. He sang each song differently, with a unique accent, intonation, and phrasing. Though Sandburg declared himself "suspicious of vocal training," he said that he missed few chances to hear great singers. "I learned from them to sing with the whole body and to make every song a role."[41] If he borrowed from the solitary, rough-hewn performance of the lone blues musician, Sandburg combined it with his skill as a storyteller and his mastery of intonation to deliver a very different kind of performance. Sandburg the radical helped invent the "folk singer," the man who sang "folk songs." So, in the midst of the machine age, his old-fashioned, homegrown performance prepared the way for an appreciation of human conflict with machines, and the song of John Henry. Sandburg made "John Henry" a popular staple in his performances.

Sandburg's performance was self-conscious—a radical intervention in debates over the artist in the machine age. His homely guitar, seemingly brought as an afterthought, projected an image of the man and his instrument who could recover the past just as the machine age was destroying it. His time as a reporter in Chicago, the center of the Great Migration, and his sympathy for black workers led him to place black music—especially black spirituals and ballads—prominently into what he called his *American Songbag*.[42] Like his other radical colleagues, Sandburg was cosmopolitan: he sang Irish drinking songs, cowboy songs, African American blues songs, and folk ballads. Men most often sang these songs to one another in sex-segregated workplaces: in mines, on the open range, in barrooms, and along railroad tracks. Sandburg conjured these places up before a mixed audience, often apologizing to "the ladies present" for the rough language. He self-consciously styled himself as an old-fashioned man of sentiment: one who posed his own craft and muscle against the looming technological age. His songs and performance conveyed the innocence of men at work. With "John Henry" in his kit bag, he became the first American folk singer.

While modern jazz looked forward and spread across America and Europe, Sandburg the "folk singer" created a different style. Sandburg became a traveling historian of music, promising to teach his listeners the ballads that stood behind the modern, jazz-age music that they knew. After each performance people in the audience would come forward to give him their own versions of old songs, which Sandburg dutifully recorded in his unique shorthand.

Sandburg redefined "folk song" from something anonymous, unprinted, and centuries old to something very different. For Sandburg, the American folk song could be less than a year old, but it had to come from the common, working people. It had to use colloquial expressions unique to a time and place, like a cowboy ditty, miner's lay, or tracklayer's chant. The performance would not be the "modern" sound of professional singers and musicians but a rough-and-ready sound, heavily accented, sung by a single person, that summoned up the song as it was originally sung. This was role-playing as high art: Listeners would be transported back to a time and place that the performer described, and sense the pathos of the common laborers who performed it there. Sandburg stood right on the margin between labor radicalism and nostalgia. Gradually he moved toward nostalgia.

After World War I, and into the 1920s, the modern Ford-like system of industrial automation that had revolutionized the North was moving south, into the textile mills. The song of John Henry emerged as an anthem there as well, creating an entirely different kind of music. Neither blues song nor folk song, the "country" song became a little bit of both. While the country song drew heavily from older ballads and fiddle songs, it relied heavily on African American work songs for stories and floating phrases. Like the folk song developed by Sandburg during World War I, the country song highlighted the experience and authenticity of the individual performer. Fiddlin' John Carson gradually merged fiddle traditions and black folk songs together to create the first and most widely disseminated version of the John Henry ballad. It was one of the first songs he ever recorded. In inventing country music, and one of its first ballads—"John Henry"—Carson made music that inspired pathos about a black man. At the same time, as he sang the songs at courthouses and on street corners in Southern textile towns, he described a conflict with machine power and the threat of early death that was disturbingly familiar to country music's first audience: cotton mill hands.

Before the Civil War, water-powered textile factories had been erected at the fall line of rivers. By the time John Henry was swinging steel, cotton bales were crowding each other along the lines of Southern railroads. The bales sat at railway terminals, awaiting transportation. In the decades after John Henry died, steam-powered factories emerged at railway hubs to process the bales, turning them into bolts of cloth, sheeting, and stockings. Steam-age mills stretched in a line from Richmond to Atlanta, with clusters at Greensboro, Gastonia, Charlotte, and Spartanburg.

Southern textile mills were segregated. Black men worked in the picker room, where bales were unloaded and unpacked. White families, with children as young as seven or eight, worked in the carding, spinning, and weaving rooms. White families worked together in the mills and lived together in company-owned houses that splayed out in the mill's shadow. Bank tellers, grocery clerks, and tradesmen called the poorly paid mill workers "lintheads." Poor by Southern standards, mill workers could nonetheless buy factory-built radios, record players, and Model T's by paying on installment. One of their heroes was a Georgia textile worker named Fiddlin' John Carson.[43]

John Carson had been uniquely situated to hear black work songs all of his life. He started life as a servant to black men. His first job was as a young waterboy for the Marietta & North Georgia Railroad in the 1880s. As a teenager he would have heard the chants of trackliners as they cursed their captains, cursed the work, and cursed the slowness of the waterboy in relieving them. By 1900, at the age of approximately twenty-six, he became a foreman in the picker room at a textile mill in Atlanta, and a part-time fiddle player. At work in the picker room, he would have heard the field hollers of black draymen as they arrived with cotton bales, and the work songs of black cotton pickers as they unloaded cotton. By the early 1910s, Carson worked after hours playing fiddle tunes at street corners and on trolley cars on Decatur Street in Atlanta. The historian Patrick Huber describes Decatur Street as a place "lined with saloons, pool halls, and back alley dives where cocaine traffickers, prostitutes, and bootleggers, white and black alike, plied their wares." On Decatur Street, Carson gradually turned the music he heard into his own brand of musical performance, part singing, part talking, part humor.[44]

Carson joined a strike at Fulton Bag and Cotton Mill in Atlanta in 1914, and when the strike failed, he was thrown out of work for good. By then his music had attracted enough attention to allow him to support himself. He played at political rallies for prominent Democrats. In 1915, he became an early member of the newly formed Ku Klux Klan. As his success as a local performer grew, he adopted an identity that disguised the largely African American environment in which he had grown up. He rewrote his past, denying having been born in nearby Cobb County, Georgia, which had a large black minority. He claimed instead to have come from the southern Tennessee mountains, where few African Americans lived. "I was born in Georgia," he told audiences, "but my maw threw her dishwater over into Tennessee." He added six years to his age and claimed to have escaped from the law, loafed about, and trafficked in moonshine. In short, Carson became the kind of man that mill workers wanted to be: dangerous, happy-go-lucky, and free. He seemed to live in a fantasy world of the distant Southern past. One critic described a performance at the Georgia Old-Time Fiddlers' Convention as "carrying the feel of the old red clay hills of Georgia and the little old cabin with the golden corn swaying in the wind across the patch and the sour mash still bubbling out its distilled sunshine just over the brow of the hill, where revenooers haven't looked yet."[45] Fiddlin' John let promoters suggest that his music came from a lost world of the white, Southern past.

In fact, Fiddlin' John was anything but. His mixture of song and storytelling resembled Carl Sandburg's, but he was decidedly high-tech. In 1922, when the *Atlanta Journal* expanded operations to operate one of the first radio stations in the South, they looked to local celebrities to perform. Fiddlin' John Carson became a regular. Soon operating at five hundred watts, the new radio station WSB (or "Welcome South, Brother") blasted music throughout the South, reaching as far as Richmond. Fiddlin' John Carson found, too, that he could take his music on the road. He bought a used Model T and traveled through mill towns throughout the Southeast, performing songs and skits in front of courthouses and on street corners. Mill workers loved his blend of folksy humor and fiddle playing, and his rendition of familiar tunes.[46]

In an often-told story, OKeh records sent artistic agent Ralph Peer to Atlanta in 1923 to record a fiddler. Peer declared Carson's singing "pluperfect awful" and nearly refused to release the records until a local records dealer offered to buy five hundred copies, the entire first pressing. Peer was shocked when the dealer sold out in a few hours and wired him for more copies. The hillbilly recording industry had begun. The following year, Fiddlin' John Carson became the first man to record a record labeled "John Henry."[47]

It may seem peculiar that a registered Klansman, who endorsed race-baiting candidates for governor in Georgia and who posed as a "hillbilly," would perform and sell a song about a black man who lived and died heroically. But we should not forget Fiddlin' John's real background and his audience. As a man who grew up in the mixed-race South near Atlanta, he would have heard the song as a waterboy for trackliners on the Marietta & North Georgia Railroad, on the picker-room floor of the textile mill, and in the mixed-race neighborhood around Decatur Street in Atlanta. In fact, in Fiddlin' John's version, John Henry is never directly referred to as a black man (though he is said to be "set on his Mammy's knee") Many white Southerners, raised on country songs, assumed that John Henry was white.

And by the 1920s, the story of John Henry seemed to suit the new environment of the modern textile mill. For the many mill workers who arrived after the turn of the century, the mill village may have seemed an inviting place. Families, after all, could work together on the floor. In older wood-and-water plants, when the millrace broke down, or a thunderstorm stopped natural light from entering the tall windows, the mill stopped. Even a minor failure in one part of the mill might stop work in other sections for hours at a time, giving workers time to chat, smoke, or play outside. There were mills that still ran on water power in the South as late as World War I.[48]

By the 1920s, though, many of the oldest factories were retooling to match the profits of Henry Ford's Michigan plant. New steam- and electric-powered firms, with indoor lighting, emerged to produce rayon hosiery. (Rayon was, of course, crucial apparel for any self-respecting flapper in the 1920s.) The new demands for workers to work more looms was called the "stretch-out." Fewer and fewer workers became responsible for more and more carding machines, spindles, and looms. Workers had to match the speed of the machines, and streamlined factories eliminated the pauses between spindles. Everything seemed to move faster and faster. The similarities between textile workers' lives and John Henry's were hauntingly similar. Workers' lungs became gummed up with microscopic cotton fibers. Over time, the fibers filled air sacs, causing silicosis and sending many mill workers to an early grave.

For mill workers, the song of a single worker dying in a headlong competition with a machine must have seemed disturbingly familiar, and "John Henry" became a country classic. Carson had successfully added the "aw shucks" style of Carl Sandburg and African American songs and stories to fiddle and mountain music, creating something called "hillbilly" or "old-time" music. By the 1950s, bluegrass music followed country. As the genre changed, the song was played faster and faster, echoing the din of the modern mill town.

"John Henry" had begun as a railroad and miners' song, transported over the lines of the South's railways, but by the 1930s it had acquired a life as a song sung by individual performers. It may have received its first imprint as a variation of the biblical story of Samson by traveling performers, particularly blind performers. Blues women at cabarets and troubadours at rent parties made it a blues song about the Great Migration and the world black men and women left behind them. Blues bands even carried "John Henry" across the Atlantic in World War I. "John Henry" also became a new kind of folk song, or a "song people have sung," in Carl Sandburg's words. This new kind of folk song was sung to summon up the past, sung with little accompaniment and a peculiar timbre in one's voice that let listeners imagine a time before the machine age had wrecked men's and women's bodies. A song of both protest and nostalgia, the ballad of John Henry became an important folk song that represented human muscle arrayed against the world of skyscrapers, assembly lines, and military machines. Finally it became a "country" song, sung not to people in the country or even from the country, but to mill workers in industrial settings *about* the country, about the world they left behind and the terrors of the world they faced in textile mills. By 1930, not everyone knew the ballad of John Henry, but it had become lodged in many places, a story sung in dialect, with old-fashioned instruments, by a single singer who let listeners imagine a past when the machine age had not yet come to swallow the world and them up with it, a dim and lamp-lit world before the monster cities came.

8

COMMUNIST STRONGMAN

By THE LATTER PART of the twentieth century, John Henry had become familiar to every schoolchild in America. My little brother and I first heard about him in 1969, on a long-playing album, sung by Burl Ives. We were at Sunday school in the Unitarian church in Orlando, Florida, and the record seemed to get perpetual rotation. The Unitarians were drawn to folk music that called on America's diverse past, and Burl Ives was a favorite. The Unitarians would have been unconcerned by conservative attacks on folk music in the 1960s that portrayed it as Communistic and subversive. In fact, that would have increased its appeal. Other albums by the Weavers and Woody Guthrie were available in our center, but Burl Ives got almost continuous play. Burl Ives had a charming, grandfatherly voice that drew our attention and hushed us, I suppose. Our teachers turned it loud enough to drown out our voices while the grown-ups drank coffee.

Five years later in Sanford, Florida, I learned a full set of the lyrics in the fifth graders' chorus. As one of the few white kids in Sanford's public schools (and the only white boy in the chorus) I learned that my classmates had a much deeper knowledge of and appreciation for the man and the legend. In the songbook for our fall pageant, we told the story of America with "John Henry" (about West Virginia) alongside "Green Grow the Laurels" (about Texas) and "If Ya Wanna Get to Heaven" (about Georgia). I don't recall that America extended north of West Virginia in those days, at least according to the songs in our fall pageant.

John Henry was more familiar to my classmates in Southside Elementary School than Thomas Jefferson, George Washington Carver, or Abraham Lincoln. He was to them the greatest of heroes. On May Day, when Southside Elementary was adjourned for running games, May Pole dancing, and the cakewalk, the girl who ran fastest was crowned Queen of May. But the boy who ran fastest in the hundred-yard dash was named our May Day John Henry. From the 1930s to the present day, tens of thousands of hopeful African American parents in the South have given their sons the first and middle names of John and Henry, in hopes that the child would fill the strongman's boots. Our middle-school football team had two John Henrys. Our track team had three.

In the orange-pickers' town of Sanford, Florida, there were many ways that the boys and girls in my schoolyard would have learned about John Henry. Sanford was a melting pot of the black South. Boys and girls in my class had great-grandparents who had come to Florida from Georgia, Alabama, and South Carolina at the end of the Civil War. Their accents were a medley of the deepest of the Deep South. The playground was filled with rhymed boasts and jump-rope songs in dialects that I could scarcely understand. The story of the steel-drivin' man would have traveled south along the Seaboard Air Line all the way to the port of Sanford, the St. Johns River town where, in the words of our school song, "the orange blossoms grow."

The difference between how my little brother and I first learned about John Henry and how my classmates did is important. The Burl Ives folk song is the more common route into American foreheads. *That* John Henry grew out of the radical movements of the Great Depression era. Radicals embraced him then as a tool for organizing workers and for pointing out the ills of the South. Fusing new modernist artistic techniques to the old songs, they turned John Henry into an icon. Oddly, this iconic image of a strong black man, put forward by the Communist Party, fed into the Communist strongman characters of Superman and Captain America. At the same time, in World War II the national government's propaganda wing in Europe had made the song of John Henry a symbol of a strong, multiracial America. That sense of John Henry continued after the war, as he became a stock character in children's books. Despite his rapid rise to national prominence, other strains of the story remained—among Black Power activists, for example—and the kids on the playground at Southside Elementary School.

It was probably Carl Sandburg's fault. Sandburg had borrowed a mode of performance and self-presentation from the blues men of Chicago. He elaborated on the formula considerably, calling himself a "folk singer," a man who collected an old song, described when and where it was originally performed, and then sang it in an old-fashioned way. Sandburg's unique style, of story combined with song, had been carefully emulated in the 1930s and forward. At one time the famous folklorist John Lomax was a "folk singer," referring to himself in promotional materials as "the ballad hunter."[1]

Another one of Sandburg's most skillful and influential imitators was the American muralist Thomas Hart Benton. Like Sandburg, Benton had traveled all over America, and like Sandburg, Benton saw himself as a delineator of the people, though Benton worked with a painter's brush rather than a typewriter. Friendly with the Mexican muralist Diego Rivera, Benton hoped to become the most famous draftsman of America's regional and rural traditions. Benton had an old guitar and gave Sandburg-like performances to friends, especially at openings for his murals. In one such performance, probably at the opening for his famous murals at the New School in New York in 1931, Benton stood underneath his fresco depicting the training of America's workers, pulled out a guitar, and belted out a version of the John Henry ballad. In the audience was the classical musicologist Charles Seeger.[2]

It was a fateful performance. Seeger, a Communist of the old school, was moved by Benton's rendition of the song. For years he had been discussing with others in the Workers Music League the possibility of using radical music to make revolutionary change. He and the other members of the league had imagined workers' orchestras and singing clubs performing revolutionary music by radical, classically trained composers like "Eisler, Wolpe, Shekhter, Davidenko, Biely, Shostakovitch, Szabo, Schaefer, Adohyman, and others." But the Workers Music League had little success in making these names into household words. *The Workers Song Book*, an early attempt at disseminating songs like "Hunger March," "Red Election Round," and "Lenin—Our Leader" had fallen on deaf ears. The league declared that in *Europe* these class-conscious fugues, marches, and strife songs were "sung everywhere by huge masses of class-conscious workers." But most workers in the United States found the tunes confusing, the tempos odd, and the vocal range required of performers to be impossible. Singing workers' groups preferred the older and familiar songs like "Battle Hymn of the Republic." Religious songs! To the Workers Music League these familiar songs smacked of "defeatist melancholy, morbidity, hysteria and triviality."[3] What was a radical to do to bring truly radical music to the masses? Then he heard the old ballad of John Henry.

Between 1931 and 1935, as the Depression in America deepened and thousands of men and women were thrown out of work, many more Americans besides Charles Seeger began to believe that radical political change was required to bring the nation back to full employment. Those in the Communist Party believed that this change had to start with a workers' movement. Seeger and the Workers Music League became convinced that, properly edited, folk songs like "John Henry" could form the basis for a truly proletarian music that would help mobilize those men and women. Abandoning classical musical forms, he and other socialists and Communists in New York eventually embraced the story and song of John Henry. While for Sandburg, and presumably Benton, the ballad of John Henry had represented workers' travails against the modern age and capitalism, Workers Music League members like Charles Seeger heard the song in very different registers. For them, the song represented more than just a challenge to modern capitalism. The ballad seemed to echo the key conflict in workers' lives that Karl Marx had identified: the intensification of work that came with the introduction of machinery. The song also seemed to speak out about the problems of Jim Crow, convict labor, and racism in the South.

Benton's performance came at an important time. By the early thirties, the Communist Party had become extremely interested in black Americans in the South, seeing them as key to any nationwide workers' movement. The Sixth World Congress of the Communist International in 1928 had declared African Americans in black-belt counties of the South to be an "oppressed nation," entitled to self-determination and the right to secede from the United States.[4] In the same year, the Communist Party had established offices in Birmingham, Alabama, campaigning for poor relief and producing the *Southern Worker,* a radical weekly aimed at black Southerners.[5] By 1930, Communists at the U.S. Pipe Company produced a newsletter celebrating black workingmen, entitled *Red Hammer.*[6] The Communist Party had terrible failings, particularly in supporting Stalin's reign of terror, but in the 1930s, socialists and Communists were among the few white people who were absorbed with direct criticism of the Jim Crow South. They attacked segregation, disfranchisement, the convict lease system, and debt peonage. And these radicals heard in "John Henry" what previous folklorists did not: an indictment of black life in the American South. Why else would John Henry be hammering? Because blacks did all the work and got nothing for it, not the vote, not housing, not freedom from debt. As Benton's performance underneath his mural suggested, new graphic art forms combined with old-time music could make a powerful point and act as a powerful force for mobilizing workers. Radicals quickly seized on the visual and aural possibilities of the John Henry legend. Three artists in the radical tradition formed indelible portraits of John Henry.

The Gellert brothers, antiwar activists from a large Jewish family in Hungary, were perhaps most important in finding and circulating the Communist Party's image of John Henry. Their father, Adolph, had fled Austria-Hungary in 1905, determined never to let his sons be forced into military service where they would be brutalized and beaten, as he had been. The Gellerts and one hundred thousand other Jews fled Austria-Hungary between 1867 and 1907, many taking advantage of inexpensive passage to the United States. Adolph first crossed under the Alps by train, in a tunnel that had been blasted through in the same years that John Henry bored through the Alleghenies. He then took a steamship to the United States. The following year he sent for his wife and their five sons. Ernest was the second son, Hugo the third, and Lawrence, only seven, was the youngest.[7] Escaping from ethnic hatred in a crumbling dynasty, they settled in New York first, where the family's import-export business thrived.[8]

In the 1910s, Ernest, Hugo, and Lawrence had become radicals, both in politics and in art. Raised in a country where liberalism was failing and a disturbing nationalism was on the rise, they saw themselves as internationalists and socialists. Hugo studied art in New York, becoming intrigued by the emerging decorative arts movement, called art deco. Deco artists reduced human forms to outlines (almost cartoons) and experimented with sharp, geometrical lines. He was influenced by the Austrian and Hungarian variations of the art deco movement, called the Vienna Secession. What the Vienna Secession artists drew from the art deco movement was its emphasis on figures in outline and the melding of human and abstract shapes. But they renounced the modernism of deco, scouring the past for usable folk traditions, especially the fables and legends of Hungarian history.[9]

In the summer of 1914, Hugo went to Paris to extend his artistic education, only to find the Julian Academy closed for the summer. All that was left was to study colorful deco posters on the fences and subway stations of Paris. He was most struck by the cartoon picture of Bibendum, an immense, heavily muscled man made of Michelin tires. Developed at the turn of the century,

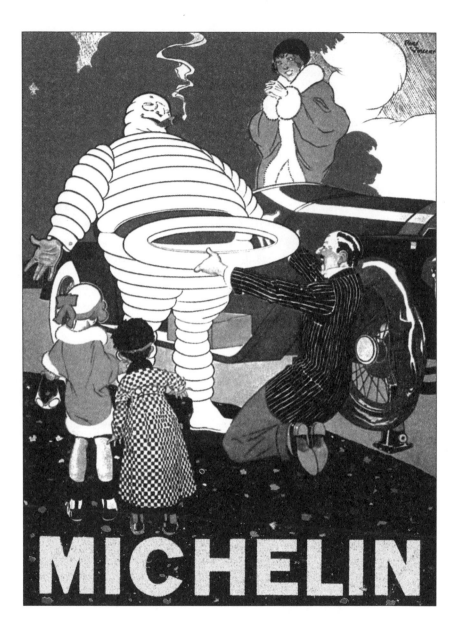

French image, circa 1914, of Bibendum, the symbol of the Michelin Corporation. (Author's private collection)

Bibendum was a mighty man, the first cartoon symbol of a corporation. "That poster was the best thing I had seen there," Hugo later said. He finished by punning, "Those tires left a big impression on me."[10]

In the years after Hugo Gellert returned from Europe, he experimented with the deco technique of sketching bodies in outline, making human forms out of a collection of boxes and circles. Gellert pressed a litho pencil onto a specially prepared stone, making posters for a commercial lithographer. These lithograph pressings onto stone were easy to mass-produce, and the commercial art Gellert did in those years let him refine techniques to capture the viewer's eye. By 1914, Gellert was a master of the litho pencil. Most of his deco contemporaries took rich young men and women at play as their subject, molding them around impossibly skinny cylinders. Gellert the socialist drew stocky, powerful men at work. Gellert's heads were boxlike; arms and thighs looked like half-inflated balloons (or tires); chests were exposed or visible in tight shirts; legs were thick and stocky, like granite pillars. Gellert's men appeared in repeating patterns, like machines, and carried workers' tools—oars, wrenches, picks, pitchforks, and hammers—that seemed extensions of their bodies. By the 1920s and 1930s, Hungarian lore and legend had faded from Hugo's artistic work, and he began exploring the legends of working-class Americans. At the end of World War I, he left commercial printing entirely and produced work almost exclusively for Communist publications like *New Masses* and the *Daily Worker*.

A tragedy struck the family at the end of World War I that forever changed how the Gellerts saw politics, violence, and the power of the state. The eldest brother, Ernest, a conscientious objector and an outspoken opponent of World War I, was arrested when the U.S. draft arrived. He was later transferred to a military prison. Within a year, Ernest died in prison from a gunshot wound. Military police glibly declared it a suicide, even though the wound came from a rifle. The family was certain it was murder.[11] As Hugo Gellert drew cartoons for rallies, concerts, and Communist Party magazines, he may have found in John Henry the perfect way of memorializing the death and martyrdom of his brother Ernest.

Hugo had first learned the legend of John Henry from his kid brother, Lawrence, who was becoming something of a folklorist. During the Depression, Lawrence had moved to Tryon, North Carolina, in hopes of recovering from a nervous condition. He soon began collecting African

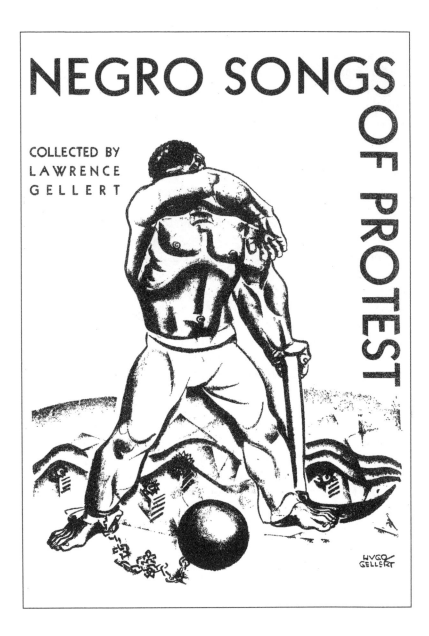

Negro Songs of Protest, collected by Lawrence Gellert (1936). Cover image by Hugo Gellert. (Swem Library, College of William and Mary)

American work songs in North Carolina, South Carolina, Georgia, and Alabama. On chain gangs and among black workers, some doubtless connected with the Communist Party, he learned a large collection of protest songs.[12] Radical magazines like *New Masses* and the *Daily Worker* soon adopted John Henry as a mascot. Brother Hugo Gellert drew the pictures.

For Gellert, the balloon-muscled John Henry represented the dangerous and revolutionary potential of the male side of America's working class. John Henry was plastered on radical posters and magazines of the 1930s and appeared on countless posters for political rallies on the Lower East Side of New York. Workers like these were shown holding back the power of police and Nazis and ushering in a workers' state.

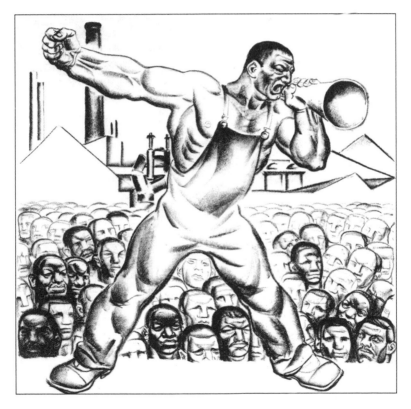

Hugo Gellert's black working-class strongman. (Swem Library, College of William and Mary)

As the Depression deepened in the 1930s, the federal government became committed to promoting and shaping a new kind of public art, one that dovetailed with radicals' fascination with the John Henry legend. Some artists, given a free rein, turned to the steel-drivin' man in part because the legend proved irresistible. Fred Becker, an African American artist born in Hollywood, California, moved to New York in September 1933 with art and architecture on his mind. He was, he wrote later, "a callow youth just turned 20." Becker found the city of New York a strange and fabulous place, and the city itself became one of his many inspirations as an artist. "The shock of this monstrous city was very difficult for me to deal with, having just come from a place that was ... an immense suburban sprawl."[13]

When offered relief in the artists' section of the Works Progress Administration (WPA) in 1935, Becker met with his supervisor, illustrator Lynd Ward. Over the 1920s, Ward had made a name for himself in art circles with a series of woodcuts that he called "Books Without Words." Ward's books, among them *Madman's Drum* and *Wild Pilgrimage,* dealt with radical themes like poverty, lynching, and police brutality. Fred Becker wrote later that he had idolized Lynd Ward, and when Ward asked him what kind of work he wanted to do for the WPA, Becker suggested a series in the tradition that Ward had begun. "I blurted out," Becker wrote later, "that I would like to do a series of engravings on the theme of 'John Henry,' the black mythological figure." Becker took Lynd's model of radical storytelling and shaped it around the stories he had read about John Henry in a folksy, dialect novel by Roark Bradford. While Becker may have started with the plight of black workers in the South, he had no particular political point to make with the images. He said later of the prints: "There are no striking workers, no miners' widows, no apple peddlers. I was simply doing my thing: the things that interested me the most."[14]

Becker's John Henry was myth, but less a Greek figure than a kind of Afro-Jamaican mythological creature with distended arms and legs and a face that was part caricature, part African sculpture. In most of the Becker images, John Henry's fingers are astonishing. Becker appeared to be thinking about the folk phrase "double-jointed," which originally referred to a kind of very powerful, articulated steam engine used in the nineteenth century. John Henry, it was said in the Bradford novel, was double-jointed and thus strong. Becker took seriously the idea that John Henry's strength came from loose joints, or perhaps no joints at all. Thus Becker's John Henry has impossibly long, supple, squidlike fingers.

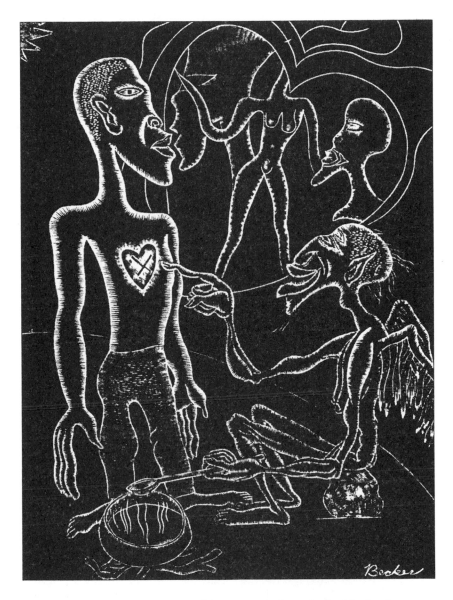

"John Henry and the Witch Woman" (1935–1939), drawn by Fred Becker for The Federal Art Project of the Works Progress Administration. (Swem Library, College of William and Mary)

Finally, the white muralist Frank W. Long, also a WPA worker, produced a memorable rendition of John Henry. Born in Knoxville, Tennessee, Long came to Berea, Kentucky, in 1930 to help his father, also a painter, reconstruct a painted canvas at a theater. Long found Berea attractive and as the Depression deepened in the 1930s, found work in the WPA. He soon became, quite against his will, a muralist. In visual composition he was influenced in part by the paintings of Thomas Hart Benton. While he disliked Benton's "commercial style," he admired the way Benton distorted physical forms. Benton "had the most admirable control of his medium and consummate knowledge of human anatomy. This allowed him to distort his figures to suit the undulating line of his style while still making them acceptable in his overcrowded compositions."[15]

In the middle of the 1930s, when little other work was available, Long continued to produce murals for post offices and public buildings. He found the conservatism of the place somewhat stifling, along with the traditional subject matter required to win contracts to produce post office murals. Yet for all of his problems with Berea, his knowledge of the folklore and traditions of the mountains granted him acceptance in the local community. In Berea he would have heard of the story of John Henry, if he had not known it before. While most of the images he drew for post offices were of white mountaineers, he continued to produce block prints that were entirely of his own making.[16] In seeking to develop a style that was all his own, and borrowing a bit from Benton's conscious distortion of bodies, Long produced one of the most memorable images of the powerful John Henry. This image, which Long gave out as a prize to a Lexington public school student, shows John Henry as impossibly large, with a body that, anatomically perfect like a Benton mural, is artificially distended to fit the triangular frame Long has chosen.

Of the three iconic images that artists made of John Henry in the Depression era, Gellert's images became the most widely diffused. This was partly an ironic result of the WPA itself. Both Becker and Long produced old-fashioned woodcuts, and as Becker noted, a WPA stamp on the back of his woodcut prints made them impossible to sell. In addition, the WPA received thousands of contracted images that it never used. Becker's woodcuts, like Long's, were preserved by the artist himself. While Becker and Long's images were seen at the time—Becker's John Henry images apparently graced the lobby for a play that Orson Welles was directing—Gellert's lithograph images had wider circulation. Partly it was the modernness of

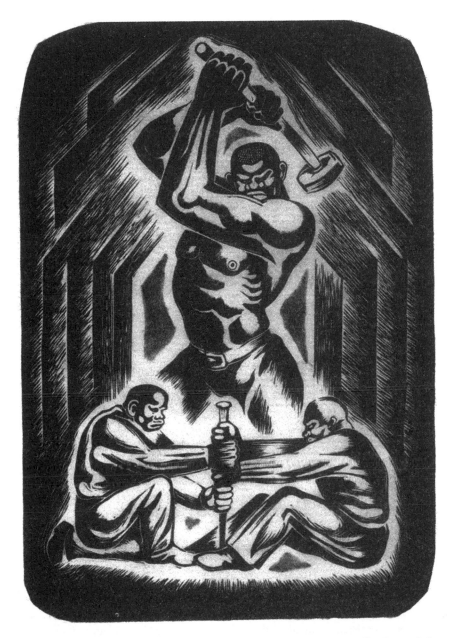

Frank W. Long's John Henry. (Warren Payne, Payne Fine Arts, Louisville, Kentucky)

Gellert's form, because lithograph on stone produced fabulous colored images. In addition, Gellert's tireless work on posters, in radical magazines, and in left-wing dailies allowed him a freer range, and as a regular member of the Party, he would have had more access to those venues. Between 1931 and 1941, the Communist Party, largely through Gellert's images, helped convert John Henry's story from a folk tale to a national symbol. An impossibly muscle-bound John Henry stood in for the powerful potential of the working class.

Folk songs by black workers about black workers proved important to socialists and Communists in the 1930s. In May 1930 Philip Schatz published an article called "Songs of the Negro Worker" in *New Masses* that discussed tracklining songs, including those that Hugo's brother Lawrence had uncovered. Schatz declared that work songs like "John Henry" expressed the genuine conflicts faced by black workers in the South. He ridiculed white interest in black spirituals. "No kind old god, smiling like a Sunday school teacher at a fish fry, comes to lighten the back breaking labors of the black worker." Instead, wrote Schatz, "his 'cap'n'... stands ready to kick new strength into every back which has reached the breaking point":

> I tol' my cap'n that my feet was col'
> "God damn yo' feet, let the car wheel roll."[17]

For Schatz, the work song "John Henry" expressed exactly the Communist Party's view of black workers' struggles. "Conscious of the strength in bodies which have industrialized the South, the Negro worker sings ... of a flesh and blood hero, a powerful worker, a giant of a black man with the muscles of a tiger rippling under his shiny black skin. A 'steel driver' who made mountains crumble with his nine-pound hammer and his rock drill, John Henry is the hero of the greatest proletarian epic ever created."[18]

It was not difficult to find a proletarian epic in the John Henry story. It was largely a matter of focus. As Communists became interested in the South and in workers' own music, they found older socialist and liberal plays that criticized the plight of black workers, and they extended them. Playwright Paul Green was a Chapel Hill colleague of Guy Johnson, John Henry's first biographer. Indeed, Green had helped Johnson collect black folk songs in the 1920s. In 1931, Green wrote *Potter's Field,* a radical play about a preacher named John Henry who visited a black community threatened by the encroachment of a railroad. Green's understanding of John

Henry was more in the mold of Carl Sandburg and Thomas Hart Benton, as a relic of a bygone era. The play used folk expressions that Green had heard among day laborers at Chapel Hill, and he used the play to condemn the relentless progress of railroads and machines that seemed to be rolling over black communities like Potter's field. "Potter's field" has a double meaning as well, as a graveyard for paupers. In the final act, John Henry is incarcerated for a crime he does not commit. Green concludes by decrying the ugliness of the convict labor system.[19]

By 1933, as left-wing theater groups in New York became interested in the John Henry legend, they updated the story. Herbert Kline, a radical from Davenport, Iowa, wrote an influential play about John Henry. The young Kline—like Sandburg—had kicked around the United States as a laborer in his teens. Kline may have learned the song at work, from Green's production, or from others in the Communist Party. In 1933, he gave his one-act revolutionary play the intentionally shocking title of "John Henry—Bad Nigger." No transcript of the play is available, but reviews suggest that the plot placed John Henry as an escaped convict. On the lam, he joined a free steel-driving gang. His white labor boss protected him from prosecution, but only if he worked impossibly hard. In this way John Henry was lured into fighting against a steam drill. Like other proletarian dramas of the time, it would have ended after a dramatic death with workers' conversion to socialism and their resolve to take up arms against the state. A Broadway producer bought the play in 1933, but it failed for lack of funds. The radical drama group Workers Laboratory Theatre gave a dramatic reading of the play in New York in March 1934, after which Kline answered questions about John Henry and his purpose in writing the piece, citing the influence of the songs that Lawrence Gellert had collected. Two other revolutionary plays borrowed from the script, one by a white Southerner named Frank B. Wells, called *John Henry*, and another by a black New York playwright named Theodore Browne, called *Natural Man*.[20]

Young Jewish artists—some from Cleveland but most from Gellert's neighborhood on the Lower East Side—absorbed the visual vocabulary of the Communist strongman from Gellert and other radical artists. They also absorbed the Communist Party's commitment to a muscular, male-centered vision of the multiracial American worker. The symbol was more than visual. As new, industrial unions emerged in the 1930s, organizers influenced by the Communist Party found Gellert's image of the heroic,

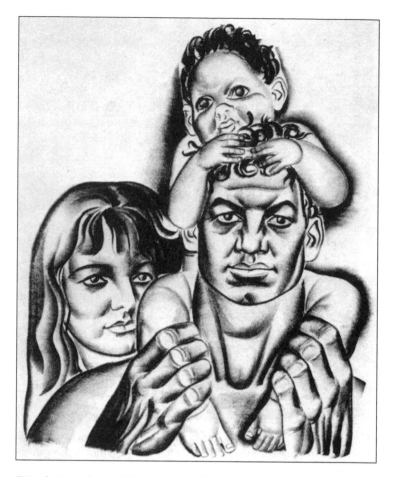

"Simple Reproduction," from Hugo Gellert's *Karl Marx's "Capital" in Lithographs*, 1934. (Swem Library, College of William and Mary)

martyred strongman a powerful organizing tool. For immigrant working-class men, the forceful working-class hero seemed to demonstrate the collective strength of workers and promise the reward of strength: political power through citizenship and economic power through union membership.[21] The strongman proved especially iconic for union organizers in the Congress of Industrial Organizations (CIO) as they organized mines, steel mills, auto factories, and sweatshops.[22] Thus when John and Alan Lomax adapted "Take This Hammer" for reproduction, they added "some

Union words" to the song: "And if he asks you what's my union/It's the C.I.O.,/It's the C.I.O."[23]

Gellert's images put strongmen like John Henry at the center of the workers' movement. Polly Ann appeared seldom, usually behind John Henry, or lifting a young John Henry as a child. This emphasis on the Communist strongman had a price, for it seemed to devalue women's contributions to organizing and their own conflicts at work.[24] While both women and men in the Communist Party pushed for women's liberation, promoted female organizers, and organized women, the Party nonetheless put up with male organizers who swaggered and harassed women. Robert Schrank, a labor organizer and Communist Party member, retold his story in *Wasn't That a Time*. He described a lifetime of male-centered organizing, punctuated by bouts of philandering. "Young communists [by which he means men] were like most other young men; any opportunity to strut our sexual stuff was not to be missed. It was just another form of boyhood pissing contests." When he lost his temper and shouted to a female Party member that she needed "a good fuck," the Party considered disciplining him but decided that he was too good a street speaker.[25] For decades, harassment may have helped solidify male power in unions and exclude or marginalize female workers.[26] The Communist Party's persistent visual image of the bare-chested John Henry may have contributed to the hyper-masculine style of the male CIO organizer.

John Henry had become an everyday part of daily life in radical circles by the late 1930s. Gellert's many drawings of the folk hero turned working-class hero appeared in calendars and in monthly magazines like *New Masses* and the *Daily Worker*, as well as in posters for rallies, concerts, plays, and film presentations. Gellert's use of lithographic crayon on stone allowed his unique bulging male surfaces to show up with dramatic colors, mostly red. Communist Party visual materials were designed to be distributed to the entire nation. In fact, the posters and magazines were more likely to be visible in the Party enclaves of Seattle, Cleveland, San Francisco, Birmingham, and New York's Lower East Side. The Lower East Side was the heart of the Jewish garment district, where CIO unions like the Amalgamated Clothing Workers and the International Ladies' Garment Workers Union were based. Some of their most committed organizers were Communists who assembled rallies, lectured on street corners, and organized demonstrations against fascism on the Lower East Side in the late 1930s.

The first American comic book artists grew up surrounded by Gellert's drawings of John Henry. In particular, comic artist Jacob Kurtzberg appeared most influenced by Gellert's style and by the muscular appeal of the CIO's symbol of the strongman. Kurtzberg was the child of Austrian Jewish garment workers. Initial plans to send Jacob to art school failed when his father lost his job during the Depression. Jacob grew up on the Lower East Side as a wayward youth, quickly becoming a member of a Jewish children's gang. Small for his age, he lifted weights, preparing for street-gang brawls that were legendary. Once Jacob was returned unconscious to the doorstep of his parents' tenement.

In his early teens, Jacob left his gang and spent his days in the Boys Brotherhood Republic, a settlement house sponsored by liberals, socialists and Communists. Children elected their own members and set their own rules of behavior. Jacob drew cartoons for the BBR newspaper. By the 1930s, he was drawing sketches for animated motion pictures. Jacob raced to meet the demands of animated movies, which required hundreds of sketches to connect static pictures together so that they moved. Like John Henry, Jacob raced to keep up with the speed of a machine. Jacob's speed at rendering images became legendary.

The bulging surfaces of the powerful manual laborer, of John Henry and the many outsized workers he represented, was an irresistible image to Jacob Kurtzberg and the other tough kids of the Lower East Side. Rounded, powerful, hairless men, men who looked as if they were smuggling balloons underneath their shirts, became a regular part of the visual vocabulary of the cartoonist. The dark-complected workers that Hugo Gellert favored were gradually lightened, their tight work clothes transformed into the tights of the circus strongman or the acrobat. The iconic, impossible John Henry would soon go on to do even greater things.

Jacob Kurtzberg never left the gritty and left-wing world of the Jewish ghetto behind him, even when he changed his name to Jack Kirby. When Britain's Prime Minister Neville Chamberlain allowed Hitler to invade Czechoslovakia, Kurtzberg drew a cartoon that showed Chamberlain patting a boa constrictor labeled Hitler. In its stomach was a bulge Kirby labeled Czechoslovakia. When Kirby's boss expressed disapproval and told him to keep his anti-Nazi politics to himself, Kirby said of Hitler, "I know a gangster when I see one!"[27]

In the late 1930s, the idea of fighting Hitler was still considered dangerous and radical. Was this America's problem, and did America need to use force? Indeed, it was not until 1941, when Germany declared war on the United States, that many isolationists committed to oppose Hitler's expansion.[28] American Jews were especially concerned about the Nazis' persecution of Jews, socialists, and Communists. After all, Adolf Hitler had built his power by stirring anti-Semitism among non-Jews in Germany leading even more Jews to leave Germany, Austria-Hungary, and Poland in the 1930s. These refugees came to settle in the Lower East Side, cheek by jowl with the Gellerts and the Kirbys.

By 1939, the team of Jerry Siegel and Joe Schuster along with Jack Kirby had pressed the Communist strongman, based in part on the folk hero John Henry, into nylon red-white-and-blue suits. And they made their strongman white. A balloon-muscled strongman, so much like the Communist symbol of workers' strength, now emerged to fight evil on the pages of comic books.[29] The evil characters in these early superhero comics were the villains we might expect in the pages of Hugo Gellert's *Daily Worker* or *New Masses*. Superman and Captain America chased down capitalists who sent miners to an early death, war profiteers, building owners who refused to maintain the buildings they operated, and above all fascists bent on twisting the minds of children. After the Japanese bombed Pearl Harbor, Japanese imperialists also became the sworn enemies of the caped crusaders. Depending on the comic franchise that sought to copyright him, the radical strongman in the mold of the CIO had different "superhero" identities. The Communist strongman became many men: Superman, Captain America, Wonder Man, and Captain Marvel. Superman was created by Jerry Siegel and Joe Schuster. Captain America and countless other iconic strongmen were created by Jack Kirby.

By the time the United States entered World War II, the golden age of comics had begun. Gradually the left-wing politics drained out of the story, just as Gellert's dark-skinned heroes lost the pigmentation in their skin. The evil characters were less often businessmen and more often agents of the Nazis or the Japanese. Jack Kirby's Captain America, for example, was Steve Rogers, a young illustrator (like Kirby himself) turned by a secret defense project into a superhuman. His enemies included Red Skull, a businessman who managed Nazi spies and saboteurs in America. Superman first fought corporate thugs but increasingly faced Nazis as the war progressed. Captain Marvel fought a superhero named Captain Nazi, who was the product of secret military experiments by the Germans.[30]

The steel-driving man of the twenties—first pressed onto stone by Hugo Gellert's lino pencil—had morphed into the man of steel in the late thirties and early forties.

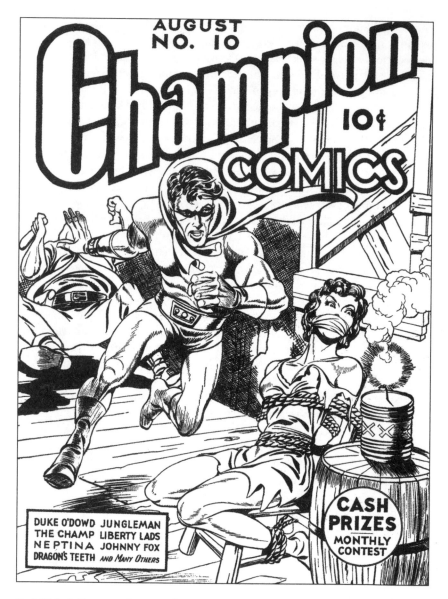

Jack Kirby's first superhero, predecessor to Captain America, as drawn in August 1940. (Author's private collection)

After Pearl Harbor, the United States entered World War II against Germany and Japan. Folk legends like John Henry became crucial in the war against fascism. Since the days of Carl Sandburg, socialists and Communists had tried to reshape the image of what constituted a representative American. They put workers—African Americans, immigrants, and native whites, usually men, but sometimes women—at the center of the American story, retelling American history in song, word, and image. The success of this new kind of story was expressed in the popularity of John Steinbeck's *The Grapes of Wrath,* a novel of Oklahoma migrants to California. It was visible too in the songs of Billie Holiday and the movies of Frank Capra.[31] The historian Michael Denning has called this broad-based movement "the Cultural Front," echoing the Communist Party policy in the 1930s of building a Popular Front of liberals and radicals to fight fascism. By the beginning of the war, this broad left-wing celebration of America's diversity became something like a national duty—a way of encouraging workers to fight and crystallizing national sentiment against Nazi Germany and Imperial Japan.

Just as the local cultural practices of black workers had been important to Communists and socialists in the 1930s, the radicals and liberals of the 1940s found African American labor songs and stories to be crucial for explaining the war over the airwaves. The radical folklorist Benjamin Botkin moved into the Library of Congress. The African American poet and devotee of black music Sterling Brown took over the black interpretation section of the Works Progress Administration. And Charles Seeger, a Communist and the key musicologist of the Workers Music League, took over the U.S. Resettlement Administration. All were folklorists and radicals who had become enamored of John Henry.

As the war progressed, the federal agencies they directed aimed to help forge a *national* identity in the United States that differed from the racial nationalism of Germany and Japan. They sought to both find and reinforce those parts of the national cultural landscape that pointed to an antiracist America. The tale of John Henry, the black workingman beloved by black and white alike, seemed the perfect story to help black and white soldiers, sailors, nurses, and merchant seamen find a common American nationalism that transcended race. Under the auspices of the federally-funded Radio Research Project (RRP), folklorists compiled songs and stories at the Library of Congress and played them to a national audience and, by 1941, to soldiers overseas. For Americans abroad, "John Henry" represented home, and the legend blossomed among those who had never heard the song before.

The Library of Congress's best material for radio proved to be its large folklore collection, including thousands of songs collected with recording equipment since the 1910s.[32] As the war began, the Radio Research Project became an important part of America's propaganda effort. The RRP was first part of the Office of Facts and Figures and then, in 1942, the Office of War Information (OWI). As the propaganda arm of the U.S. government, the OWI was designed to promote "American" values abroad and to encourage English allies and French resistance fighters that the United States was committing all of its powers to the war effort. In particular, the Voice of America, the radio arm of the OWI, assured Britons, the French resistance, and German deserters that the United States was a vibrant, diverse, multiracial democracy that was fighting along with them to end the power of fascist, racially hierarchical states run by dictators like Hitler, Mussolini and Hirohito. Indeed, the American propaganda campaign of the OWI incorporated much of the romantic and democratic idealism of liberals and radicals.[33]

In this newly crafted vision of a diverse and vitally democratic America, American folklore and folk songs helped to make the case. Thus Charles Seeger, who had helped assemble the *Workers Song Book* in 1934 and 1935, was asked in 1941 to write the *Army Song Book,* including folk songs from around the country. Seeger did not carry over "Lenin—Our Leader" and "Red Soldiers Singing" from the *Workers Song Book,* but he did add "I've Been Workin' on de Railroad," "Aloha Oe," and "The Boll-Weevil Song" to the army's collection, giving the official songs of the army a multiracial, folk flavor.[34] ("John Henry" was a favorite, but it apparently did not make the final cut with the secretary of war.) The American composer Marc Blitzstein assembled a chorus of two hundred black soldiers to sing patriotic and folk songs for the American Broadcasting Station in Europe (ABSIE). The ABSIE transmitted these American songs, sung by African Americans, to shortwave radios across the continent.[35]

By the end of World War II, radicals of various stripes had appropriated and transformed the John Henry story. Rather than a struggle against technology, John Henry represented everyday workers' struggles against the forces of capitalism. While for playwrights he represented a fight against the evils of the Jim Crow South, overseas he had become an emblem of a new kind of multiracial America.

American schools became the last holding place for the John Henry legend. While Southern history and geography textbooks would not and did not embrace the legendary black hammer man, the song of John Henry crept into new subjects like chorus and music appreciation. As early as the 1950s, music teachers were dropping hymns and classical music from the curriculum and seeking more popular and accessible songs for elementary schools. Prevented by copyright law from reproducing modern music, book publishers borrowed heavily from the folk songs in Carl Sandburg's *American Songbag*, Benjamin Botkin's *Treasury of American Folklore*, and *Our Singing Country* by John and Alan Lomax. All showcased "John Henry." Folk songs allowed teachers to teach rhythm (a new emphasis in music education) and allowed students to enjoy singing without learning to read music. "John Henry" became especially popular for teaching English as a second language, because it introduced students to Southern and African American dialects while simultaneously teaching a little American history.[36] With the rise of a broader American interest in folksongs, "John Henry" became an entirely new kind of tool. Once a tool to line railway track, it now became a tool to teach music, an arrow in the quiver of music teachers everywhere.

Children's books also absorbed the John Henry legend. By the early 1950s, New York writers in informal writing groups had seized upon the story of John Henry as a new weapon in the war against segregation in the South. Many had written and illustrated dramatic biographies of famous black Americans, as well as stories of African American legends. While segregationist school boards throughout the South would never accept such books as textbooks, black biography and folklore nonetheless seeped into school libraries. The reason was complicated. School boards chose textbooks but left stocking the school libraries to school librarians, usually women. Apparently because they were women, school boards treated them as proxy mothers and let them choose the books they wanted. To school librarians, the legend of a man who died in a race against a steam drill suited the new postwar emphasis on good stories featuring gritty realism and social significance. Indeed, despite the anti-Communist hysteria of the 1950s, radical writers who had been raised on the legend of John Henry found a haven in the world of children's book publishing. By 1955, more than a dozen children's library books made frequent use of John Henry, the famous steel-driving man.[37]

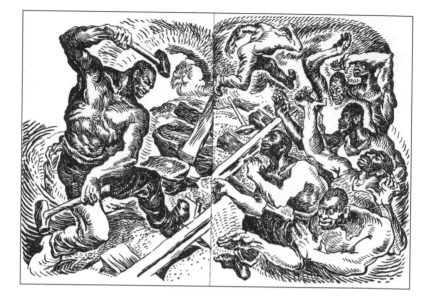

A James Daugherty illustration from Irwin Shapiro's children's book *John Henry and the Double-Jointed Steam Drill.* (Swem Library, College of William and Mary)

So, after radicals had seized upon John Henry during the Depression, his iconic status had been assured. Whether in comic books or on Armed Forces Radio, he came to symbolize America itself. John Henry became so domesticated, in fact, that his story became a standard in children's books. While the Communist Party's version of John Henry endured, sustained in the Popular Front, in comics, and on the Burl Ives record in our Sunday school, competing interpretations of and stories about John Henry remained, particularly among African Americans.

The song of John Henry followed a somewhat different course through African American schools. For segregated black schools in the South, teachers and principals built year-long lesson plans for elementary and secondary schools that showcased the histories of famous black Americans, including black legends like John Henry.[38]

Whether in the North or the South, it would be difficult to predict how that story would be taught. An African American drinking companion of mine, a man in his late thirties, said he heard the story of John Henry "on day one" of his American history class in a predominantly African American public middle school in Cleveland. It was the early 1970s, and there were tough boys in his school, many of whom had no interest in an American history course. Their teacher was new. Stories circulated that she had been a black activist, possibly in the Black Panther Party. On that first day she told the boys in the class that their history, the history of the black man in America, could be told with the story of John Henry. It was a story about the strongest black man in America, tougher and faster than any of the boys in that classroom, but he ended up "working for the man" and died an early death. Would they like to hear that story? The class gave her a resounding YES. That story, she said, was the story of American history, and it would take them an entire year to learn it.[39]

Like the unnamed teacher in the Cleveland public schools, countless other African American storytellers, schoolteachers, and political activists found a different kind of John Henry, relying on him as a source for building black pride and exploring black history. Ed Cabbell, an advisor for the Black Student Union at Concord College in Athens, West Virginia, counseled the African American students there. He later wrote that they came to him one day in 1971 to report that as African Americans who came from the Appalachian Mountains, they were troubled by the "emerging curriculum of Afro-American studies and Appalachian studies programs." In these programs, black men and women from the mountains were "virtually invisible."[40] Cabbell vowed to organize a festival to celebrate their tradition. The person that sprang to Ed's mind was the legendary John Henry, a man who represented both the mountains of West Virginia and black pride. His efforts culminated in the creation of the John Henry Memorial Authentic Blues and Gospel Jubilee at Beckley Park, West Virginia, on Labor Day weekend 1973. He created an organization called the John Henry Center to continue festival activities from year to year. It has gone on for over thirty years to inspire black students and to honor black men's and women's contribution to the history of West Virginia. In the last few years it has moved to Morgantown, West Virginia, and presented dozens of black musicians from all over the country, including black yodelers, folk singers, blues musicians, and the occasional beat poet.

As the Black Power movement of the 1970s faded, the ballad of John Henry gradually became emptied of its racial and political significance. My elementary school abandoned the May Day cakewalks and the John Henry races by the end of the decade. The most important sponsor of our May Day contests had been our history teacher, a tall and barrel-chested African American man named Mr. Haynes. But a stroke killed Mr. Haynes on the last day of our spring semester in 1975.

CODA

John Henry was a little baby
Sittin' on his Mammy's knee
He picked up a hammer and a little piece of steel
Said, "Hammer's gonna be the death of me
Hammer's gonna be the death of me."

John Henry went up on the mountain
Came down on the other side
The mountain was so tall, John Henry was so small
He laid down his hammer and he cried,
Laid down his hammer and he cried

John Henry was a railroad man
He worked from six till five
"Raise 'em up bullies and let 'em drop down,
I'll beat you to the bottom or die
I'll beat you to the bottom or die."

John Henry had a little woman
Her name was Polly Ann
John Henry took sick and had to go to bed
Polly Ann drove steel like a man
Polly Ann drove steel like a man

The Captain said to John Henry
"Gonna bring that steam drill 'round
Gonna bring that steam drill out on the job
Gonna whop that steel on down
Whop that steel on down."

John Henry told his captain
"A man ain't nothin' but a man
Before I let your steam drill beat me down
I'll die with this hammer in my hand
I'll die with this hammer in my hand."

They placed John Henry on the right hand side
The steam drill on the left
He said "Before I let that steam drill beat me down
I'll hammer my fool self to death
I'll hammer my fool self to death."

John Henry told his shaker
"Shaker you had better pray
For if I miss this six-foot steel
Tomorrow will be your buryin' day
Tomorrow will be your buryin' day."

The man that invented that steam drill
Thought he was mighty fine
John Henry sunk her fourteen feet
And the steam drill only made nine
Steam drill only made nine

Sun shine hot an' burnin',
Weren't no breeze at all
Sweat ran down like water down a hill
The day John Henry let his hammer fall
Day John Henry let his hammer fall

John Henry was lyin' on his death bed,
He turned over on his side

And these were the last words John Henry said
"Bring me a cool drink of water 'fore I die
Cool drink of water 'fore I die."

John Henry's woman heard he was dead
She could not rest on her bed
She got up at midnight, caught that No. 4 train,
"I'm goin' where John Henry fell dead
Goin' where John Henry fell dead."

John Henry had a little woman
The dress she wore was blue
She went down the track and never looked back
Saying "Johnny I been true to you
Johnny I been true to you."

They took John Henry to the white house
And buried him in the sand
And every locomotive come roarin' by
Says, "There lays that steel-drivin' man
There lays that steel-drivin' man."[1]

By 1979, John Henry had simply become a shorthand symbol for size and strength. The textile company J. P. Stevens put John Henry's name on a line of chambray shirts for big and tall men. He appears as a statue at the Big Bend Tunnel, and at dozens of historical signposts throughout the Southeast, as nearly every Southeastern state has claimed him. DC Comics staged the death of Superman in 1993, then resurrected him in four different incarnations, with one version that turned the Man of Steel back into Steel-Drivin' Man. In the comic version Dr. John Henry Irons, an inventor and ballistics expert, makes a fortune building military hardware that stuns rather than kills. When a demonstration goes awry, Irons is wounded, fakes his own death, and rebuilds himself as a mechanically powered superhero. Shaquille O'Neal starred in the regrettable 1997 movie adaptation.

Yet there are reasons to still have faith. It is true that recordings of "John Henry" crested between 1955 and the 1970s. Among its most famous exemplars were Charles Seeger's son Pete Seeger, who apparently also learned the song from Thomas Hart Benton. Woody Guthrie and Pete Seeger carried on the tradition of the traveling radical troubadour that blues musicians, and more directly Carl Sandburg, had laid out for them, and "John Henry" was a standard.[2] It was a standard too for Johnny Cash, who donated a portion of the funds to build the statue in Talcott, West Virginia. Yet recordings of "John Henry" have shot up again since the mid-1990s. Almost a hundred versions of the John Henry song have appeared in the past decade, among artists as diverse as nerd-pop idols They Might Be Giants, the grunge-country band Drive-by Truckers, and a jazz-trance-folk band called Snakefarm. For scores of fiddle bands, especially in the musical tradition called alt.country, the song is a staple. Finally, by the end of the century, the novelist Colson Whitehead turned John Henry's story into an allegory for artists' attempts to make a life in a society that constantly revolutionizes production and reproduction. For Whitehead, artists, whether jazz musician or writer, must race to live on the edge of a constant demand for both novelty and authenticity while corporations use, demean, and cheapen every expression they produce. That artistic race to find novelty in the mundane world, to keep up with corporate demands to write or paint or sing for less and less, echoes John Henry's attempt to keep up with a steam drill in a race that would kill him. The machine of selling, of popularity, is intangible, yet is the greatest steam drill of all.

Nailing down the song to a single interpretation is impossible. This is largely because John Henry died without leaving us a written testament, making his story almost infinitely mutable. The last words he is said to have spoken ("cool drink of water 'fore I die") are little help in letting us decide what his life and death was about. We need, finally, to grasp the entire song and story of John Henry, though it is a sharp nettle. We need to see it for all its complexity: It is a story of murder, and of the unnamed dead buried in the sand without gravestones. It is a story of the rage of a Yankee soldier with a terrible wound who consigned a black man to his death. It is a story of state laws that appeared just but let Virginia's assemblymen cuff and slap down the black men who strode about them like conquerors, let them hurt the John Henrys who had seen haughty planters run away from the ramparts of Petersburg, had seen the planters surrender, had watched them beg for mercy. It is a story of Collis Potter Huntington's fantasy of transcendence by money and machinery: of magical steam drills, impossible shortcuts, and the real story about the men who got the job done. It is a story of a man robbed of his dignity and his life, who in death claimed victory. It is a story of an octopus built and sustained by forty thousand aching hands, and arms, and backs, an octopus whose origins are remembered in the breath of forty thousand men. It is a story of women who carried the work forward in some of the darkest days of African American history, of women who remembered, and did the work of any man. It is a story that let people tell their own sorrows in the sorrows of another human being who lived and died. It is a blues story to chase hurt away. It is a story of the blind biblical prophet Samson, reborn to overpower the mighty Philistines. It is a story of the power that God could put into a man with a hammer, while letting him die a natural man. It is a story of the injuries that hide in tunnels, mines, and cotton factories, unacknowledged, ignored, and fatal as a bullet. It is a story of a perilous race to the bottom against impossible odds. It is a story about the ills of capitalism and Jim Crow and about the power of revolution. It is a story about terrible adversity that somehow produces marvelous things, like a rumor that was terrible and true, a song.

Even today, as those songs and stories are pushed down fiber-optic pathways, they still travel along the path laid out by the nation's railroads, along channels bored by John Henry and hundreds of other men like him.[3] If John Henry's bones—first in the penitentiary and now at the Smithsonian—could speak to us today, he might have two words to share with us.

Slow down.

NOTES

1. The Search for John Henry

1. Joe Hickerson and Jennifer Cutting, personal conversation, American Folklife Center, Library of Congress, 25 Sept. 2003.

2. Fisk & Hatch, "Chesapeake and Ohio Railroad . . . The Security for the First Mortgage Bonds of the Company, January, 1872," C&O Railroad Papers, Western Reserve Historical Society, Cleveland, Ohio. On bond marketing in Prussia, see John Moody and George Kibbe Turner, "Masters of Capital in America" *McClure's Magazine* 36 (Jan. 1911): 334ff. On Huntington's experiences, see *American National Biography* q.v. "Huntington, Collis Potter" (New York: Oxford University Press, 1999).

3. Norman E. Tutorow and Evie LaNora Tutorow, *The Governor: The Life and Legacy of Leland Stanford, a California Colossus* (Spokane, Wash.: Arthur H. Clark, 2004), chapter 6; David Haward Bain, *Empire Express: Building the First Transcontinental Railroad* (New York: Viking, 1999).

4. Louis C. Hunter, *A History of Industrial Power in the United States, 1780–1930,* 3 vols. (Charlottesville: University Press of Virginia, 1979).

5. On George Washington's survey, see James Poyntz Nelson, "A State Railway," *Outlook,* Sept.–Dec. 1904, 78; and Walter Buell, "Geo. Washington's First Experience as Surveyor," *Magazine of Western History,* Nov. 1884, 62.

6. Five million: Virginia Senate Committee on Finance, *Report on the Public Debt of Virginia to the Senate,* report prepared by Bradley T. Johnson, 1878, Senate Doc. No. 24, 2–6; Robert F. Hunter and Edwin L. Dooley, *Claudius Crozet: French Engineer in America, 1790–1864* (Charlottesville: University Press of Virginia, 1989).

7. Socks versus pipes: "Rambling Sketches," *Southern Literary Messenger,* Dec. 1854, 721. Shotgun: [Jedidiah Hotchkiss], "New Ways in the Old Dominion II: The Chesapeake and Ohio Railroad," *Scribner's Monthly* 5 (Jan. 1873): 277.

8. Henry S. Drinker, *Tunneling, Explosive Compounds, and Rock Drills* (New York: John Wiley & Sons, 1878), 965.
9. See the many reports to Huntington in Chesapeake & Ohio Company Correspondence, 1869–74, Western Reserve Historical Society, Cleveland, Ohio.
10. Engineer's Report, Greenbrier Division, in "Fifth Annual Report of the President and Directors of the Chesapeake & Ohio Railroad Company, Annual Meeting, December 1872," in *Annual Reports of the Chesapeake & Ohio Railroad Co. 1867&8–1877&8,* microfilm 25, Library of Virginia, Richmond.
11. Engineer's Report, Greenbrier Division, in "Proceedings of the Fourth Annual Meeting of the Stockholders of the Chesapeake & Ohio RR Co, . . . 1871," ibid.

2. To the White House

1. Grady Family Papers, Southern Historical Collection, University of North Carolina, Chapel Hill.
2. "Report of the Board of Directors of the Virginia Penitentiary, with Accompanying Documents for the Year ending Sept. 30, 1872," bound in *Annual Reports of Officers, Boards, and Institutions of the Commonwealth of Virginia,* Library of Virginia, Richmond. Before 1999, the Library of Virginia was called the Virginia State Library.
3. *Staunton Spectator,* 14 Feb. 1871. On railroads' purchase of Southern newspapers, see Scott Nelson, *Iron Confederacies: Southern Railways, Klan Violence and Reconstruction* (Chapel Hill: University of North Carolina Press, 1999).
4. Thus a reporter in New Jersey describes African American hammer men from Virginia who "never seem to tire, and will dance like children after a day's work that would use up two or three ordinary men." See "New York's New Lake," *New York Times,* 5 Jan. 1896. On African American dance generally, see Jacqui Malone, *Steppin' on the Blues: The Visible Rhythms of African American Dance* (Urbana: University of Illinois Press, 1996).
5. Howard Washington Odum, *Rainbow Round My Shoulder: The Blue Trail of Black Ulysses* (Indianapolis: Bobbs-Merrill, 1928).
6. John Lomax, "Some Types of American Folk-Song," *Journal of American Folklore* 28 (Jan.–March 1915): 14.
7. Bruce Michael Harrah-Conforth, "Laughing Just to Keep from Crying: Afro-American Folksongs and the Field Recordings of Lawrence Gellert" (master's thesis, Indiana University, 1984), appendix, page 50.
8. Guy Benton Johnson, *John Henry: Tracking Down a Negro Legend* (Chapel Hill: University of North Carolina Press, 1929), 79.
9. Louis Watson Chappell, *John Henry: A Folk-Lore Study* (1933; rpt. Port Washington, N.Y.: Kennikat, 1968), 14.
10. Victor Chikezie Uchendu, *The Igbo of Southeast Nigeria* (New York: Holt, Rinehart & Winston, 1965); Northcote Whitridge Thomas, *Anthropologi-*

cal Report on the Ibo-Speaking Peoples of Nigeria, 6 vols., vol. 1 (1913–14; rpt. New York: Negro Universities Press, 1969); R. E. Bradbury, P. C. Lloyd, and International African Institute, *The Benin Kingdom and the Edo-Speaking Peoples of South-Western Nigeria*, Ethnographic Survey of Africa: Western Africa, pt. 13 (London: International African Institute, 1964).

11. Chappell, *John Henry*, 13–14.

12. Johnson, *John Henry*, 73.

13. Ibid., 76.

14. Ibid., 99.

15. Author's transcription of "22" and Group, "John Henry," *Prison Songs (Historical Recordings from Parchman Farm, 1947–48), vol. 2: Don'tcha Hear Poor Mother Calling?* Rounder Select CD 611715.

16. "Long John," *Afro-American Spirituals, Work Songs, and Ballads*, Rounder Select CD 1510.

17. Author's transcription of Willie Williams and Group, "The New Burying Ground," 31 May 1936. Original sound recording made by John Lomax, Virginia Penitentiary, Richmond, AFS 725 A1. For provenance, see Field Recordings Geographical Cardfile s.v. "Virginia: Richmond," American Folklife Center, Library of Congress. Available on *Afro-American Spirituals, Work Songs, and Ballads*, Rounder Select CD 1510.

18. Carl Smith and Anderson, South Carolina, chain gang, recorded 9–12 June 1939, at http://memory.loc.gov.

19. The two standard accounts of John Henry are Johnson, *John Henry*, and Chappell, *John Henry*.

20. *Washington Post* reporter Linda Wheeler helped me find Katherine Beidleman.

21. The buildings I saw in the postcard were in different places. In 1878, for example, the workshops had burned in a fire that consumed shops and machinery and were replaced by a new white house. Mary Agnes Grant, *History of the State Penitentiary of Virginia* (master's thesis, College of William and Mary, 1936), 94–101, 146.

22. The archivist opened the records for me on 23 Dec. 2003.

23. Prison Register, Penitentiary Records, Department of Corrections, Library of Virginia, Richmond.

24. Ibid. See the last dozen pages for labor contracts with railroads and canals.

25. *Staunton Vindicator*, 1 Nov. 1872.

26. OCLC accession number 22370122 in FirstSearch. According to the director, Michael McCormick, much of the material was uncataloged and unavailable to researchers until 1972, when a comprehensive catalog was released. The catalog states that the society initially had no staff to catalog the collection and thus "bring under control efficiently the documents that had been accumulated. Until this was done, however, a large portion of the material would remain unserviceable." Whitcomb's correspondence might

have arrived through William Pendleton Palmer, a collector who had previously worked at the Virginia State Library. Michael McCormick, personal conversation, 13 Dec. 2002. Quotation from Kermit J. Pike, *A Guide to the Manuscripts and Archives of the Western Reserve Historical Society* (Cleveland: Western Reserve Historical Society, 1972).

3. Wiseman's Grocery

1. "The Bone Question," *Petersburg Daily Index*, 20 March 1866.
2. J. A. Yeckley, Reports of Operations and Conditions, 31 Aug. 1866, BRFAL, Records of the Asst. Commissioner for Virginia, M1048, reel 45.
3. *Petersburg Daily Index*, 8 June 1866.
4. *Petersburg Daily Index*, 1 March 1866.
5. On groceries, see Ted Ownby, *Subduing Satan: Religion, Recreation, and Manhood in the Rural South, 1865–1920* (Chapel Hill: University of North Carolina Press, 1990). On Wiseman, see Auditor of Public Accounts, Land Tax Books, 1871, reel 608, Library of Virginia, Richmond.
6. Freedman's Bureau Circular No. 10, issued March 12, 1866, ordered bureau officials to turn over criminal cases to civilian officials. See J. M. Tracy to Capt. Barnes, 14 April 1866, BRFAL, Records of the Asst. Commissioner for Virginia, M1048, reel 44: Reports of Operations and Conditions, Monthly narrative, frame 482.
7. John Wm. Henry appears on a bill from the county clerk for keeping black men and women in the city jail in Richmond. His internment is listed from April 26 to May 10, 1866. No record of his arrest is in county court records, though the case appears in the Order Book, Justice Court. See the bill in 1866 April Term Papers, County Court Papers, 1867 [*sic*] to 1869, Prince George Circuit Court Clerk's Office, Prince George, Va.
8. U.S. Patent No. 32,510; Joseph Williamson, *History of the City of Belfast in the State of Maine: From Its First Settlement in 1770 to 1875* (Portland: Loring, Short & Harmon, 1877), 462, 468–69.
9. Pete Dalton, *With Our Faces to the Foe: A History of the 4th Maine Infantry in the War of the Rebellion* (Union, Me.: Union Publishing, 1998).
10. *Medical and Surgical History of the Civil War, Part 1* 2:181. The surgical report refers to him as Charles W. Burd, Company F, Fourth Maine Volunteers, from Belfast, Maine. The special request from Thomas, however, refers to him as Lieutenant Charles H. Burd, Company F, Fourth Maine Volunteers. *Official Records of the War of the Rebellion* 116:203. For diagnosis, see George Alexander Otis, *Reports on the Extent and Nature of the Materials Available for the Preparation of a Medical and Surgical History of the Rebellion* (Philadelphia: Printed for the Surgeon General's Office by J. B. Lippincott, 1865), 18. On the final procedure, see Jonathan Mason Warren, *Surgical Observations, with Cases and Operations* (Boston: Ticknor & Fields, 1867), 543–44.

11. *Medical and Surgical History of the Civil War, Part 1,* 2:181. On lead, see National Institute of Environmental Health Sciences circular, "Lead and Your Health," April 2005.

12. J. A. Yeckley, Reports of Operations and Conditions, 10 Aug. 1866, BRFAL, Records of the Asst. Commissioner for Virginia, M1048, reel 45.

13. Charles H. Burd, Reports of Operations and Conditions, 31 March 1866, BRFAL, Records of the Asst. Commissioner for Virginia, M1048, reel 44.

14. *Petersburg Daily Index,* 15 May 1866.

15. J. A. Yeckley, Reports of Operations and Conditions, 10 Aug. 1866, BRFAL, Records of the Asst. Commissioner for Virginia, M1048, reel 45.

16. "Outrageous conduct": J. A. Yeckley, Reports of Operations and Conditions, 10 Aug. 1866, BRFAL, Records of the Asst. Commissioner for Virginia, M1048, reel 45.

17. Charles H. Burd, Reports of Operations and Conditions, 28 Feb. 1866, BRFAL, Records of the Asst. Commissioner for Virginia, M1048, reel 44.

18. Ibid.

19. *Petersburg Daily Index,* 13 March 1866; "strike for higher wages": Charles H. Burd, Reports of Operations and Conditions, 1 May 1866, BRFAL, Records of the Asst. Commissioner for Virginia, M1048, reel 45.

20. See Yeckley's complaint about Burd's previous procedure in J. A. Yeckley, Reports of Operations and Conditions, 10 Aug 1866, BRFAL, Records of the Asst. Commissioner for Virginia, M1048, reel 45.

21. Report of O. O. Howard in 39th Cong., 1st sess., House Executive Document 120, pp. 44, 46.

22. *Petersburg Daily Index,* 16 March 1866.

23. *Petersburg Daily Index,* 15 March 1866; the man who cut prisoners free was Levi Boone, mentioned by name on 16 March 1866.

24. Charles H. Ambler, *Francis H. Pierpont* (Chapel Hill: University of North Carolina Press, 1937), 283; Eric Foner, *Reconstruction: America's Unfinished Revolution, 1863–1877* (New York: Harper & Row, 1988).

25. "Immigrants," *Petersburg Daily Index,* 10 July 1866; see Secretary of the Commonwealth, Executive Papers, Library of Virginia, Richmond, box 9 (Feb.–May 1868) for letters written by Virginia citizens describing the weak evidence used for rounding up black men and women in 1865.

26. "Rogues": *Petersburg Daily Index,* 6 March 1866; chapters 13, 22–25, 28, *Session Laws of the American States and Territories,* Virginia, fiche 159.

27. See the many petitions for pardon for black code convictions in H. H. Wells, Secretary of the Commonwealth, Executive Papers, Library of Virginia, Richmond, boxes 9–13.

28. Sarah and Lucy Thomas to H. H. Wells, mislabeled "25 Mar. 1864" but entered 15 May 1868, box 9, Secretary of the Commonwealth, Executive Papers, Library of Virginia, Richmond.

29. The Freedmen's Bureau actually made the decision to turn over all criminal cases to the state courts in late March, after the Milligan case had been heard but before the verdict had been delivered. See *Petersburg Daily Index,* 19 March 1866.

30. Charles H. Burd, Reports of Operations and Conditions, 1 May 1866, BRFAL, Records of the Asst. Commissioner for Virginia, M1048, reel 45.

31. See the bill in 1866 April Term Papers, County Court Papers, 1867 [*sic*] to 1869, Prince George Circuit Court Clerk's Office, Prince George, Va.

32. On court days, see Ownby, *Subduing Satan;* Edward L. Ayers, *The Promise of the New South: Life After Reconstruction* (New York: Oxford University Press, 1992); and D. W. Meinig, *The Shaping of America: A Geographical Perspective on 500 Years of History,* vol. 2: *Continental America* (New Haven: Yale University Press, 1986). On fistfights in groceries, see Charles C. Bolton and Scott P. Culcasure, eds., *The Confessions of Edward Isham: A Poor White Life of the Old South* (Athens: University of Georgia Press, 1998), 1–18. W. H. Wiseman appears in the 1860 census with his wife, Lucy, as a forty-two-year-old white farmer, born in Germany and living in Prince George County. Virginia Manuscript Census, series M653, roll 1372, page 412. Lucy appears as head of household in 1870, in the township now labeled Bland, but is listed as a retired grocer. Virginia Manuscript Census, series M593, roll 1673, page 177. "Wiseman, Wm. Mrs." appears in the Prince George section of "Saloons" and "Country Stores and Merchants" in *Boyd's Directory of Richmond City, and a Business Directory of about Fifty Counties of Virginia* (Richmond: Bates & Waddy Brothers, 1869–70).

33. "Underwood," *Petersburg Daily Index,* 11 May 1866; "Circuit Court Presiding," *Petersburg Daily Index,* 23 May 1866.

34. "Commonwealth of Virginia against John Wm. Henry, 17th of May 1866," Order Book, Circuit Court, Prince George County, Prince George Circuit Court Clerk's Office, Prince George, Va. "Wiseman, Mrs. Lucy J.," Auditor of Public Accounts, Personal Property Tax Books, Powhatan, Prince Edward, Prince George Counties, 1871, reel 865, Library of Virginia, Richmond.

35. William Wiseman died before 1869. "Wiseman, Wm. H. Est.," Table of Tracts of Land for the Year 1871, Prince George County Within the Township of Bland, Auditor of Public Accounts, Land Tax Books, 1871, reel 608, Library of Virginia, Richmond.

36. "Commonwealth of Virginia against John Wm. Henry, 17th of May 1866," Order Book, Circuit Court, Prince George County, Prince George Circuit Court Clerk's Office, Prince George, Va.

37. Charles A. Burd to Capt. Stuart Barnes, 1 June 1866, BRFAL, Records of the Asst. Commissioner for Virginia, M1048, reel 44. Howard circular: 39th Cong., 1st Sess. House Executive Document 120, p. 3.

38. Yeckley's arrival: J. A. Yeckley, Reports of Operations and Conditions, 10 Aug. 1866, BRFAL, Records of the Asst. Commissioner for Virginia, M1048,

reel 45. "Seemed to me" and "sentence seems a long one": J. A. Yeckley to Brevet Brig. Genl. O. Brown, BRFAL, reel 58, City Point Trials, 30 Nov. 1866. "We of the jury": 12 Nov. 1866, Minute Book, Circuit Court, Prince George County, 1866–70, Prince George Circuit Court Clerk's Office, Prince George, Va.

39. County Court Order Book, 1865–67, Prince George Circuit Court Clerk's Office, Prince George, Va. Burd was gone before John Henry's final trial in November. Criminal cases were turned over to civil courts in April 1866: *New York Times*, 13 May 1866. Andrew Johnson ordered investigations of Bureau operations in late April of 1866. Paul Skeels Pierce, *The Freedmen's Bureau* (Iowa City, Iowa: The University, 1904), 63–65. Superintendent O. O. Howard began his own investigation into allegations of misconduct on May 21, 1866, declaring that court-martials "are to be deprecated" and that after an inspection he would simply remove "every unfaithful officer." 39th Cong., 1st sess., House Executive Document 120, p. 3. Burd was replaced between August 1 and 10, by special order 139. J. A. Yeckley to Bvt. Lt. Col. Jas. A Bates, 10 Aug. 1866, BRFAL, Records of the Asst. Commissioner for Virginia, M1048, reel 45.

40. J. A. Yeckley to Brevet Brig. Genl. O. Brown, BRFAL, reel 58, City Point Trials, 30 Nov. 1866.

4. Ward-Well

1. On the necessity for convicts in the physical reconstruction of the South, see Alex Lichtenstein, *Twice the Work of Free Labor: The Political Economy of Convict Labor in the New South* (New York: Verso, 1996).

2. "Report of William Crawford, Esq., on the Penitentiaries of the United States, addressed to His Majesty's Principal Secretary of State for the Home Department. Ordered by the House of Commons, to be Printed, 11 August 1834," available at Special Collections, Library of Virginia, Richmond; *Richmond Dispatch*, 17 Oct. 1866; Burnham Wardwell to H. H. Wells, 4 May 1868, box 9, Secretary of the Commonwealth, Executive Papers, Library of Virginia, Richmond. For "neatly cropped" prisoners, see *Richmond Dispatch*, 17 Oct. 1866.

3. *Richmond Dispatch*, 25 Oct. 1866.

4. On the role of secret fraternities in Richmond, see Peter J. Rachleff, *Black Labor in the South: Richmond, Virginia, 1865–1890* (Philadelphia: Temple University Press, 1984).

5. Heritage Quest Online s.v. "John Henry," U.S. Federal Census, 1870.

6. *Richmond Dispatch*, 31 Aug. 1866.

7. The best treatment of the rise of Radical Reconstruction is Eric Foner, *Reconstruction: America's Unfinished Revolution, 1863–1877* (New York: Harper & Row, 1988).

8. Of the 761 in the penitentiary in 1870 (the first year statistics were tabulated after the war), approximately 600 were in jail for burglary, theft,

housebreaking, horse and mule stealing, or grand larceny. "Report of the Board of Directors of the Virginia Penitentiary . . . 1870," bound in *Annual Reports of Officers, Boards, and Institutions of the Commonwealth of Virginia*, Library of Virginia, Richmond, 5.

9. Leasing contracts in unnumbered rear pages, Book 1, Prisoner Register, Penitentiary Records, Department of Corrections, Library of Virginia, Richmond.

10. The best current biography of Schofield is Donald B. Connelly, "Political Soldier: John M. Schofield and the Politics of Generalship" (dissertation, University of Houston, 2003).

11. See John M. Schofield to U. S. Grant, 2 April 1868, Letters Sent, container 48, John M. Schofield Papers, Manuscripts Division, Library of Congress.

12. Elizabeth Wardwell Stay, *Wardwell: A Brief Sketch of the Antecedents of Solomon Wardwell* . . . (Greenfield, Mass: E. A. Hall, 1905), 7–8; genealogy posting by J. Bragdon Hutter (Hutter@montana.com) on Genealogy.com dated 29 Oct. 2002, http://genforum.genealogy.com/wardwell/messages/117.html, viewed 8 Nov. 2005.

13. Army Records 117:367, 117:529, 123:765. On the oath, see [H. H. Bigelow], "Burnham Wardwell Vindicated in His Work for Humanity" (Worcester, Mass.[?]: s.n., 1882), available on microfilm in *Pamphlets in American History,* 2–3, 5.

14. Army Records 117:862–63.

15. [Bigelow], "Burnham Wardwell."

16. John M. Schofield apparently spoke directly with Underwood about this issue, convincing him not to go forward. See Schofield to Stoneman, 29 Aug. 1868, Letters Sent, container 49, John M. Schofield Papers, Manuscripts Division, Library of Congress. On the treason trial, see [Bigelow], "Burnham Wardwell."

17. Michael B. Chesson, *Richmond After the War, 1865–1890* (Richmond: Virginia State Library, 1981), 110–11.

18. Obituary, *Journal of Prison Discipline and Philanthropy,* Jan. 1876, 47.

19. "Present State of the Prison Question in the United States," *Hours at Home,* April 1869, 546.

20. Wardwell to H. H. Wells, 30 April 1868, box 9, Secretary of the Commonwealth, Executive Papers, Library of Virginia, Richmond.

21. The Virginia Assembly had already made it possible back in April 1867, a month after Radical Reconstruction had begun. Contract with Claiborne R. Mason in box 11, Secretary of the Commonwealth, Executive Papers, 31 Aug. 1868, Library of Virginia, Richmond. The enabling legislation was "An Act to authorize the Governor to hire out the convicts at the penitentiary to learn stone-cutting or other mechanical trades," passed by the General Assembly on 29 April 1867.

22. Wardwell to H. H. Wells, 25 May 1868, box 9, Secretary of the Commonwealth, Executive Papers, Library of Virginia, Richmond.

23. Leasing contracts in unnumbered rear pages, Book 1, Prisoner Register, Penitentiary Records, Department of Corrections, Library of Virginia, Richmond.

24. *Virginia Acts of Assembly, 1867,* 789–91.

25. *New York Times,* 25 March 1886, 8.

26. For complaints to Stoneman, see the letters of October and November 1868 in entry 127, C&O Railroad, folder 1, 1868–75, Board of Public Works Records, Library of Virginia, Richmond. The envelope for Stoneman's original, confidential letter to Schofield is in Letters Received, container 8, John M. Schofield Papers, Manuscripts Division, Library of Congress. The letter itself is not in the collection. Schofield's response is in Schofield to Stoneman, 12 Oct. 1868, and Schofield's reassurance to James Lyon is in Schofield to Lyon, 20 Nov. 1868, both in Letters Sent, container 48, Schofield Papers.

27. "An act to provide for the completion of a line or lines of Railroad from the waters of the Chesapeake to the Ohio River," passed March 1, 1867, fiche 166, chapter 280, *Session Laws of the American States and Territories.*

28. The best chronology for the use of Chinese workers is William F. Chew, *Nameless Builders of the Transcontinental* (Victoria, B.C.: Trafford, 2004).

29. David Haward Bain, *Empire Express: Building the First Transcontinental Railroad* (New York: Viking, 1999), 273.

30. J.[?] M. Hall, Washington, D.C., to H. D. Whitcomb, 13 April 1870, Chesapeake & Ohio Company Correspondence, 1869–74, Western Reserve Historical Society, Cleveland, Ohio.

31. Herman Haupt, *Tunneling by Machinery: Description of Perforators and Plans of Operations in Mining and Tunneling. Devised by Herman Haupt, Civil Engineer . . . Prepared . . . by Blanchard & McKean* (Philadelphia: H. G. Leisenring's Steam Printing House, 1867), 27, in folder 75, Herman Haupt Papers, Yale University.

5. Man Versus Mountain

1. "The Hoosac Tunnel," *Scientific American* 22 (12 Feb. 1870): 106–7; Graham West, *Innovation and the Rise of the Tunnelling Industry* (New York: Cambridge University Press, 1988), 60.

2. Frank Aaron Edson, *Diamond Drilling with Special Reference to Oil-Field Prospecting and Development,* U.S. Bureau of Mines, Bulletin 243 (Washington: USGPO, 1926). John Tilsby to H. D. Whitcomb, 15 Sept. 1869, 5 Oct. 1869; C. P. Durham to H. D. Whitcomb, 3 April 1870; William J. Holt to H. D. Whitcomb, 9 April 1870, Chesapeake & Ohio Company Correspondence, 1869–74, Western Reserve Historical Society, Cleveland, Ohio (hereafter cited as WRHS).

3. The term allegedly derives from an intricate tangle of cams and driveshafts called a "Kluge paper feeder" that fed paper into mechanical printing presses in the 1930s.

4. Herman Haupt, *Tunneling by Machinery: Description of Perforators and Plans of Operations in Mining and Tunneling. Devised by Herman Haupt,*

Civil Engineer... Prepared... by Blanchard & McKean (Philadelphia: H. G. Leisenring's Steam Printing House, 1867), 20, in folder 75, Herman Haupt Papers, Yale University.

5. "Trip to the Coal Mines, from the Richmond Compiler," *Niles' Register* 65 (Oct. 1843): 108–9.

6. Discussion of African American miners from Chesterfield at tunneling sites in 1871 is in *Richmond Dispatch*, 14 Nov. 1871.

7. I have added line breaks to identify the drilling process. Bruce Michael Harrah-Conforth, "Laughing Just to Keep from Crying: Afro-American Folksongs and the Field Recordings of Lawrence Gellert" (master's thesis, Indiana University, 1984), 162.

8. I depart slightly from, but rely a great deal on, Archie Green, *Only a Miner: Studies in Recorded Coal-Mining Songs* (Urbana: University of Illinois Press, 1972).

9. See previous chapter. Wardwell to H. H. Wells, 25 May 1868, box 9, Secretary of the Commonwealth, Executive Papers, Library of Virginia, Richmond.

10. "Short, stout": *Staunton Vindicator,* 7 Feb. 1872; *Richmond Dispatch*, 13 Jan. 1885.

11. G.F.R. Henderson, *Stonewall Jackson and the American Civil War* (London: Longmans, 1898), 2:48–49; Secretary of the Commonwealth, Executive Journal, 1868–70, Minute Book, 31 Aug. 1868, Library of Virginia, Richmond; *Richmond Dispatch*, 13 Jan. 1885; Thomas Frazier, "Four Years of My Life During the War Between the States," excerpted from *The Olive Branch* (Earleysville, Va.: the author, 1896), http://www.geocities.com/~jcrosswell/Hist/obranch.html, accessed 22 March 2004.

12. Leasing contracts in unnumbered rear pages, Book 1, Prisoner Register, Penitentiary Records, Department of Corrections, Library of Virginia, Richmond.

13. Burnham Wardwell to H. H. Wells, 22 May 1868, box 9, Secretary of the Commonwealth, Executive Papers, Library of Virginia, Richmond; "Escape and Recapture of Convicts," *Richmond Dispatch*, 1 Aug. 1868.

14. Written below message from J. R. Goodloe to H. H. Wells, 20 Oct. 1868, box 12, Secretary of the Commonwealth, Executive Papers, Library of Virginia.

15. [Nelson Hotchkiss], "New Ways in the Old Dominion: The Chesapeake and Ohio Railroad," *Scribner's Monthly* 5 (Dec. 1872): 137–60.

16. Peyton Randolph to HDW, 24 Feb. 1870, WRHS; Alleghany County, Common Law Order Book, vol. 6, 1859–73, Library of Virginia, Richmond.

17. On the overstint, see *Virginia Acts of Assembly, 1867,* 790–91.

18. Manuscript Census, Town of Staunton, Augusta County, Virginia, U.S. Census of Population, 1860, p. 24 in National Archives Microfilm Collection; "Social Events and Announcements," *Washington Post*, 24 Jan. 1890. On Whitcomb's wartime activities, see Henry C. Parsons Papers, Manuscripts Division, Virginia Tech, Blacksburg. Elizabeth R. Varon, *Southern Lady, Yankee Spy: The True Story of Elizabeth Van Lew, a Union Agent in the Heart of the Confederacy* (New York: Oxford University Press, 2003).

19. James Poyntz Nelson, *Address: The Chesapeake and Ohio Railway. The Realization of the Dream of George Washington, the Surveyor on the Banks of the Kanawha*, 2d ed. (Richmond: Mitchell & Hotchkiss, 1916), 3; "Second Annual Report of the Chesapeake & Ohio Railroad Company," 25 Nov. 1869, p. 30, film 25, Library of Virginia, Richmond.

20. C. A. Sharp, Rollinsburgh, W.Va., to H. D. Whitcomb, 22 Feb. 1869, WRHS.

21. *Richmond Dispatch*, 10 April 1872; Francis Earle Lutz, *Chesterfield, an Old Virginia County* (Richmond: W. Byrd Press, 1954), 260; leasing contracts in unnumbered rear pages, Book 1, Prisoner Register, Penitentiary Records, Department of Corrections, Library of Virginia, Richmond.

22. In May 1871, David Tucker, the engineer in charge of machinery for the Big Bend Tunnel, wrote the Tanner steam engine company that their engine "is now in operation and works beautifully," but noted that he had two others "of inferior patterns and workmanship" that had given him trouble. These two were hoisting engines that came from a factory in Newark, and were not steam drills. Wm. E. Tanner, *Price List of Portable, Stationary, and Agricultural Steam Engines* (Richmond, 1872), 46; Bolen and Crane to Whitcomb, 14 Nov. 1870, WRHS. Chief engineer Whitcomb described the two thirty-pound hoisting engines from Tanner as doing "all that were required or expected of them." Tanner, *Price List of Steam Engines*, 35.

23. John Tilsby to HDW, 15 Sept. 1869, WRHS.

24. Jos. F. Nounnan to HDW, 16 Oct. 1869, WRHS.

25. C. P. Durham to HDW, 5 April 1870, WRHS.

26. [Peyton Randolph] to HDW, 6 April 1870, WRHS.

27. John Tilsby to HDW, 5 Oct. 1869, C. P. Durham to HDW, 3 April 1870, Wm. J. Holt to HDW, 9 April 1870, WRHS.

28. Wm. J. Holt to HDW, 12 April 1870, WRHS.

29. C. P. Durham to HDW, 29 April 1870, WRHS; *Staunton Spectator*, 14 June 1870; Durham & Co. to HDW, 18 June 1870, C. P. Huntington to HDW, 25 June 1870, WRHS.

30. C. P. Huntington to HDW, 28 July 1870, WRHS.

31. Cerinda W. Evans, *Collis Potter Huntington* (Newport News, Va.: Mariners' Museum, 1954), 2:513; Durham & Co., Lewis Tunnel, Va., to HDW, 4 July 1870, WRHS.

32. Peyton Randolph to HDW, 23 May 1870, WRHS.

33. C. P. Durham to HDW, 15 July 1870, WRHS.

34. George McKendree to HDW, 2 June 1870, WRHS.

35. Martin Cherniack, *The Hawk's Nest Incident: America's Worst Industrial Disaster* (New Haven: Yale University Press, 1986).

36. U.S. Congress, *Report of the Joint Special Committee to Investigate Chinese Immigration. February 27, 1877* (Washington: USGPO, 1877); David Haward Bain, *Empire Express: Building the First Transcontinental Railroad* (New York: Viking, 1999).

37.   C. P. Huntington to HDW, 7 July 1870, WRHS.

38.   C. P. Huntington to HDW, 10 Aug. 1870; Lee & Hustons, Thorndike P.O., Cabell Co., W. Va., to HDW, 20 Aug. 1870, WRHS.

39.   "Report of the Board of Directors of the Virginia Penitentiary . . .1870," bound in *Annual Reports of Officers, Boards, and Institutions of the Commonwealth of Virginia*, Library of Virginia, Richmond (hereafter cited as VPR), 4; Secretary of the Commonwealth, Executive Journal, 1864–67, Minute Book, Feb. 1870, Library of Virginia, Richmond.

40.   VPR 1870, 4.

41.   Leasing contracts in unnumbered rear pages, Book 1, Prisoner Register, Penitentiary Records, Department of Corrections, Library of Virginia, Richmond; VPR 1872, 5–6; 1873, 3–5.

42.   Leasing contracts in unnumbered rear pages, Book 1, Prisoner Register, Penitentiary Records, Department of Corrections, Library of Virginia, Richmond.

43.   Harrah-Conforth, "Laughing Just to Keep from Crying," 165.

44.   Three hundred eighty prisoners worked on the railroad for the year Septepber 30, 1871, to September 30, 1872. VPR 1872, 13.

45.   *Richmond Dispatch,* 12 Oct. 1871

46.   *Staunton Vindicator,* 1 Sept. 1871.

47.   "Excursion of Northern Editors," *Staunton Vindicator,* 2 June 1871; N. J. Watkins and Nelson H. Hotchkiss, *The Pine and the Palm Greeting; or, the Trip of the Northern Editors to the South in 1872, Under the Leadership of Maj. N. H. Hotchkiss* (Baltimore: J. D. Ehlers, 1873), 27–28. The writer describes a tunnel "three thousand nine hundred feet in length," on page 27. This can only be the Lewis Tunnel, with a final length of 4,033 feet. See H. S. Drinker, *Tunneling, Explosive Compounds and Rock Drills,* 3d ed. (New York: John Wiley & Sons, 1893), appendix, table 123.

48.   Watkins and Hotchkiss, *Pine and the Palm,* 27–28.

49.   "The Tunnel," *The Friend: A Religious and Literary Journal,* 22 April 1871, 273.

50.   Chappell, *John Henry,* 108.

51.   *Richmond Dispatch* 12 Oct 1871.

52.   J. J. Gordon to HDW, 3 Oct. 1871, WRHS.

53.   Louis Watson Chappell, *John Henry: A Folk-Lore Study* (1933; rpt. Port Washington, N.Y.: Kennikat, 1968), 108.

54.   Huntington to HDW, 30 Aug. 1871, WRHS.

55.   Peyton Randolph to HDW, n.d. [Oct. 1871], WRHS.

56.   John Henry is the only man from New Jersey in the census for the penitentiary. A man listed as "colored" and from New Jersey appeared in the "nativity of convicts" table in the penitentiary reports in September 1870, 1871, 1872 and 1873. In the next report, of 1875, when all convicts had been returned from the railroad, he was no longer listed. The nativity table was probably compiled at the penitentiary, suggesting that John Henry was kept on the books until it was obvious that he had not returned alive.

57. Guy Benton Johnson, *John Henry: Tracking Down a Negro Legend* (Chapel Hill: University of North Carolina Press, 1929), 94.

58. Many were shifted to the James River and Kanawha Canal and continued to die in large numbers through 1878. *Medical and Surgical Reporter*, 21 Dec. 1878, 547.

59. Chappell, *John Henry*, 14.

60. VPR 1872, 21.

61. "The Origins of Rock Drilling," *Digging Deeper: Newsletter of Australian Mining Consultants, Pty. Ltd.*, July 1998, 2–3.

62. "A Rockman's Work in Tunnel Building," *New York Times*, 5 May 1901, 28.

63. Cherniack, *Hawk's Nest Incident*.

64. P. Dee, P. Surratt, and W. Winn, "The Radiographic Findings in Acute Silicosis" *Radiology* 126 (Feb. 1978): 359–63 (abstract viewed); U.S. Department of Labor, Mine Safety and Health Administration, "Dust—What You Can't See CAN Hurt You!" 1999; E. Edward Bittar, *Pulmonary Biology in Health and Disease* (New York: Springer, 2002), 403–4.

65. Kari Bruwelheide, e-mail communication with author, 17 May 2005.

66. This process is described in detail in Cherniack, *Hawk's Nest Incident*.

67. VPR 1872; VPR 1873.

68. Johnson, *John Henry*, 118.

6. The Southern Railway Octopus

1. Louis Watson Chappell, *John Henry: A Folk-Lore Study* (1933; rpt. Port Washington, N.Y.: Kennikat, 1968), 106.

2. The Western North Carolina Railroad, built by convicts in the 1880s, gave the Southern Railway its own route through the Allegheny Mountains.

3. Edward L. Ayers, *The Promise of the New South: Life After Reconstruction* (New York: Oxford University Press, 1992).

4. William Henry Hotzclaw, *The Black Man's Burden* (New York: Neale, 1915); Nate Shaw and Theodore Rosengarten, *All God's Dangers: The Life of Nate Shaw* (New York: Knopf, 1974).

5. Allen Reid, "Bad Laz'us," sung at State Penitentiary, Raiford, Fla., 3 June 1939, in "The John and Ruby Lomax 1939 Southern States Recording Trip," American Folklife Center, Library of Congress, http://memory.loc.gov/ammem/lohtml/lohome.html, accessed 8 Aug. 2002.

6. On the geography of plantations, see Merle Prunty Jr., "The Renaissance of the Southern Plantation," *Geographical Review* 45 (1955): 459–91; Roger L. Ransom and Richard Sutch, *One Kind of Freedom: The Economic Consequences of Emancipation* (New York: Cambridge University Press, 1977).

7. Luther Porter Jackson, *Negro Office-Holders in Virginia, 1865–1895* (Norfolk: Guide Quality Press, 1945), 74–75. On the continuity of Reconstruction past 1877, see Laura F. Edwards, *Gendered Strife and Confusion: The Political Culture of Reconstruction* (Urbana: University of Illinois Press, 1997).

8. See Scott Nelson, *Iron Confederacies: Southern Railways, Klan Violence, and Reconstruction* (Chapel Hill: University of North Carolina Press, 1999). The actual mechanics of this process are still a matter of considerable debate. On whether Hayes or Congress removed troops, see Matthew Wayne Shepherd, "Ten Tumultuous Months: Rutherford B. Hayes and the Limitations of 'Home Rule' in the Post-Reconstruction South, September 1878– June 1879" (honors thesis, College of William and Mary, 1998).

9. Nelson, *Iron Confederacies*, chapter 8.

10. Josephus Daniels, *Tar Heel Editor* (Chapel Hill: University of North Carolina Press, 1939); Jeffrey J. Crow and Robert Franklin Durden, *Maverick Republican in the Old North State: A Political Biography of Daniel L. Russell* (Baton Rouge: Louisiana State University Press, 1977).

11. Eber Carle Perrow, "Songs and Rhymes from the South," *Journal of American Folklore* 26 (April–June 1913): 164.

12. Nelson, *Iron Confederacies*, chapter 8.

13. Alexander Boyd Andrews, comp., "Scrapbook of Newspaper Clippings on North Carolina Railroads," North Carolina Collection, University of North Carolina, Chapel Hill.

14. On catalogs, see Thomas Dionysius Clark, *Pills, Petticoats, and Plows: The Southern Country Store* (Norman: University of Oklahoma Press, 1964). On black and white schooling, see Neil R. McMillen, *Dark Journey: Black Mississippians in the Age of Jim Crow* (Urbana: University of Illinois Press, 1989). On a school without walls, see Holtzclaw, *Black Man's Burden*.

15. On investors' interest in the coalfields, see Amasa Mason to H. D. Whitcomb, 1 Oct. 1869, Chesapeake & Ohio Company Correspondence, 1869–74, Western Reserve Historical Society, Cleveland, Ohio. On the C&O's promotion of coal seams, see [Nelson Hotchkiss], "New Ways in the Old Dominion II: The Chesapeake and Ohio Railroad," *Scribner's Monthly* 5 (Jan.): 278–80. On Huntington's mining investment in the West, see Salvador A. Ramirez, ed., *The Octopus Speaks: The Colton Letters* (Carlsbad, Calif.: Tentacled Press, 1982).

16. *Journal of the Western Society of Engineers* 2 (1897): 61, cited in Chappell, *John Henry*, 81.

17. On the mining industry in eastern Virginia, see Sean P. Adams, *Old Dominion, Industrial Commonwealth: Coal, Politics, and Economy in Antebellum America* (Baltimore: Johns Hopkins University Press, 2004). On ballad formation and transformation, see Tristram P. Coffin, " 'Mary Hamilton' and the Anglo-American Ballad as an Art Form," *Journal of American Folklore* 70 (July 1957): 208–14.

18. Chappell, *John Henry*, 109, 114.

19. Author's transcription from "22" and Group. "John Henry," *Prison Songs (Historical Recordings from Parchman Farm, 1947–48), vol. 2: Don'tcha Hear Poor Mother Calling?* Rounder Select CD 611715.

20. Norm Cohen, *Long Steel Rail: The Railroad in American Folksong*, 2d ed. (Urbana: University of Illinois Press, 2000), 70. Child ballad no. 76 in Francis James Child, *English and Scottish Ballads* (Boston: Little, Brown, 1857).

21. Cohen, *Long Steel Rail*, 70.

22. A. M. Bacon, "Proposal for Folk-Lore Research at Hampton, Va.," *Journal of American Folklore* 6, no. 23 (1893): 305–9; Alice Mabel Bacon, "Work and Methods of the Folk-Lore Society," *Journal of American Folklore* 11, no. 40 (1898): 17–21.

23. Natalie Curtis-Burlin, *Negro Folk Songs, Hampton Series, Book IV: Work and Play Songs* (New York: G. Schirmer, 1919), 126.

24. Ibid., 141.

25. Virginia Steele, "Legends of John Henry, Part II," *Wonderful West Virginia* 36, no. 9 (1972): 18–21, 29.

26. Chappell, *John Henry*, 109.

27. Ibid., 110.

28. Ibid., 119.

29. On the continued use of convicts for high-tech labor, see Alex Lichtenstein, *Twice the Work of Free Labor: The Political Economy of Convict Labor in the New South*, Haymarket Series (London and New York: Verso, 1996). The best account of the Asheville tunnel experience is John Ehle's novel, based on research at the North Carolina Division of Archives and History in Raleigh. See John Ehle, *The Road* (New York: Harper & Row, 1967).

30. Bascom Lamar Lunsford, "Ballads, Banjo Tunes and Sacred Songs of Western North Carolina," Smithsonian Folkways SF CD 40082.

31. William Aspenwall Bradley, "Song-Ballets and Devil's Ditties," *Harper's Monthly Magazine* 130 (May 1915): 901–14.

32. Johnson, *John Henry*, 124.

33. Ibid., 101.

34. On the fascination for and fear of black men's bodies, see Hazel V. Carby, *Race Men* (Cambridge: Harvard University Press, 1998) and bell hooks, *We Real Cool: Black Men and Masculinity* (New York: Routledge, 2004). On women, see Evelyn Brooks Higginbotham, *Righteous Discontent: The Women's Movement in the Black Baptist Church, 1880–1920* (Cambridge: Harvard University Press, 1993); and Glenda Elizabeth Gilmore, *Gender and Jim Crow: Women and the Politics of White Supremacy in North Carolina, 1896–1920* (Chapel Hill: University of North Carolina Press, 1996).

35. Cotton mills had a large workforce, but their most explosive growth was after 1909. Clarence Heer, *Income and Wages in the South* (Chapel Hill: University of North Carolina Press, 1930).

36. Holtzclaw, *Black Man's Burden*, 20.

37. "I'm Running a French Railroad," *New York Times*, 31 Dec. 1944.

38. David T. Courtwright, "The Rise and Fall and Rise of Cocaine in the United States," in *Consuming Habits: Drugs in History and Anthropology*, ed. Jordan

Goodman, Paul E. Lovejoy, and Andrew Sherratt (New York: Routledge & Kegan Paul, 1995), 206–28.

39. Guy Benton Johnson, *John Henry: Tracking Down a Negro Legend* (Chapel Hill: University of North Carolina Press, 1929), 92.

40. Chappell, *John Henry,* 108.

41. Lawrence W. Levine, *Black Culture and Black Consciousness: Afro-American Folk Thought from Slavery to Freedom* (New York: Oxford University Press, 1977).

42. Mississippi John Hurt, "Stagolee."

43. "Shack Rouster Holler," AFS 3143B:1, American Memory Project at http://memory.loc.gov.

44. On the abuse of black workers, see Brian Kelly, *Race, Class, and Power in the Alabama Coalfields, 1908–21* (Urbana: University of Illinois Press, 2001), 91–97.

45. I have corrected the transcriber somewhat, replacing "dem" with "them," etc. Ben Lewis, Mississippi Slave Narratives, on *Slave Narratives,* Ancestry.com CD-ROM 1950.

46. Leon R. Harris to Dewey R. Jones, 23 March 1927, series 5.4, folder 102, Guy Benton Johnson Papers, Southern Historical Collection, University of North Carolina, Chapel Hill.

47. Archie Green, *Only a Miner: Studies in Recorded Coal-Mining Songs* (Urbana: University of Illinois Press, 1972), 332; Brett Williams, *John Henry: A Bio-Bibliography* (Westport, Conn.: Greenwood Press, 1983), 47. Louise Bascom was born c. 1885 in Highlands, North Carolina. Her first published play was *Masonic Ring, or the Adventures of a College Bride,* printed in 1910. She also published stories in *Harper's Monthly Magazine* between 1913 and 1915.

48. Bascom's "informant," a "certain woman" she has "known . . . for a dozen years or more," is probably the family's servant listed in the 1900 census, Naomi Wilson, who would have been fifty-five at the time that Louise's article came out. The informant notes having a number of boys who are fiddle players, and Naomi is listed in that census as having five boys. From Louise's obituary it is clear that Louise went to boarding school in Salt Lake City and then to Wellesley, probably graduating in 1907, and came home to North Carolina for the summers. Census and obituary come from John M. Stewart, a descendant, "Research Notes on Louise Rand Bascom," in author's possession. Bascom was unique among collectors, noting the methods of transmission of songs. Later scholars have noted the problem of how collecting worked: Most collectors in the early years were university professors. These collectors "seldom surprised the folksong; he [*sic*] had it recalled for him by self-conscious informants on their best behavior and without their instruments of the devil [i.e., fiddle or guitar, thus losing the tune]. He collected not just half the folksong, as often charged, but sometimes only a third of it."

Donald K. Wilgus, *Anglo-American Folksong Scholarship Since 1898* (New Brunswick: Rutgers University Press, 1959), 154.

49. Eber Carle Perrow, "Songs and Rhymes from the South," *Journal of American Folklore* 26, no. 100 (1913): 163; Green, *Only a Miner*, 333; Cohen, *Long Steel Rail*, 65. I have found no biography of Perrow. Born in 1880, he was a student of William Ellery Leonard at the University of Wisconsin. He taught at the University of Louisville but retired around 1919 to live on a farm in Talking Rock, Georgia. See Eber Carle Perrow, *Unto the Hills* (privately printed, 1955), pamphlet collection, Duke University Library.

50. Williams, *John Henry*, 47–48; Archie Green, *Wobblies, Pile Butts, and Other Heroes* (Urbana: University of Illinois Press, 1993), 53. Duke University was still called Trinity College when Brown began collecting.

51. Perrow had versions from correspondents in Mississippi and Kentucky; Curtis-Burlin had a version from a student who heard the song in the mines of Virginia; Lomax had the songs of C&O trackliners. A ballad stanza usually has four lines with an *xaxa*, *xbxb* structure, where *a* rhymes with *a*, *b* with *b*, and the *x* lines do not rhyme. The first and third lines usually have four beats, and the second and fourth have three. The ballad has a regular pattern, but a free enough form to allow considerable variation. Some versions of the John Henry song double the last line.

52. Chappell and Green believe these hammer songs to be unrelated to the ballads. Johnson believed that the ballad evolved from work songs. See Green, *Only a Miner*, 337.

53. William Powell Jones, *The Tribe of Black Ulysses: African American Lumber Workers in the Jim Crow South* (Urbana: University of Illinois Press, 2005); Howard Washington Odum and Guy Benton Johnson, *Negro Workaday Songs* (Chapel Hill: University of North Carolina Press, 1926); Lynn Moss Sanders, *Howard W. Odum's Folklore Odyssey: Transformation to Tolerance Through African American Folk Studies* (Athens: University of Georgia Press, 2003).

7. Songs People Have Sung: 1900–1930

1. Howard Washington Odum and Guy Benton Johnson, *Negro Workaday Songs* (Chapel Hill: University of North Carolina Press, 1926); Paul A. Cimbala, "Black Musicians from Slavery to Freedom: An Exploration of an African-American Folk Elite and Cultural Continuity in the Nineteenth-Century Rural South," *Journal of Negro History* 80 (Winter 1995): 15–29.

2. Leonard P. Curry, *The Free Black in Urban America, 1800–1850: The Shadow of the Dream* (Chicago: University of Chicago Press, 1981).

3. Guy Benton Johnson, *John Henry: Tracking Down a Negro Legend* (Chapel Hill: University of North Carolina Press, 1929), 110.

4. Ibid., 111.

5. Anonymous, liner notes for *Stovepipe No. 1: Complete Recorded Works (1924–1950) and the Jug Washboard Band (1928)*, Document Records 5269.

6. Paul Oliver, *Songsters and Saints: Vocal Traditions on Race Records* (New York: Cambridge University Press, 1984), 199–221.

7. "Blind Tom, Singing," *Southern Workman,* May 1901, 258. Corrothers may have been referring archly to the story of Samson, in which Samson was blinded and paraded before the Philistines. As they watched, Samson stood between the two central pillars of the house. After praying to God, he pushed on the pillars and brought the building down around him, killing all the Philistines.

8. Oliver, *Songsters and Saints,* 199–221.

9. Norm Cohen, *Long Steel Rail: The Railroad in American Folksong* (Urbana: University of Illinois Press, 2000), 74.

10. Johnson, *John Henry,* 111.

11. John Wesley, *Sermons on Several Occasions in Four Volumes* (London: printed for G. Whitfield, 1796), sermons 7 and 9, pp. 100–112, 127–43.

12. Ibid., sermon 9.

13. 1 Cor. 2:14, King James Version: "Now the natural man receives not the things of the Spirit of God: for they are foolishness unto him; and he cannot know them, because they are spiritually judged."

14. "Sampson," Golden Gate Quartet, *Travelin' Shoes,* RCA 66063.

15. Louis Watson Chappell, *John Henry: A Folk-Lore Study* (1933; rpt. Port Washington, N.Y.: Kennikat, 1968), 116.

16. Ibid., 112.

17. Ibid., 117.

18. Ibid., 120.

19. *New York Times,* 4 Aug. 1881.

20. *Chicago Daily Tribune,* 30 Sept. 1894.

21. Thomas N. Maloney and Warren C. Whatley, "Making the Effort: The Contours of Racial Discrimination in Detroit's Labor Markets, 1920–1940," *Journal of Economic History* 55 (Sept. 1995): 465–93.

22. Darlene Clark Hine, "Black Migration in the Urban Midwest," in *The New African-American Urban History,* ed. Kenneth W. Goings and Raymond A. Mohl (Thousand Oaks, Calif.: Sage Publications, 1996), 242.

23. William J. Collins, "When the Tide Turned: Immigration and the Delay of the Great Black Migration," *Journal of Economic History* 57 (Sept. 1997): 607–32.

24. Eric Arnesen, *Black Protest and the Great Migration: A Brief History with Documents* (Boston: Bedford/St. Martin's, 2003), 1.

25. "*Freight Train Blues,*" Trixie Smith, *Complete Recorded Works, vol. 1 (1922–1924),* Document Records 5332.

26. Big Bill Broonzy and Yannick Bruynoghe, *Big Bill Blues* (New York: Da Capo Press, 1992), 37–38.

27. Lieut. William N. Colson, "The Social Experience of the Negro Soldier Abroad," *Messenger,* Oct. 1919, 26–27.

28. On floating verses, see Lynn Abott and Doug Seroff, "'They Certl'y Sound Good to Me': Sheet Music, Southern Vaudeville, and the Commercial Ascendancy of the Blues," *American Music* 14 (Winter 1996): 411–12.

29. Michael Taft, *Blues Lyric Poetry: An Anthology* (New York: Garland, 1985), preface; "Drop That Sack," ibid., 118.

30. Katrina Hazzard-Gordon, *Jookin': The Rise of Social Dance Formations in African-American Culture* (Philadelphia: Temple University Press, 1990), chapter 2; Chris Albertson, *Bessie* (New Haven: Yale University Press, 2003); Marshall Winslow Stearns and Jean Stearns, *Jazz Dance: The Story of American Vernacular Dance* (New York: Macmillan, 1968).

31. "John Henry," Big Bill Broonzy, *On Tour in Britain, 1952*, Jasmine Music B0000799IH.

32. W. Astor Morgan, "Music," *Messenger*, Feb. 1924, 57.

33. "Operas and Cabarets," *Messenger*, Feb. 1924, 71.

34. Oliver, *Songsters and Saints*, 44.

35. Jacqui Malone, *Steppin' on the Blues: The Visible Rhythms of African American Dance* (Urbana: University of Illinois Press, 1996).

36. "The Nickel Under the Frenchman's Foot," *Messenger*, Sept. 1922, 478.

37. "The Nickel Under the Dutchman's Foot," *Messenger*, Jan. 1923, 597.

38. Penelope Niven, *Carl Sandburg: A Biography* (New York: C. Scribner's Sons, 1991), 116–17.

39. Lloyd Lewis, *It Takes All Kinds* (New York: Harcourt Brace, 1947), 78.

40. Ibid., 74.

41. Ibid., 80.

42. Ibid., 80.

43. Jacquelyn Dowd Hall et al., *Like a Family: The Making of a Southern Cotton Mill World* (Chapel Hill: University of North Carolina Press, 1987).

44. Patrick Joseph Huber, "The Modern Origins of an Old-Time Sound: Southern Millhands and Their Hillbilly Music, 1923–1942" (dissertation, University of North Carolina at Chapel Hill, 2000), 27–46. While most people give a birth date for Carson of 1868, Huber demonstrates (28) that he was probably born in 1874 in Cobb County, Georgia.

45. Ibid.: "dishwater," 28; swaying, 49.

46. Ibid., 54.

47. Ibid., 50–52.

48. Hall, *Like a Family*.

8. Communist Strongman

1. Only in later years did John Lomax restrict himself to collecting songs.

2. David King Dunaway, "Unsung Songs of Protest: The Composers' Collective of New York," *New York Folklore* 5 (Summer 1979): 6.

3. Quotes from Workers Music League, *Workers Song Book*, vol. 1 (New York: Workers Music League, 1934), foreword. The *Workers Song Book* represents

an effort by the league to accommodate both the classically inspired songs of European composers and more "humorous" and "catchy" songs.

4.   Robin D. G. Kelley, *Hammer and Hoe: Alabama Communists During the Great Depression* (Chapel Hill: University of North Carolina Press, 1990), 13.

5.   Robert Ingalls, "Antiradical Violence in Birmingham During the 1930s," *Journal of Southern History* 47 (Nov. 1981): 522.

6.   Kelley, *Hammer and Hoe*, 17.

7.   Bruce Michael Harrah-Conforth, "Laughing Just to Keep from Crying: Afro-American Folksongs & the Field Recordings of Lawrence Gellert" (master's thesis, Indiana University, 1984), 21–22; James Weschler, "From World War I to the Popular Front: The Art and Activism of Hugo Gellert," *Journal of Decorative and Propaganda Arts* 24 (2002): 198–229; James Weschler, "Embracing the Specter of Communism: The Art and Activism of Hugo Gellert" (dissertation, City University of New York, 2003), 15–17.

8.   Weschler, "Embracing the Specter," 15–17.

9.   Weschler, "From World War I to the Popular Front."

10.   On Gellert's trip, see Hugo Gellert, "Europe Summer of 1914," in *This Noble Flame: Portrait of a Hungarian Newspaper in the USA, 1902–1982: An Anthology,* ed. Zoltán Deák, ([New York?]: Heritage Press, 1982), 72–74, Jeff Kisseloff, *Hugo Gellert: Catalogue of Prints and Drawings* (New York: Mary Ryan Gallery, 1986), 1.

11.   Hugo and his brother Lawrence both joined the Party after Ernest's death. See Harrah-Conforth, "Laughing Just to Keep from Crying."

12.   Steven Garabedian, "Reds, Whites, and the Blues: Lawrence Gellert, 'Negro Songs of Protest,' and the Leftwing Folksong Revival of the 1930s and 1940s," *American Quarterly* 57 (2005): 179–206.

13.   Fred Becker, "The WPA Federal Art Project, New York City: A Reminiscence," *Massachusetts Review* 39, no. 1 (1998): 74–92; quotes on 74.

14.   Ibid., 79–80.

15.   Frank W. Long, *Confessions of a Depression Muralist* (Columbia: University of Missouri Press, 1997), 40.

16.   Long, *Confessions of a Depression Muralist.*

17.   Philip Schatz, "Songs of the Negro Worker," *New Masses,* May 1930, 6.

18.   Ibid., 6–8.

19.   I have relied on a later edition of Green's play. Paul Green, *Roll Sweet Chariot: A Symphonic Play of the Negro People; in Four Scenes* (New York: S. French, 1935).

20.   William Alexander, *Film on the Left: American Documentary Film from 1931 to 1942* (Princeton: Princeton University Press, 1981), 159–60.

21.   Gary Gerstle, *Working-Class Americanism: The Politics of Labor in a Textile City, 1914–1960,* 1st Princeton ed. (Princeton: Princeton University Press, 2002).

22.   The CIO was a group of eight unions that broke away from the American Federation of Labor in 1935 to organize mass-production industries. Immi-

grants and African Americans were especially important in these industries and had been largely ignored by the older unions. Many of the newest organizers recruited came from the radical parties.

23. "Take This Hammer" (copyright 1941), reproduced in Alan Lomax, Woody Guthrie, and Pete Seeger, *Hard-Hitting Songs for Hard-Hit People* (New York: Oak Publications, 1967), 84-85.

24. Elizabeth Faue, *Community of Suffering and Struggle: Women, Men, and the Labor Movement in Minneapolis, 1915–1945*, Gender and American Culture (Chapel Hill: University of North Carolina Press, 1991).

25. Robert Schrank, *Wasn't That a Time: Growing Up Radical and Red in America* (Cambridge: MIT Press, 1998); "strut our sexual stuff," 123; "a good fuck," 135.

26. On the way in which hypermasculinity contributed to male solidarity, see Daniel Bender, *Sweated Work, Weak Bodies: Anti-Sweatshop Campaigns and Languages of Labor* (New Brunswick: Rutgers University Press, 2004).

27. William A. Christensen and Mark Seifert, "A Look at the Life and Career of Jack 'King' Kirby," *Wizard* 36 (Aug. 1994).

28. While socialists opposed Hitler, Communists changed positions when Stalin and Hitler signed the Ribbentrop-Molotov Pact, which lasted from August 1939 until June 1941, when Germany invaded the Soviet Union.

29. As many commentators have noted, the strongman and trapeze artists of the circus were also models for superheroes.

30. Bradford White, *Comic Book Nation: The Transformation of Youth Culture in America* (Baltimore: Johns Hopkins University Press, 2001), 9–13.

31. Michael Denning, *The Cultural Front: The Laboring of American Culture in the Twentieth Century* (London and New York: Verso, 1996).

32. Benjamin Filene, *Romancing the Folk: Public Memory and American Roots Music*, Cultural Studies of the United States (Chapel Hill: University of North Carolina Press, 2000), 133–59. Filene, however, contends that while many RRP and OWI programs were created by the Library of Congress, they were not played overseas. Continuity between Library of Congress folklorists like Philip Henry Cohen, who became chief of the Domestic Radio Bureau and later chief of the OWI's American Broadcasting Station in Europe, may suggest otherwise.

33. Holly Cowan Shulman, *The Voice of America: Propaganda and Democracy, 1941–1945*, History of American Thought and Culture (Madison: University of Wisconsin Press, 1990), 53–74.

34. Workers Music League, *Workers Song Book*, vol. 1 (New York: Workers Music League, 1934); ibid., vol. 2 (New York: Workers Music League, 1935); U.S. Adjutant General's Office, *Army Song Book* (Washington: Library of Congress, 1941).

35. Eric A. Gordon, *Mark the Music: The Life and Work of Marc Blitzstein* (New York: St. Martin's Press, 1989).

36. Margaret Bradford Boni, *The Fireside Book of Favorite American Songs* (New York: Simon & Schuster, 1952); Lois Raebeck, *New Approaches to Music in the Elementary School* (Dubuque, Iowa: W. C. Brown, 1969); George A. Luvenia, *Teaching the Music of Six Different Cultures in the Modern Secondary School* (West Nyack, N.Y.: Parker, 1976); Olive Ashby, personal conversation, 28 March 2005.

37. Julia Lynn Mickenberg, "Educating Dissent: Children's Literature and the Left, 1935–1965" (dissertation, University of Minnesota, 2000).

38. W. Fitzhugh Brundage, *The Southern Past: A Clash of Race and Memory* (Cambridge: Belknap Press, 2005).

39. Pierre Priest, personal conversation, Cleveland, Ohio, 13 Dec. 2002.

40. [Ed Cabbell], "John Henry Center for Culture and History Exchange" (Morgantown, W. Va.: John Henry Center, n.d.), 1.

Coda

1. The song quoted here is a compilation of many of the versions of the John Henry ballad. "The John Henry shirt," John Henry Vertical Files, American Folklife Center, Library of Congress; see "V.I.P Comfort," *New York Times,* 8 Sept. 1974, 287.

2. David King Dunaway, "Unsung Songs of Protest: The Composers' Collective of New York," *New York Folklore* 5 (Summer 1979): 1–19; Richard A. Reuss, "The Roots of American Left-Wing Interest in Folksong," *Labor History* 12 (1971): 259–79.

3. The name of the first competitor to American Telephone and Telegraph, Sprint, is an acronym for Southern Pacific Railroad International. The Southern Pacific, because it had trunk lines through many of the corridors in the South and Southwest, was able to claim rights to cable that its technicians had laid down, and associated rights of eminent domain. Much of the fiber-optic cable laid by corporations in the 1990s was laid and is maintained by the nation's railroads.

ACKNOWLEDGMENTS

IT IS IRONIC, I suppose, that a (reformed) hacker who can't do a pull-up should find the true story behind the legend of John Henry, but it is not *that* ironic. The digitization of manuscript-finding aids helped make his story understandable, but scholarly work still relies on physical strength: eyes to pore over documents, hands to sort materials into categories, and strong sitting muscles, what historians called "sitzfleisch." But these are not my strengths, they are the strengths of others, those who helped me. Many hands, backs, and shoulders made this book possible. So I must first thank archivists at the Library of Virginia, the University of North Carolina's Southern Historical Collection, the Western Reserve Historical Society in Cleveland, and Swem Library in Williamsburg. They preserve, they winnow, they explain, and historians ignore their advice at their peril. The *real* history is impossible without them. William and Mary reference librarians, as always, saved my fanny, especially Hope Yelich, who helped me navigate difficult manuscript census materials.

This book would have been impossible without colleagues, and I have the greatest in the world. In particular I remember two dozen lunches in the 1998–99 academic year eating sardines and cheese with Rhys Isaac, Kris Lane, and Kelly Gray. They helped me understand the legend of John Henry. They provoked and prodded me, asking disturbing, impossible questions. They knew, the three of them, more than I did about mining, folklore, slavery, abolition, songs, violence, crime, and unpaid debts. This book is a long-delayed payment—they helped me hear the murder in a song that seemed to be about man and machine. A larger community in my department made it possible to write. They dropped in at lunchtime, accepted my buttonholing in the halls, or shot back questions at the Greenleafe (the pub next door). I remember help at critical points from Ron Schechter, Lisa Swartout, Chandos Brown, Kim Phillips, Charlie McGovern, Leisa Meyer, Carol Sheriff, Judy Ewell, Mel Ely, and Ed Crapol, but I am certain that I have left many others out. Scholars outside my department also helped me enormously: Rick Halpern in Toronto, Alex Lichtenstein in Texas, Ed Cabbell in Morgantown, Gunther Peck in North Carolina, Jennifer Luff in D.C., Bruce Baker in Britain, Selina Lewis-Davidson in New York, Seth Bruggeman in Kansas, and Harold Forsythe in New York each read or heard drafts at various points. They sharpened arguments and poked holes in my simplistic conclusions. Bill Walker and Amy Ruth at William and Mary's Office of University Relations told the world about my first scholarly paper about John Henry, hooking me up with many of the people I needed to know but could not have thought to call. Linda Wheeler at the *Washington Post* tracked down the details that I could not about the bones at the white house.

Paul Heideman, a biologist with a heart of gold, read most of this manuscript and taught me a great deal about storytelling. Cindy Hahamovitch, my wife and the better historian in our family, also read every word and forced me to make some sense. She tried to excise the "hoot owls" and every other strained metaphor in this book. I left some in just to tick her off. Back in 1997, Leon Fink, my graduate advisor and now at the University of Illinois–Chicago, was working on a labor folklore course. He asked me what I knew about John Henry and suggested that I take a look at the story. That it took me nine years to answer the question probably does not surprise him—I always turned in things late.

I did not see a book in the true story of John Henry. Deirdre Mullane, first as an editor and then as an agent, did see one. She showed me how to write in the first person, a kind of writing that most historians regard as just below pool-hustling or prostitution. She showed me what I should have known all along, that history is still a branch of storytelling. She is the bomb.

Furaha Norton, my editor at Oxford, told me that my story about the life and death of John Henry made her cry. She immediately won me over. When I chose an academic press over a popular one, I asked her to edit me harshly, because I worried that academic presses sometimes refuse to really criticize scholars for their writing. When I sent her the manuscript, I received seventeen single-spaced pages of comments, and more than a hundred marginal comments. She radically recast this book, tore out its foundations and built them up again, chided me for my foibles, and praised (as I recall) only two or three sentences. The comments were perfect. I have edited student papers, theses, and dissertations for twelve years and cannot imagine the energy, focus, and critical power that Furaha used to reshape this book. She is my hero.

I have other heroes too. Susan Ferber took over the project when Furaha went on to Vintage and is a master at all the details of turning a good book into a better one. Joellyn Ausanka made al the gears click together without breaking any hearts. India Cooper, my copy editor, knows my voice better than I do, and took great hunks of slovenly prose and beat them into shape.

INDEX

Note: Page numbers in *italics* indicate photographs and illustrations.